A BRIEF HISTORY OF THE

Late Ottoman Empire

A BRIEF HISTORY OF THE
Late Ottoman Empire

M. Şükrü Hanioğlu

PRINCETON UNIVERSITY PRESS

PRINCETON AND OXFORD

Published by Princeton University Press, 41 William Street, Princeton,
New Jersey 08540

In the United Kingdom: Princeton University Press, 3 Market Place, Woodstock,
Oxfordshire OX20 1SY

Frontispiece: Spectators watching a military balloon given the name *Osmanlı* (Ottoman)
in Istanbul (1909). *Resimli Kitab*, 2/9 (June 1909), p. 872.

Library of Congress Cataloging-in-Publication Data

Hanioğlu, M. Şükrü.
A brief history of the late Ottoman empire/M. Şükrü Hanioğlu.
p.   cm.
ISBN 978-0-691-13452-9 (alk. paper)
1. Turkey—History—19th century.   2. Turkey—History—Ottoman Empire,
1288–1918.   I. Title.
DR557.H36 2008
956'.015—dc22   2007061028

British Library Cataloging-in-Publication Data is available

This book has been composed in Minion Typeface

Printed on acid-free paper. ∞

press.princeton.edu

Printed in the United States of America

1   3   5   7   9   10   8   6   4   2

For Arsev

Mazi ve müstakbel ahvâline vakıf ve belki ezel ve ebed esrarını
ârif olmağa insanda bir meyl-i tabiî olduğundan ale-l-umum nevʿ-i
beşerin bu fenne [tarih] ihtiyac-ı maʿnevîsi derkârdır.

Since man has a natural aptitude for comprehending past and future
affairs, and perhaps also for unlocking the secrets of eternities past and
future, humanity's spiritual need for this science [history] is evident.

—AHMED CEVDET, *Tarih-i Cevdet*, 1 (Istanbul: Matbaa-i
Osmaniye, 1309 [1891]), pp. 16–17

Contents

Figures

Acknowledgments

I HAVE INCURRED numerous debts of gratitude while engaging in the research and writing of this book. First and foremost, I should express my deepest gratitude to Michael A. Cook and Jesse Ferris, who have read successive drafts of the entire manuscript and offered generous help in organizing the text. They also drew my attention to points which I might otherwise have overlooked. I am also grateful to my learned colleagues András P. Hámori and Stephen Kotkin, who read the final draft and provided excellent remarks and suggestions. Likewise, I am indebted to my colleagues Mustafa Aksakal, Nancy Coffin, Robert P. Finn, Said Öztürk, İskender Pala, and Milen Petrov for answering numerous inquiries and supplying valuable information. I would also like to express my thanks to the two anonymous reviewers for offering insightful comments toward improving this book.

Special thanks are due to Princeton University Press for its careful execution of a difficult task. At the Press, editors Brigitta van Rheinberg and Sara Lerner answered a myriad of questions with competence and good humor, accommodated all requests, and coordinated the publication. Dimitri Karetnikov, the illustration specialist, managed to produce illustrations that look better than the originals. Karen M. Verde, with her extremely thorough and professional work, considerably exceeded my expectations in a copyeditor. I would also like to express my thanks to Dr. Christopher L. Brest for his help in drawing the maps and to Dr. Lys Ann Weiss for preparing the index.

I am indebted to the administrations of the Başbakanlık Osmanlı Arşivi and Müftülük Arşivi, both in Istanbul, not only for access to their collections but also for many of the illustrations that appear in this book. I likewise wish to thank Mr. Mehmet Darakçıoğlu, Dr. Fatmagül Demirel, Ms. İffet Baytaş, and Mr. Sabit Baytaş for their help in obtaining some of the illustrations. Thanks are also due to the managers and office staff of the Near Eastern Studies Department: Kathleen O'Neill, Christine Riley, Angela Bryant, Danette Rivera, Pınar Gibbon, and Tammy M. Williams for their continuous technical support during the preparation of this study.

It is my pleasant duty to record my gratitude to the University Committee on Research in the Humanities and Social Sciences for making grants toward the cost of my research in Istanbul in 1994 and 2001. I collected all the data regarding books read by members of the Ottoman ruling (*askerî*) class and Ottoman constitutionalism during these two research trips.

Last but not least, I thank my wife Arsev for once again sacrificing the time it took me to work on another book.

MŞH

Princeton, NJ

May 2007

Note on Transliteration,
Place Names,
and Dates

NAMES AND TITLES in Ottoman Turkish are rendered according to modern Turkish usage and not by strict transliteration. Arabic names and titles are transliterated according to a slightly simplified system based on that of the *International Journal of Middle East Studies (IJMES)*. Sources in Slavic languages are transliterated using the modified Library of Congress transliteration system. For geographical names frequently encountered in material in the English language, common English usage is preferred. Thus we have Damascus, Monastir, and Salonica, not Dimashq, Bitola, and Thessaloniki. For all other place names, to avoid confusion, the designations current in the contemporary Ottoman successor states of the Balkans and Near East have been employed. In accordance with *The Chicago Manual of Style*, frequently used foreign terms are italicized only on their first appearance. Gregorian equivalents of both Muslim *Hicrî (Hijrī)* and the *Rumî (Rūmī)* dates are provided in square brackets where considered necessary. The *Hicrî* calendar is lunar and starts from the Hijra in A.D. 622; the *Rumî* calendar was a solar version of the *Hicrî* calendar based on the Julian calendar.

A BRIEF HISTORY OF THE

Late Ottoman Empire

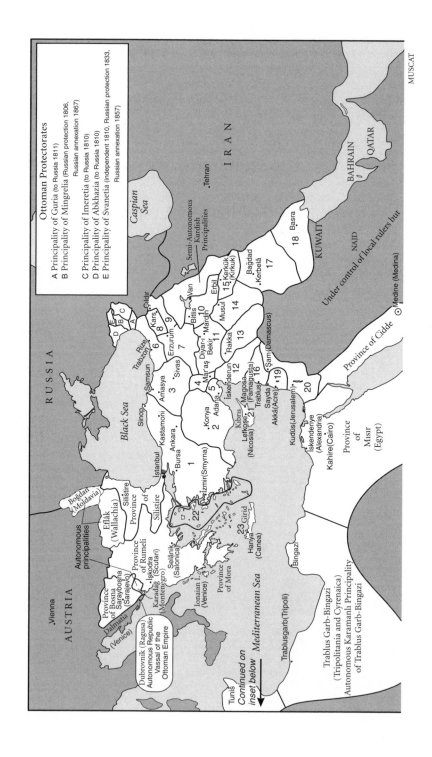

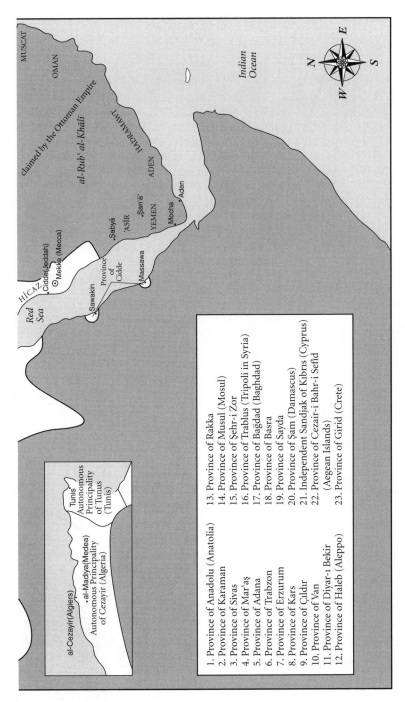

1. Province of Anadolu (Anatolia)
2. Province of Karaman
3. Province of Sivas
4. Province of Marʿaş
5. Province of Adana
6. Province of Trabzon
7. Province of Erzurum
8. Province of Kars
9. Province of Çıldır
10. Province of Van
11. Province of Diyar-ı Bekir
12. Province of Haleb (Aleppo)
13. Province of Rakka
14. Province of Musul (Mosul)
15. Province of Şehr-i Zor
16. Province of Trablus (Tripoli in Syria)
17. Province of Bağdad (Baghdad)
18. Province of Basra
19. Province of Sayda
20. Province of Şam (Damascus)
21. Independent Sandjak of Kıbrıs (Cyprus)
22. Province of Cezair-i Bahr-i Sefid
    (Aegean Islands)
23. Province of Girid (Crete)

al-Cezayir(Algiers)
• al-Madiya(Medea)
Autonomous Principality
of Cezayir (Algeria)

Tunis •
Autonomous
Principality
of Tunus
(Tunis)

claimed by the Ottoman Empire

MUSCAT
OMAN
al-Rubʿ al-Khālī
HADRAMAWT
ADEN
YEMEN
ASİR
•Şabyā
•Sanʿāʾ
•Mocha
Aden
Indian Ocean

HİCAZ
Red Sea
Cidde(Jeddah)
⊙Mekke (Mecca)
Province of Cidde
Massawa
Sawakin

N E W S

FIGURE 1. The Ottoman Empire ca. 1795.

Introduction

THIS BRIEF HISTORY aspires to cover a period of almost one-and-a-half centuries, during which enormous changes took place over a vast geographic area. As if this were not ambitious enough, the need to place the events of 1798–1918 in context requires a description of Ottoman reality in the late eighteenth century by way of background, as well as some discussion of the legacy bequeathed by the late Ottoman Empire to the new nation-states that emerged on its ruins. The compression of so much history into a concise book naturally necessitates certain choices and omissions, as well as the privileging of trends and analyses over facts and figures. The general nature of this work thus precludes a thorough discussion of any particular issue or field. Specialists—whether of cultural, diplomatic, intellectual, literary, military, political, social, or economic history—may thus be somewhat disappointed with the result. But they may find some compensation in the attempt to integrate the advances made in multiple subfields into a general framework that offers a new approach to the study of late Ottoman history.

There is also a more ideological problem. The usual human failure to take account of historical contingency has been reinforced by prevalent nationalist narratives in the Ottoman successor states, producing a conception of late Ottoman history that is exceedingly teleological. It is often assumed that the emergence of the Republic of Turkey in Anatolia, and of the neighboring nation-states in the surrounding territories of the disintegrated Ottoman polity, was the inevitable and predictable result of the decline of a sprawling multinational empire. This retrospective approach to late Ottoman history has become, it seems to me, a major obstacle to viewing the period as it really was. In particular, it distorts key historical processes by pulling them out of their historical context and placing them in a contrived chain of events leading up to the familiar post-imperial world. The point is not to deny the significance of the link between the successor nation-states—especially Turkey—and their Ottoman past; on the contrary, retrieving the historical roots of modern phenomena is a vital and worthy undertaking. But the attempt to frame late Ottoman history in a narrative of imperial collapse to the relentless drumbeat of the march of progress—usually associated with Westernization, nationalism, and secularization—prevents a clear understanding of the developments in question. Rectifying this error is a major goal of this book.

An illustration may help clarify this point. Any deep, evocative understanding of Turkish Republican ideology necessarily entails retrieving its intellectual progenitors of the late Ottoman period. But a nuanced, contextualized examination of the ideological debates of late Ottoman times should avoid projecting this later historical reality of a struggle between revolutionary secularists and religious conservatives onto an earlier, altogether different one. Nor will it do to simplify historical reality by depicting two imaginary camps upholding the contending banners of scientific progress and religious obscurantism—as is too often the case with modern commentators blinded by the modern Republican reality. The importance of a work like *The Genesis of Young Ottoman Thought*,[1] in this context, is the corrective insight that the Young Ottomans were not secularist opponents of religious obscurantism, forming a link in the chain leading to secular republicanism; rather, they were the proponents of a uniquely Islamic critique of the new Ottoman order of the 1860s.

Thus, in order to locate the origins of modern Turkish official ideology in late Ottoman history, I have first tried to provide an account of late Ottoman history that does not assign it a teleological mission. More generally, I have avoided the fashionable but misleading tendency to see late Ottoman history primarily in terms of a struggle between competing ideologies. Although one of the tasks I have set myself has been to fill one of the more glaring lacunæ in the study of the late Ottoman period—intellectual history—I conclude that the ideas debated did not, in the final analysis, serve as the engines of historical change. A contextual analysis of the most important historical developments of the period places a premium not on ideologies as the driving force of history, but on the oppressive weight of circumstances, which inhibited the freedom of realistic policy makers who sought to innovate. For example, if we are to explain the Islamist policies adopted by the staunch secularists of the Committee of Union and Progress (hereafter CUP), we must first recognize that such contradictions exist (which is impossible from the Republican perspective), and then look to structural realities—like the increasing proportion of Muslim citizens in the empire that the CUP leadership inherited from its pious predecessor—to help us explain them. Likewise, if we are to make sense of the modernizing policies of Abdülhamid II, we must first avoid the trap of associating his rule with backward religiosity, and then look to imperial parallels in Europe, inter alia, to understand his reaction to the challenges of the day.

---

[1] Şerif Mardin, *The Genesis of Young Ottoman Thought: A Study in the Modernization of Turkish Political Ideas* (Princeton: Princeton University Press, 1962).

My narrative emphasizes historical trends and processes more than single events, placing them within an analytical framework with four principal dimensions: the persistent imperial ambition to centralize, the shifting socioeconomic context, the key challenge of forging an Ottoman response to modernity, and the need to integrate Ottoman history into world history. Let me take each of these in turn.

First, where the nationalist narrative portrays the struggle of an oppressed people to liberate themselves from the Turkish yoke, I introduce a paradigm of struggle between the imperial drive to centralize and a variety of centrifugal forces. As the imperial center took advantage of the possibilities afforded by modern technology to launch an ambitious attempt to centralize and modernize the mechanisms of control over the loosely held periphery, nationalist movements, the aspirations of local rulers, and international encroachments exerted an ever-stronger pull in the other direction. Seen in this light, nationalism provided a powerful new ideological framework for the mobilization of the masses in the perpetuation of an older and more fundamental struggle between center and periphery.

Second, the struggle between center and periphery involved a wholesale transformation of the old order of the empire. Administrative reform entailed radical changes to economic relations, to Ottoman culture, and to the fabric of society. Thus, I have found it necessary to treat social, cultural, and economic developments within this larger context, and not as phenomena occurring in a vacuum. As with the question of ideas, here, too, I have avoided the tendency to ascribe historical developments to a single social or economic cause. Just as, for example, it is unhelpful to seek the origins of the Young Turk Revolution in the rise in inflation, it is equally misleading to ascribe opposition to the printing press to "religious fanaticism" alone, while ignoring the socioeconomic basis of this opposition among thousands of individuals who made a living from manuscript production. Historical developments in the late Ottoman period did not stem from simple economic, social, or cultural reasons, but were affected by all three.

Third, instead of the worn-out paradigms of modernization and Westernization, I have tried to write in terms of the Ottoman response to challenges brought on by the onset of modernity. The Ottoman state was not unique in adapting to modernity, though its task was perhaps more arduous than that of European states, if only because modernity was initially a European phenomenon (although a uniquely Ottoman version of modernity had emerged, arguably, by the late nineteenth century). Similar challenges confronted European contemporaries and provoked similar responses, of which the Ottoman establishment was not unaware. More important, analyzing societal transformation as the response of state and society to external challenge once again helps us avoid seeing change as driven by an ideology of modernization. This is not to deny that over time the concepts of modernization and Westernization became slogans in their own right. But it is to assert that the simplistic picture of an uncompromising hostility to modernity confronting enthusiastic support for its wholesale adoption across an unbridgeable divide is to a large extent a fiction. The similarities between Young Ottoman constitutionalism, rooted as it was in Islamic principles, and later Young Turk constitutionalism, grounded in an intensely secular outlook, are greater than many would care to admit. Similarly, the "pious Caliph" Abdülhamid II's responses to the challenge of modernity did not differ significantly from those of his grandfather Mahmud II, nicknamed the "infidel sultan" by devout Muslims ever since. Westernization, too, was not just a matter of importation. Rather, it was a complex process of acculturation, in which Western ideas, manners, and institutions were selectively adopted, and evolved into different forms set in a different context.

Fourth, I have attempted to portray Ottoman history as an integral part of the larger histories of Europe and the world. Integrating Ottoman history into world history does not mean situating it in grandiose theoretical frameworks, such as the "World Systems theory," or reducing it to a matter of trade statistics. It does, however, involve the reintroduction of a long-neglected, now out-of-fashion area of study: diplomatic history. After the Congress of Vienna in 1815, the Ottoman Empire became fully integrated into the struggle for power in Europe. This makes late Ottoman history incomprehensible in isolation from European history. The story of European colonialism, of Anglo-Russian strategic rivalry, of the Austrian quest for stability—all hold vital keys to understanding Ottoman policy in the nineteenth century. Viewing Ottoman foreign policy through the lens of the centralization paradigm outlined above restores relations between the Ottoman government and the Great Powers of Europe to the proportions they held in the perspective of contemporary statesmen. It highlights the tension between the European wish to see a weak Ottoman entity subdivided into autonomous zones open to European commerce and influence on the one hand, and the Ottoman center's wish to extend the area under its direct control on the other. Moreover, to understand the final collapse of the empire in the twentieth century, one must also look abroad. After all, it was not the internal dynamics of the empire but the new international order brought about by the Great War that sounded the death knell of the "Sick Man of Europe." Although the Ottoman state lacked the innate power to transform itself into a new kind of empire, more suited to the modern age—as was the case for a while in the neighboring Soviet Union—its leaders might have prolonged the life of the empire considerably had they opted for armed neutrality in 1914.

Finally, a word on sources. The dearth of local sources that might aid in the reconstruction of late Ottoman history from the vantage point of the periphery compels the student to accept the well-preserved records of the central bureaucracy. The best one can do to avoid the obvious pitfalls of reliance on such evidence is to treat imperial documents not as reliable mirrors of events on the ground but as filtered interpretations of them. The general nature of this study has necessarily reinforced this emphasis on the state, its agencies, and its communities—rather than on the individual. Still, I have tried where possible to present the average person's view of the sweeping changes under way around him or her, however briefly.

Despite the general nature of the study, I have found it valuable to incorporate material from original archival sources in conjunction with histories and treatises produced during the late Ottoman period. Although the book in no way pretends to revolutionize the field with new archival discoveries, this approach, it is hoped, will enrich the reader's perspective on late Ottoman history. I have also drawn on major monographs devoted to various aspects of late Ottoman history, while staying away from extensive consultation of general studies of the period, so as to avoid producing a mere summary of these secondary works. Finally, while refraining from turning the text into a series of statistics and tables, I have tried to provide a measure of quantitative information to amplify the central themes of this narrative.

4 mins –
1) Imperial drive to centr. v. centrifugal forces
2) → transform. of whole Emp. une
   – econ. admin. & social.
3) modernity not wholly re. Westernisation
4) Part of larger hist. of Eu. & world

The Ottoman Empire at the Turn
of the Nineteenth Century

Shortly before his death in 1774, Sultan Mustafa III (r. 1757–74) composed a quatrain describing the state of the Ottoman Empire:

> The world is turning upside down, with no hope for better during our
> reign,
> Wicked fate has delivered the state into the hands of despicable men,
> Our bureaucrats are villains who prowl through the streets of Istanbul,
> We can do nothing but beg God for mercy.[1]

Whether or not fate was responsible for the desperate situation of the empire, both Mustafa III and his brother Abdülhamid I (r. 1774–89) spared no effort in the attempt to reform it. But it was Mustafa III's son Selim III (r. 1789–1807) who would make the most significant effort yet to reverse the seemingly inexorable process of decline. It was not that the empire had regressed in its administration, economy, or culture, as is often assumed; on the contrary, many of its provinces were thriving in all these respects. But from the perspective of its rulers, the decreasing ability of the empire to compete militarily and economically with its continental rivals was cause for considerable alarm.

A Tour of the Ottoman Lands at the Turn
of the Nineteenth Century

The most salient characteristic of the Ottoman Empire at the end of the eighteenth century was its decentralization. In fact, the Ottoman state can

---

[1] Ahmed 'Ataullah, *Tarih-i 'Ata'nın Eş'ar Faslına Dair Olan Dördüncü Cildidir* (Istanbul, s.n., 1293 [1876]), p. 67.

only be considered an empire in the loose sense in which the term is used to refer to such medieval states as the Chinese under the late T'ang dynasty. Its administrative establishment, economic system, and social organization all call to mind the structure of a premodern state. On paper, Ottoman territory at the turn of the nineteenth century stretched from Algeria to Yemen, Bosnia to the Caucasus, and Eritrea to Basra, encompassing a vast area inhabited by some 30 million people.[2] In practice, the reach of the Ottoman government in Istanbul rarely extended beyond the central provinces of Anatolia and Rumelia, and then only weakly.

The remainder of the "sultanic domains" displayed a rich variety of administrative patterns, the common theme of which was the dominance of quasi-independent local rulers. Strong governors who controlled vast swathes of territory with the help of private armies naturally had their own styles of administration. Institutions that looked the same on paper worked quite differently in practice; the formal bureaucratic structure in Egypt under Mehmed Ali, for instance, might seem nearly identical with that of Ali Pasha of Tepelenë. In reality, however, Mehmed Ali's relentless efforts to transform the Egyptian bureaucracy in the early years of the nineteenth century turned it into a modern, effective machine of government, whereas Ali Pasha of Tepelenë's despotic administration was rigid and inefficient by comparison.[3] In the periphery, particularly in Africa and the Arabian Peninsula, fluid boundaries fluctuated in tandem with the vicissitudes of tribal loyalty. Everywhere, population data, even vital information on taxpaying households, was hopelessly out of date. The first comprehensive modern Ottoman census did not take place until 1831.

In Europe, the empire faced imperial competitors who were steadily eroding the Ottoman gains of the fifteenth and sixteenth centuries. Of these, Russia and Austria posed perhaps the most formidable threats to the integrity of the empire. By the terms of the Küçük Kaynarca Treaty of 1774, the Crimean Khanate—the only de jure autonomous Muslim administrative unit in the empire—became an ostensibly independent state, only to be swallowed by Russia nine years later. The two other autonomous Ottoman principalities, Wallachia and Moldavia, came under Russian protection. Thereafter, they drifted steadily away from Ottoman control. Local hospodars had ruled Wallachia and Moldavia on behalf of the Ottoman sultan until 1715–16, when the Ottoman center began to award these positions to imperial dragomans belonging to the major Greek Phanariot families in Istanbul.[4] This practice provoked considerable discontent in the

[2] Charles Issawi, "Population and Resources in the Ottoman Empire and Iran," *Studies in Eighteenth Century Islamic History*, eds. Thomas Naff and Roger Owen (Carbondale: Southern Illinois University Press, 1977), pp. 155–6.

[3] Ahmed Cevdet, *Tarih-i Cevdet*, 11 (Istanbul: Matbaa-i Osmaniye, 1309 [1891]), p. 44.

[4] Ibid., 1, p. 300.

principalities. Local resentment grew when the Ottoman administration introduced new trade regulations that required the sale of grain and animals to the imperial government at a set price. Russia, by contrast, came to be seen as the beneficent Orthodox protector. This sentiment acquired a legal basis in Article 16 of the Küçük Kaynarca Treaty. Thus emboldened by Russian support, notables and intellectuals demanded that the Ottomans grant further autonomy to the principalities. In 1790, Ioan Cantacuzino submitted a petition to the Ottoman government in which, inter alia, he asked that they be granted the right to elect rulers according to local traditions. The Ottomans responded to such requests with a number of formal concessions, embodied in the New Law of 1792, which regulated relations between the imperial center and the principalities.[5] In practice, however, the Ottomans conceded little, and consequently failed to win the support of local notables.

The tributary city-republic and major port of Ragusa (Dubrovnik)—an Ottoman Hong Kong on the Adriatic, linking the imperial heartlands with Europe—was the center of endless Ottoman, Habsburg, and Venetian diplomatic maneuvers and bargains. Although Vienna became the second protector of Ragusa in 1684, the Ottomans succeeded in reestablishing sole protection in 1707 and kept this city-republic in the Ottoman fold until the French occupation in 1806. The French integrated Ragusa into their *Provinces illyriennes* in 1808, but ceded it to Austria at the Congress of Vienna, whereby the Ottomans lost this vital trade link forever.[6]

The remaining Ottoman provinces were divided into two major groups. The provinces in which the distribution of land was effected according to the *timar* system formed the first group. In these territories, Ottoman viziers, princesses, governors, and subgovernors administered royal fiefs (timars), collecting revenues through tax farmers. In principle, these provinces operated as autonomous financial units charged with maintaining a balanced budget. Examples of this type of province are Anatolia, Rumelia, Bosnia, Erzurum, and Damascus.

The second major group of provinces comprised those in which the timar system was not applied. Here the state claimed all tax revenues, paying governors a yearly salary in cash (the *salyâne*), while local authorities were responsible for the collection of taxes and the payment of all local salaries. The best examples of such provinces are the North African domains, Basra, Egypt, several Mediterranean islands, and parts of Baghdad province. Of these, Baghdad, Basra, and Egypt transferred surpluses to the

---

[5] Mustafa A. Mehmet, "O nouă reglementare a raporturilor Moldovei și Țării Românești față de Poartă la 1792 (O carte de lege—*Kanunname*—în limba turcă)," *Studii* 20/4 (1967), pp. 695–707.

[6] M[aren] M[ikhailovich] Freidenberg, *Dubrovnik i Osmanskaia Imperiia* (Moscow: Izdatel'stvo Nauka, 1989), pp. 252ff.

central government on a yearly basis, whereas other provinces of this type merely submitted gifts.

The Arab provinces had another distinctive administrative-economic characteristic. Following the conquest in the sixteenth century, the Ottoman authorities had decided not to alter the preconquest systems of land tenure and taxation, in order to ease the incorporation of these provinces into the empire. Accordingly, the inhabitants continued to pay taxes in the particular manner to which they had been accustomed for centuries. For instance, in Sayda (modern-day Syria and Lebanon with the exclusion of Aleppo province), the inhabitants paid a cash tax on saplings to the imperial treasury and another in kind on wheat and barley to local state depots. In Mosul, farmers paid half of their harvest as a tithe (öşür), while tribesmen paid taxes based on the number of tents or herds they owned. In Cyrenaica, the determining factor was the number of wells in a given tribe's territory.[7]

Among the Arab provinces, the North African dominions of Algeria, Tunis, and Tripoli of Barbary enjoyed varying degrees of self-rule. These provinces had been incorporated into the empire in the sixteenth century by leading corsairs, such as Hayreddin Barbarossa, who pledged allegiance to the sultans and served in the Ottoman navy. Tunis and Algeria were subsequently ruled by Ottoman governors in consultation with councils led by Janissary commanders of the local army. The leaders, or *Dayıs*, of these councils gradually encroached on the authority of the governors. They even seized power in Tunis and Algeria in 1582 and 1670, respectively. Although a later governor, Ramaḍān Bey, managed to reestablish central control in Tunis, one of his followers, Ḥusayn Bey, founded a hereditary governorship in 1705. Thereafter, Tunis became a virtually independent state with only loose ties to the imperial center. However, even after the establishment of French colonial rule in Algeria in 1830 and the declaration of the French protectorate in Tunisia in 1883, the Ottoman administration continued to claim a border with Morocco, considered Tunisia an autonomous province, and classified Algeria as an imperial region (the Ottoman term *hitta* refers to a territory with vague boundaries).[8]

In 1711, a Janissary officer by the name of Karamanlı Ahmed became governor of Tripoli of Barbary and Cyrenaica (forming the Ottoman province of Tripoli). He subsequently established a hereditary governorship that lasted more than a century. Thereafter, Tripoli too became an essentially

[7] Abdurrahman Vefik, *Tekâlif Kavâidi*, 1 (Istanbul: Kanaat Kütübhanesi, 1328 [1910]), pp. 47–9.

[8] See the official maps and explanations in *Memâlik-i Osmaniye Ceb Atlası: Devlet-i Aliyye-i Osmaniye'nin Ahvâl-i Coğrafiyye ve İstatistikiyyesi*, eds. Tüccarzâde İbrahim Hilmi and Binbaşı Subhi (Istanbul: Kütübhane-i İslâm ve Askerî, 1323 [1905]), pp. 267, 283–5; and p. 64 (map section).

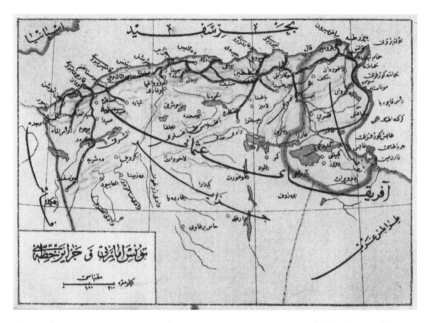

FIGURE 2. A map showing "Ottoman Africa" including the "Principality (*Emaret*)
of Tunis" and the "Region (*Hıtta*) of Algeria," from the *Memâlik-i Osmaniye Ceb
Atlası: Devlet-i Aliyye-i Osmaniye'nin Ahvâl-i Coğrafiye ve İstatistikiyesi*, eds.
Tüccarzâde İbrahim Hilmi and Binbaşı Subhi (Istanbul: Kütübhane-i
İslâm ve Askerî, 1323 [1905]), p. 64 (map section).

independent province. Ahmed Bey and his successors went so far as to assume the title "commander of the faithful," a label hitherto restricted to the
Ottoman Sultan as Caliph. The local economy thrived on piracy in the
Eastern Mediterranean. But state-sponsored piracy and the regular holding
of hostages for ransom inevitably led to trouble with foreign governments.
In 1798, for instance, the governor demanded 100,000 French francs from
the Swedish government, in addition to a yearly payment of 8,000 French
francs, in return for safe passage for Swedish vessels. The Swedes' refusal
prompted an all-out attack on their shipping, and only Napoleon's personal intervention secured the release of hundreds of hostages at a reduced
rate of 80,000 French francs on top of the annual fee.[9] In 1801, a spate of
attacks provoked the U.S. government to launch its first naval expedition
to the Mediterranean. This conflict, known as the Tripolitan War, ended
with a peace treaty signed on June 4, 1805. American terms were harsh and

[9] Mehmed Nuri and Mahmud Naci, *Trablusgarb* (Istanbul: Tercüman-ı Hakikat Matbaası,
1330 [1912]), pp. 140–44.

dealt a shattering blow to a state that was heavily dependent on ransom revenue. The Anglo-Dutch expedition of 1816 against Algiers and the resultant pressure applied by the Congress of Aix-la-Chapelle (1818) worsened the economic situation and paved the way for the reestablishment of Ottoman central control in 1835.

In the province of Egypt, conquered by the Ottomans in 1517, local Mamluk houses held almost all the bureaucratic positions by the end of the eighteenth century. The leader of the strongest of these houses would be elected Shaykh al-Balad (Chief of the City). He ruled the country from Cairo in spite of the continued presence of an Ottoman governor.[10] Over the course of the eighteenth century, Ottoman frustration at this indignity gave way to a policy of restraint and accommodation[11]—an approach bolstered, no doubt, by the substantial tax revenues remitted from the province by local *amīr*s, who increasingly took over the duties of tax collection from the imperial authorities.[12] Bonaparte's invasion in 1798 reinforced the separatist drift of Egypt, completing the foundations for virtual independence under a hereditary dynasty.

The province of Ethiopia included parts of modern-day Eritrea and the Sudan, and was established in 1555 to preempt Portuguese domination of the region. But by 1800, it had lost so much territory to the Ethiopian emperors that in practice it had been reduced to the major port cities of Massawa and Sawakin with their environs; this territory was governed together with Jeddah and Mecca.[13] The port of Sawakin, now in the Sudan and formerly part of the province of Egypt, was later entrusted to a sea captain and attached to the new Province of Ethiopia. A customs director collected duties with the help of a local amīr and a handful of soldiers. In the early years of the nineteenth century, 3,200 Spanish silver dollars were remitted annually from Sawakin to Jeddah.[14] However, this amount did not even cover the governor's salary.

Ottoman control of the Arabian Peninsula was no better. Despite claims to the entire peninsula, based on pledges of allegiance made by tribal leaders in the sixteenth and seventeenth centuries, central rule was limited to the coastal areas along the Red Sea and Persian Gulf, and to the Ḥijāz. Control

[10] Stanford J. Shaw, *Ottoman Egypt in the Age of the French Revolution by Ḥuseyn Efendi* (Cambridge, MA: Harvard University Press, 1964), pp. 10–11.

[11] Michael Winter, *Egyptian Society under Ottoman Rule, 1517–1798* (London: Routledge, 1992), p. 61.

[12] Stanford J. Shaw, *The Financial and Administrative Organization and Development of Ottoman Egypt, 1517–1798* (Princeton: Princeton University Press, 1962), p. 348.

[13] Cengiz Orhonlu, *Osmanlı İmparatorluğu'nun Güney Siyaseti: Habeş Eyaleti* (Istanbul: Edebiyat Fakültesi Yayınları, 1974), pp. 37ff.

[14] [John Lewis Burckhardt], *Johann Ludwig Burckhardt's Reisen in Nubien* (Weimar: Landes-Industrie-Comptoirs, 1820), pp. 608–13.

of the Ḥijāz was essential for the legitimacy of the Ottoman sultans who, unable to trace their lineage back to the Prophet Muḥammad, based their claim to the Caliphate on their custodianship of the Two Holy Sanctuaries of Mecca and Medina. The Ottomans administered the Ḥijāz through the Sharifs of Mecca, and distributed large sums of money and handsome gifts on a regular basis in an effort to gain favor with the local population.

But Ottoman rule of the peninsula met a vigorous challenge at the turn of the century. The influence of the teachings of the eighteenth-century scholar Muḥammad ibn ʿAbd al-Wahhāb spread following their adoption by Muḥammad ibn Saʿūd, sheikh of a local dynasty in Najd. The Wahhābīs, who called themselves al-Muwaḥḥidūn (Affirmers of the Unity of God), based their theology on the teachings of the controversial fourteenth-century Syrian scholar, Ibn Taymīyah, and those of his famous disciple, Ibn Qayyim al-Jawzīyah. They followed the Ḥanbalī legal doctrine—the strictest of the four Sunnī schools of law. The Wahhābīs, who frowned on ostentatious displays of spirituality, espoused a puritanical and scripturalist interpretation of the Qurʾān and the sayings of the Prophet Muḥammad, and advocated their stringent application to Muslim society. They mounted a deft challenge to the orthodoxy sponsored by the Ottoman state, denouncing traditional Ottoman religious practices as polytheistic innovations. The Wahhābīs condemned such Ottoman traditions as the construction of tombs and shrines, the decoration of holy buildings in Mecca and Medina, and various religious ceremonies, including pilgrimages to shrines and tombs and the celebration of the Prophet's birthday. For the Wahhābīs—who forbade all forms of music but the drum and viewed decorative arts as un-Islamic— Ottoman high culture represented the worst form of idolatry, toward which they harbored a visceral hatred reminiscent of Protestant attitudes toward Catholic religiosity.

During the last years of the eighteenth century, Muḥammad ibn Saʿūd's son ʿAbd al-ʿAzīz led campaigns against the Ottomans, pillaging towns in the Ḥijāz and Iraq. In 1798, following the defeat of his forces, the Sharif of Mecca signed an agreement permitting the Wahhābīs to come to Mecca on pilgrimage.[15] In 1803, Saʿūd ibn ʿAbd al-ʿAzīz occupied the holiest city of Islam on behalf of his father. He extracted oaths of allegiance from the local tribes and, with their assistance, destroyed numerous tombs revered by the Ottoman authorities. The Wahhābīs seized control of the Two Holy Sanctuaries, prevented pilgrims from the Ottoman lands from performing the pilgrimage, and demanded that clerics not deliver the Friday sermons in the name of the Ottoman sultan—thereby undermining the most significant manifestation of Ottoman authority at the time.[16] In addition, until their

---

[15] *Tarih-i Cevdet*, 7, p. 197.
[16] Ibid., 8, pp. 123–4.

initial defeat in 1813, they refused to allow the sultan's *Mahmil* (Mahmal), the special litter that carried the Ottoman sultan's yearly offerings to Mecca and Medina at the time of the pilgrimage, to enter the Ḥijāz. In their words: it was "not permissible for us . . . to approve a symbol of polytheism."[17]

The transformation of the Wahhābī movement into a state stretching from the borders of Yemen to the outskirts of Basra prompted Ottoman statesmen to entertain the radical idea of seeking help from the British Royal Navy.[18] In the event, however, the Governor of Egypt Mehmed Ali Pasha and his sons İbrahim (Ibrāhīm) and Tosun (Tūsūn) Pashas launched successive military campaigns between 1811 and 1818 to eradicate the Wahhābī threat. That the reestablishment of Ottoman rule in the Ḥijāz, however tenuous, was seen as crucial to Ottoman legitimacy is shown by the fact that Mahmud II (r. 1808–1839) adopted the title of *ghazi* (holy warrior) upon receiving the key of the Kaʿbah in 1813.[19]

In many other parts of the peninsula Ottoman rule was a fiction, as illustrated by the following anecdote. In 1917, the Ottoman Foreign Ministry charged two ambassadors with the preparation of an official memorandum on the history of the Southern Arabian region of Hadramawt in order to substantiate Ottoman claims to this territory after the war. As an exhaustive search through the Ottoman archives yielded no data whatsoever on the area, the ambassadors resorted to composing their memorandum on the basis of the entry in the *Encyclopædia Britannica*. If their research experience was any guide, they concluded, the region should be considered part of the British sphere of influence.[20] Similarly, into the twentieth century, the Law Bureau of the Grand Vizier's Office was still relying heavily on a sixteenth-century compilation of letters exchanged between Ottoman sultans and local leaders in Arabia in order to divine the nature of a given region's relationship with the imperial center.[21] Despite the evident weakness or nonexistence of Ottoman rule, over the course of the nineteenth century the Ottoman authorities developed an uncompromising claim to the entire Arabian Peninsula—including such regions as Oman, where there had never been any Ottoman administration, and whose rulers had signed international treaties with European powers.[22] This claim became one of the

---

[17] BOA-HH 19550 J. Saʿud ibn ʿAbd al-ʿAzīz's letter to Yusuf Pasha [January 1809].

[18] BOA-HH 3831. Undated letter from the Governor of Baghdad, Süleyman Pasha, to Sufyan Ağa.

[19] *Tarih-i Cevdet*, 10, p. 102.

[20] Mehmed Nâbi and Rumbeyoğlu Fahreddin, *Hadramut Mes'elesi* (Istanbul: Matbaa-i Âmire, 1334 [1917]), pp. 1–6.

[21] BOA-BEO/ file 353914 [February 6, 1912].

[22] However, in letters sent to the Ottoman authorities, the Omani leaders professed "sincerity and respect." See *Tarih-i Cevdet*, 2, p. 148.

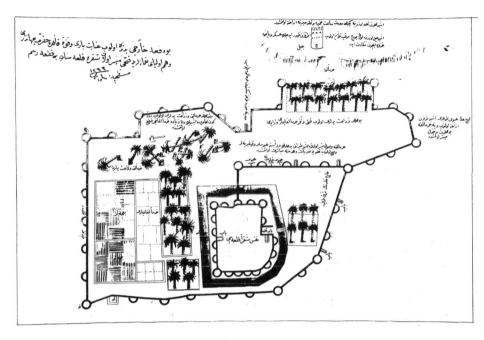

FIGURE 3. An Ottoman sketch dated January 23, 1818, depicting how the Shaqrā' fortress fell to the Ottoman-Egyptian expeditionary force during the campaign against the Wahhābīs. BOA, HH. 19533 (1818).

basic tenets of Ottoman foreign policy, tenaciously upheld until the end of the empire.[23]

In much of the rest of the empire, we find a pattern of strong governors compelling the central government to grant them various degrees of autonomy. In Baghdad, successive governors appointed an ever-growing number of slaves (Mamluks) imported in this case from Georgia, to important positions in government. The able Süleyman Pasha, appointed by the central government in 1749 to stem the rising tide of disorder, did so with the help of a massive influx of slaves. Ömer Bey, who eventually succeeded him as governor, further institutionalized the Mamluk role in Baghdad, which came to resemble the Mamluk position in Egypt, particularly in terms of the extent of autonomy from the Ottoman center and the strong local impulse toward modernization. A later governor, also named Süleyman Pasha, employed one John Raymond, a British military adviser from India, to reform the local military organization.[24] Like Mehmed Ali in

[23] Mehmed Nâbi and Rumbeyoğlu Fahreddin, *Maskat Mes'elesi* (Istanbul: Matbaa-i Âmire, 1334 [1917]), pp. 5–6.

[24] *Tarih-i Cevdet*, 7, p. 289.

Egypt, the Mamluks of Baghdad expanded the area under their direct or indirect rule. In time, the area from Basra to Mosul fell under the control of semi-autonomous Mamluk governors allied to a powerful Mamluk bureaucratic class in Baghdad. The last Mamluk governor of Baghdad, Davud Pasha, was not defeated by the central government until 1831.

In Scutari in Albania, Kara Mahmud Pasha, a local governor whose grandfather Mehmed Pasha had established hereditary rule, went so far as to enter into cordial relations with Austria and Venice, the two archenemies of the Ottoman state during the last decade of the eighteenth century.[25] In southern Albania and northern Epirus, Ali Pasha of Tepelenë, a former brigand whose ruthless regime Lord Byron described as "lawless law,"[26] enjoyed a similar autonomy verging on independence. With the help of the French, to whom he promised that he would be their "best and most faithful ally," Ali Pasha managed to extend the area under his administration to the Peloponnese and Aetoloacarnania. Unlike his kinsman to the north, he worked against the Venetians.[27]

In Syria and modern-day Palestine the nature of local government and of relations with Istanbul hinged on the character of the man or group in power. The family governorship of the ʿAẓms in Damascus (beginning in the 1730s and continuing intermittently until the early nineteenth century) never questioned the authority of the imperial center.[28] The ʿAẓms' power over much of the Syrian hinterland rested on a strong local military and economic base coupled with a strategic partnership with the center: the family helped the central government keep the region in the Ottoman fold in return for a free hand in the conduct of local affairs. They were exceptionally adept at accommodating the changing expectations of the center while satisfying the demands of local elites and the broader populace. The ʿAẓms brought prosperity to Syria by increasing exports to Europe. A more independent local ruler emerged in Acre: Ẓāhir al-ʿUmar al-Zaydānī, who introduced an effective commercial monopoly system[29] later emulated by Mehmed Ali and the Ottoman center, forged independent trade deals with European consuls, straining ties with the imperial government. But the resulting economic prosperity garnered popular support for his rule. His army

[25] Ibid., 6, pp. 101ff.

[26] [George Gordon] Byron, *Childe Harold's Pilgrimage*, ed. A. H. Thompson (Cambridge: Cambridge University Press, 1931), p. 60.

[27] [Alphonse de Beauchamp], *The Life of Ali Pacha of Janina, Vizier of Epirus, Surnamed Aslan, or the Lion from Various Authentic Documents* (London: Lupton Relfe, 1822), pp. 68–9.

[28] See *al-Usra al-ʿAẓmīya*, ed. ʿAbd al-Qādir al-ʿAẓm (Damascus: Maṭbaʿat al-Inshāʾ, 1960), pp. 25ff.

[29] Thomas Philipp, *Acre: The Rise and Fall of a Palestinian City, 1730–1831* (New York: Columbia University Press, 2001), pp. 102ff, 128.

was notable for the role played in it by the Lebanese Shīʿites, now the military base of Ḥizballāh. His reign was followed by the iron rule of the dreaded Cezzar Ahmed Pasha (Aḥmad Pasha al-Jazzār, "the butcher") in the 1770s; his methods were so cruel that the locals named his rough successor Süleyman Pasha "al-ʿĀdil" ("the just"), by comparison. Unlike Ẓāhir al-ʿUmar, Ahmed Pasha, a Bosnian, did not have a local power base, but he succeeded in winning imperial favor by restoring order in Syria and weakening the notable houses. In return for his distinguished service, Ahmed Pasha was rewarded with noteworthy appointments, as governor first of Sidon and then of Damascus. His defense of Acre against Bonaparte earned him enormous fame. Once in power, Ahmed Pasha enhanced his authority by a policy of oppression and assiduous efforts to crush the independent power bases in the region, including that of the ʿAzms. Possessing a private army and navy, he ruled like an independent prince, although he never acquired popular support. Ahmed Pasha's deafness to orders from above and appeals from below made him tremendously unpopular with subjects and overlords alike.[30] Yet he remained in power until his death in 1804.

Abuse of imperially sanctioned power was rampant throughout the empire. In several regions, individuals actually obtained official appointments through the threat or use of force against the imperial authorities. In Vidin in 1795, Pazvandoğlu Osman, a former mercenary in the service of the Wallachian prince, took advantage of being the son of a former notable who had been executed by the central administration, and subjected a vast area in present-day Serbia and western Bulgaria by force, dismissing local administrators and installing his own men. Two years later, the central government dispatched an army to put an end to this situation, but Bonaparte's invasion of Egypt in 1798 compelled it to grant Pazvandoğlu Osman an imperial pardon and appoint him governor of Vidin with the rank of vizier.

In areas that had never fallen under direct Ottoman control, like Mount Lebanon, rival groups vied for power and recognition from Istanbul. The Bashīr clan in Lebanon reemerged victorious from a protracted period of internecine strife in the late seventeenth century. When, in 1788, Lebanese notables and other local leaders elected Bashīr Shihāb II as the new governor of Mount Lebanon,[31] the central government had no alternative but to recognize his rule (which he sustained, with brief interruptions, until 1840). As governor, Bashīr Shihāb II consistently resisted any Ottoman diktat: when Bonaparte attacked the empire in 1798, he declared his neutrality; and when İbrahim Pasha laid siege to Acre in 1832, he aided him. A similar situation existed in Ottoman Kurdistan, where rival tribal leaders fought

---

[30] *Tarih-i Cevdet*, 7, p. 47.
[31] Ibid., 6, p. 110.

each other for dominance without much interference from the center. Mere rumors of Ottoman troop mobilization were sufficient to trigger a revolt by a major Kurdish tribe.[32] Nevertheless, both in Lebanon and Kurdistan, local chieftains never went as far as the outright rejection of Ottoman suzerainty, and the Ottoman authorities carefully monitored the local political scene.

All the same, Ottoman understanding of the local dynamics of power was not always very accurate, as the following incident from the ostensibly vassal principality of Montenegro illustrates. In 1797, a man named Vinčić appeared at the imperial capital with a letter of introduction from the Ottoman ambassador to Prussia, claiming that he was a Montenegrin aristocrat duly elected by a local council. He furnished an election document, dated 1795, and promised to raise a 35,000-man army and collect the poll tax on behalf of the central government. The Ottoman authorities seriously entertained the idea of recognizing this person as the new ruler of Montenegro until the French ambassador informed them that he was a charlatan who had already attempted to dupe the French authorities by posing as a Croat prince.[33]

Even in the central provinces of Anatolia and Rumelia, imperial control was far from effective. Two social groups in particular gained considerable power vis-à-vis the state: local dynasts and notables. In many regions, local dynasts became so powerful that they exercised feudal control over large areas. Contemporaries termed such leaders "Mütegallibe," meaning usurpers or oppressors. Men such as Çaparoğlu Süleyman or Karaosmanzâde Ömer in Anatolia, or İsmail Bey of Serez in Rumelia, continued to contribute to military campaigns and did not challenge the authority of the state directly (e.g., by withholding taxes). In return, they secured the freedom to administer the territory under their control according to their desires, and often bequeathed their power to members of their own families.

The power of the *âyân*, or local notables, increased over the eighteenth century, as governors opted to appoint influential locals as tax collectors. A parallel development that reinforced this trend in 1726 was the end of the Ottoman practice of dispatching subgovernors from the center. This decision paved the way for the appointment of local notables as administrators to combat brigandage, safeguard tax collection, and recruit soldiers.[34] The notables thus emerged as a significant social class mediating between the central government and its subjects. Despite the official abolition of the title

---

[32] Ahmed Vâsıf, *Mehasinü'l-Âsâr ve Hakaikü'l-Ahbâr*, ed. Mücteba İlgürel (Ankara: Türk Tarih Kurumu Yayınları, 1994), p. 349.

[33] *Tarih-i Cevdet*, 6, pp. 274–7.

[34] Yücel Özkaya, *Osmanlı İmparatorluğu'nda Âyânlık* (Ankara: Türk Tarih Kurumu Yayınları, 1994), pp. 141–68.

âyân in 1786, notables—such as Tirsinikli İsmail and Alemdar Mustafa Pasha in Rumelia, and Cizyedârzâde Hüseyin of Bursa in Anatolia—continued to represent a powerful social group in the empire until the success of the centralization policies in the mid-nineteenth century. The concentration of power in the hands of local dynasts and notables brought about a de facto change in the land tenure system, compelling the government to agnize private ownership of land, albeit unofficially. This significantly altered the relationship between landholders and peasants, providing impetus for peasant revolts, particularly in the European provinces of the empire.

The Ottoman Legal System

Ottoman law was based on two major sources: traditional Islamic *sharī'a* law and sultanic law, the latter produced through legislation issued by the sultans. The sharī'a served as the sole base for adjudicating issues concerning individual rights, family law, inheritance, commerce, and the rights of foreign subjects. In practice, standard works of *fiqh* (canonical jurisprudence) were used to settle disputes on such matters. Although Ottoman practice employed Muslim fiqh as a penal code, imperial *kanunnâmes* (code books) were also used as a major reference in this field. Numerous *fatwās*, issued by the highest judicial authorities, invested the sultan with the authority to legislate based on the principle of protecting the public interest.[35] The exercise of the sultan's right to issue laws in areas outside the sharī'a led to the creation of a considerable body of law regulating administration, taxation, and international relations, as well as special rules for taxation and administration in the various provinces; these provincial regulations took local customs and traditions into account. The sultan, as legislator, could issue *yasaknâmes* (laws banning certain acts or establishing regulations for new circumstances), *adaletnâmes* (decrees requiring the authorities to act within the boundaries of the sharī'a, sultanic law, or custom), and decrees for implementation by *qāḍīs*. These accepted forms of *lex principis* (sometimes based on *ius commune*) generated the Ottoman *örfî* (customary, sultanic) law.

In theory, all laws and practices conformed to the sharī'a, and were applied by qāḍīs in a uniform manner throughout the empire. In practice, however, the dualistic character of the legal system, the different administrative regulations for the various provinces, and their somewhat arbitrary implementation resulted in uneven application of the law. This phenomenon was exacerbated by the seepage of power to the periphery, as qāḍīs

---

[35] Halil İnalcık, "Osmanlı Hukukuna Giriş: Örfi-Sultanî Hukuk ve Fatih'in Kanunları," *Ankara Üniversitesi Siyasal Bilgiler Fakültesi Dergisi* 13/2 (1958), pp. 104ff.

yielded to the authority of notables and imperial uniformity to local variation. One need not agree with Max Weber's depiction of *Kadijustiz* as the anti-thesis of Western legal formalism and substantive rationality to recognize that the uniform application of justice was severely disrupted by the rise of local notables. Another impediment to uniformity was the decline of the ulema as a class. As the foremost Ottoman court historian of the nineteenth century put it, religious scholars who could not even mount a coherent re-sponse to the challenge of Wahhābism[36] "existed only in name."[37] Selim III's angry remark—"May God help us and relieve us of our dependence on them!"[38]—attests to the waning respect for the ulema in official circles. The fragmentation of legal practice and the decline of legal practitioners con-tributed much to the disintegration of the empire as a whole.

In addition to the legislative latitude granted to the sultan, the Ottoman sharī'a tolerated the existence, within limits, of parallel systems of law ap-plicable to non-Muslims. Up to 1839, the Ottoman legal system recognized three major groups among the inhabitants of the empire: Muslims, *dhimmīs* (scriptuaries, or people of the Book, living under Muslim rule), and *musta'mins* (non-Muslim foreigners residing in the empire). The sharī'a applied to all issues involving Muslims. But when it came to the adjudication of internal matters, such as family law, non-Muslims had a choice: they could submit cases either to their own religious institutions (e.g., Christian ecclesiastical courts or Jewish rabbinical courts) or to sharī'a courts. By and large, non-Muslims preferred the former course of action. Cases between individuals of the same foreign nationality were settled according to the law of their country of origin by special magistrates located within their embassies or consulates. Legal conflicts between a non-Muslim foreigner and a Muslim were settled in sharī'a courts with the presence of dragomans.

THE OTTOMAN ECONOMY

At the turn of the nineteenth century, the Ottoman economy was still pre-mercantilist and agrarian. Circulation and use of money was mostly lim-ited to large towns. Like many other pre-industrial European economies, the Ottoman system was founded on local self-sufficiency, and state policy had a distinctly provisionist character. Production first satisfied local de-mand; any surpluses were either consumed by the state (especially the mil-itary) or sent to other provinces. The domestic and international customs

[36] *Tarih-i Cevdet*, 7, p. 195.
[37] Ibid., 1, p. 117.
[38] Ibid., 5, p. 31.

regime discouraged long-distance trade, including exports, while providing an incentive for local distribution. At the same time, the state encouraged the import of scarce products and protected the merchants concerned by means of capitulations. Not surprisingly, the combination of state-sponsored imports and restrictions on exports was producing soaring trade deficits by the eighteenth century, giving rise to strong pressures to borrow money.[39] The persistence of provisionism as the cornerstone of economic policy in the Ottoman Empire up to the middle of the nineteenth century stands out in contrast to Europe, where criticism of its tenets had already emerged by the end of the seventeenth century (e.g., Pierre le Pesant sieur de Boisguilbert's *Le détail de la France; la cause de la diminution de ses biens et la facilité du remède*, 1695), and sophisticated alternatives were being suggested in the eighteenth century (e.g., by the Physiocrats).

Because the Ottoman economy was founded on agriculture, the structure of land tenure lay at the heart of the Ottoman economic system. In principle, the state recognized three primary types of landholding: private property belonging to Muslims (*öşrî* land), private property belonging to non-Muslims (*haracî* land), and conquered land under state control (*mirî* land). But in practice the first two types were rare, and were largely confined to Syria, Arabia, and various Mediterranean islands. Registration of a piece of land as *haracî* by a non-Muslim was irrevocable, even if the owner subsequently converted to Islam or sold the land to a Muslim. The same rigidity applied to land registered as *öşrî*. But almost all of the Ottoman heartland was state-owned property, on which peasants worked as tenants. Beginning in the sixteenth century, and based on some famous fatwās of Şeyhülislâm Mehmed Ebu'ssu'ud Efendi, all conquered territory here was considered state property. In practice, however, there was no consistent policy on the question whether landowners in conquered lands should be allowed to retain ownership of their property. Practical and economic considerations usually determined the status of a particular piece of land. For instance, although the state recognized the islands of Mitilíni and Crete as privately owned land belonging to non-Muslims, it considered Cyprus to be state-owned land.

Roughly 20 percent of Ottoman agricultural land belonged neither to private individuals nor to the state, but rather to pious foundations (*waqfs*). These foundations were established by sultans, members of the royal family, statesmen, ulema, and other wealthy individuals. The income from land (and buildings) owned by the foundations was earmarked for social purposes and for cash foundations that operated like banks. Although the state did receive a minuscule portion of the income derived from foundations

[39] Mehmet Genç, *Osmanlı İmparatorluğunda Devlet ve Ekonomi* (Istanbul: Ötüken, 2000), pp. 88–9.

(the *divanî* share), the control of a huge part of the empire's agricultural land by charitable institutions represented a serious limitation on state revenue. Sultan Mustafa III once remarked that his forefather Bayezid II (r. 1481–1512) had "turned everything into pious foundations."[40] Beginning in the nineteenth century, the state strove to centralize the administration of pious foundations (eventually through the Ministry of Imperial Pious Foundations, established in 1826), and sought to transform vast amounts of land into state property by recourse to sometimes dubious legal arguments.

On state-owned lands, the most significant structural feature of the Ottoman economy was the ancient timar system, through which the state funneled agricultural taxes directly to its agents and the military. This institution continued to decay, but it still functioned, and as late as 1777 and 1790 the center was still producing proposals to reform it.[41] By the eighteenth century, a substantial portion of state-owned (mirî) land that had been distributed as timars had in effect become private land. In the later seventeenth and eighteenth centuries, a significant portion of the remaining timars was transferred to *mültezims*, who practiced a system of public tax farming (*iltizam*). This did little to halt the steady decline in state revenues.

In 1695, in an effort to improve efficiency and increase revenue, the state launched a major change in the method of tax collection. Instead of allocating the collection of public revenues (including various taxes, stamp duties, and customs revenues) to members of the ruling class for life, the state began to sell these rights to revenue farmers, usually gentry and urban notables, at public auctions. By doing so, the state extended prerogatives hitherto reserved for officialdom to the public at large, in an attempt to foster shared interests with a large, geographically dispersed sector of the population.[42] As a result of this new practice, called *malikâne*, between 1698 and 1774 the number of tax revenue farms administered through the chief accounting office increased by 209 percent and their revenues rose by 88 percent. In the same period, the tax revenues sold to tax farmers increased by 1,400 percent.[43] By 1780, however, the major sources of state income available for auction were largely exhausted, and investors displayed little interest in the minor public revenues pathetically put on the market by the state.[44]

[40] *Tarih-i Cevdet*, 8, p. 277.

[41] Ibid., 2, pp. 85, 317–24; and 5, pp. 289–91.

[42] Ariel Salzmann, "An Ancien Régime Revisited: 'Privatization' and Political Economy in the Eighteenth-Century Ottoman Empire," *Politics and Society* 21/4 (December 1993), p. 409.

[43] Genç, *Devlet ve Ekonomi*, p. 117.

[44] Yavuz Cezar, *Osmanlı Maliyesinde Bunalım ve Değişim Dönemi: XVIII. yy dan Tanzimat'a Mali Tarih* (Istanbul: Alan Yayıncılık, 1986), p. 104.

Despite the advantages of the malikâne, the overall benefit of the system was cancelled out, for the most part, by the decline of central power and the concomitant reduction in the state's capacity to raise taxes. As a result, tax income increased by only 10 percent between 1700 and 1800, during a period in which prices quadrupled.[45] Inflationary pressures naturally gave rise to social discontent. Moreover, the malikâne often had a negative impact on local economies, because the farming out of many local fiscal resources by the central treasury deprived many provincial administrations of traditional sources of income.

A major debilitating factor for the Ottoman economy was war. Loss of territory and population reduced available sources of revenue; enormous war indemnity payments, such as the 7.5 million *gurushes* paid to Russia in 1775—equivalent to almost half of all state revenues for that year—bloated expenditure; and the need for a bigger and better military required an increasing flow of funds for investment and upkeep.

To address these economic problems, the state adopted new commercial, fiscal, and monetary policies. Adjusting trade imbalances was probably the most difficult problem for the Ottoman authorities to control. The state's ability to restrict imports was severely hampered by the capitulations granted to foreign powers. Accordingly, the state attempted to limit exports, reasoning that every bit of local production was needed to support domestic needs. But this too proved next to impossible to achieve. Many measures directed at the trade deficit were predictably futile: an imperial decree of 1783 requesting that officials and citizens of the empire wear only domestic products had little effect,[46] while restrictions on exports led only to a dramatic rise in the smuggling of banned products to Europe.

In order to increase state revenues, the government established new internal customs duties. To the dismay of the population, many new taxes, initially introduced as extraordinary wartime taxes, turned into regular dues after the war in question was over. State confiscations of property and assets became increasingly common during times of war or economic crisis. From the late eighteenth century, the state no longer restricted sequestrations to the estates of deceased members of the ruling *askerî* class, and began to seize the property of dead businessmen as well.[47] In 1775 the state resorted to internal borrowing, creating a hefty debt in a short period of time. Although the threat of economic instability led the government to begin liquidation of this debt in 1792, the French occupation of Egypt prompted a fresh round of domestic borrowing. To cover the deficit, the

[45] Genç, *Devlet ve Ekonomi*, p. 27.
[46] *Tarih-i Cevdet*, 2, pp. 245, 359–60.
[47] Cezar, *Osmanlı Maliyesi*, p. 110, n. 86.

state was compelled for the first time to consider borrowing money from foreign powers. But efforts to secure a foreign loan in 1784–86 proved inconclusive.[48] By 1812, annuities paid on the internal debt had reached 25 percent of total revenues.[49]

Attempts to restrain expenditure complemented the efforts to increase state revenues in order to balance the budget. The greater part of the budget went on salaries and other compensation payments to state officials and members of the armed forces; the second principal item was expenditure on military provisions and equipment. The traditional principle of fiscal responsibility restricted budgetary sources to current revenues, thereby preventing irresponsible allocations of future income. The most prevalent drawback of this basic principle was that it made budgets enormously sensitive to the annual vicissitudes of production. Ottoman budgetary planning already suffered from the unpredictability of war, which always sparked an extraordinary rise in spending, and the unforeseeable lifespan of sultans, whose accession ceremonies were accompanied by enormous outlays of *cülûs bahşişi* (accession money) and salary raises.[50] Renewal of state licenses and certificates under the new sultan's name eventually covered part of the accession costs, but failure to grant these traditional gifts on time often resulted in Janissary revolts. Another tool used by the state to control spending was the practice of "public purchases," which allowed the state to buy goods at a special price set by the government; this price was always lower than the market price, and sometimes even below the cost of production.[51] But this practice naturally led producers to cut supplies, lower quality, or even abandon the production of goods needed by the state.

Inefficient purchasing by the state was only one of an array of factors working against the Ottoman manufacturing sector in the eighteenth century. Persistent deficits led to minuscule investment, the provisionist nature of the economy thwarted a shift to mass production, the capitulations favored foreign merchandise, efficient European manufacturing meant intensified competition from cheaper European products, war losses entailed the shrinking of the domestic market, difficulties in technology transfer stunted productivity growth, and poor infrastructure inhibited

---

[48] Ahmed Vâsıf, *Mehâsinü'l-Âsâr*, pp. 191–2; *Tarih-i Cevdet*, 5, pp. 295–6.

[49] Genç, *Devlet ve Ekonomi*, p. 192.

[50] During the time frame covered by this study, Sultan Mustafa III paid accession money but not salary increases; Sultans Abdülhamid I and Selim III disbursed neither due to ongoing military campaigns; and Sultan Mustafa IV was forced by the rebellious Janissaries who had put him on the throne to make an accession payment, despite the dire financial situation prevailing at the time. He was the last Ottoman sultan to grant accession money.

[51] Genç, *Devlet ve Ekonomi*, p. 89.

transportation and development. Although the state invested heavily in military-related industries, such as silk and wool for the production of sail-cloth for the navy, the overall picture from the mid-eighteenth century on-ward was one of stagnation and decline relative to Europe. Many Ottoman manufacturers were bankrupt by the end of the century.[52]

Debasement remained the mainstay of Ottoman monetary policy. In the late seventeenth century an experiment with minting cheaper copper coins along with the traditional silver proved unsuccessful, primarily because provincial suspicion of the new coinage precipitated the flight of gold and silver to the periphery and the accumulation of copper in the cities. The Ottoman silver currency, the *akçe*, which contained 0.860 grams silver in 1469, had only 0.290 in 1600, 0.132 in 1700, 0.121 in 1750, and 0.050 in 1801.[53] In 1789, a major devaluation marked the beginning of a forty-year run of debasement that fed rising inflation. Despite repeated attempts (dating back to the late seventeenth century) to preserve monetary unity and ban the circulation of foreign gold coins,[54] at the turn of the nineteenth century all kinds of European and North African coins (and their counterfeits) circulated freely in the Ottoman market. In a classic illustration of Gresham's law, the more valuable gold and silver coins flowed out from the central lands of the empire to Egypt, Iran, and India. To combat the flood of foreign gold and silver and enrich the Ottoman mint, the state often resorted to the collection and confiscation of gold and silver artifacts for coin production. In 1789, the government sought and obtained a fatwā declaring the use of any kind of gold and silver artifacts (with the exception of women's jewelery) to be "un-Islamic."[55]

OTTOMAN SOCIETY

Straddling three continents and encompassing an extraordinary diversity of ethnic and religious groups, the Ottoman Empire at the turn of the century was perhaps the most cosmopolitan state in the world. On paper, the major division among the empire's estimated 30 million subjects was that between the ruling askerî class and the subjects, the *re'aya*. The ruling class had three components: the ulema, the bureaucracy, and the army—itself

---

[52] Ibid., pp. 226ff.

[53] Şevket Pamuk, *İstanbul ve Diğer Kentlerde 500 Yıllık Fiyatlar ve Ücretler, 1469–1998* (Ankara: Devlet İstatistik Enstitüsü, 2000), pp. 14–16.

[54] Mehmed Raşid, *Tarih-i Raşid*, 2 (Istanbul: s.n., [1865]), pp. 383–4.

[55] *Tarih-i Cevdet*, 5, pp. 33–4.

composed of the janissaries and timariot cavalry.[56] Society at large was traditionally organized along religious lines, the principal division being that between Muslim and non-Muslim. An estimated 80 percent of the population was rural. The overwhelming majority of the subjects was illiterate.

The Muslim community, though far from monolithic, was regarded as the dominant one by virtue of the Islamic ideology of the state. Although there are no reliable population figures, Muslims clearly formed a majority over non-Muslims. Most Ottoman Muslims were Sunnīs who belonged to various legal schools and Ṣūfī orders; the rest of the Muslim population was a colorful mix of mainstream Shīʿites, Alevîs, and less significant sects (considered Muslim only by non-Muslims) such as the Druzes and the Nuṣayrīs. Among the Christians of the empire, various strands of Eastern Christianity predominated, comprising almost one-third of the subjects. Armenians, belonging to the Armenian Apostolic (Lusavorchakan) Church, existed in significant numbers. The Jewish population was small but prominent. Pockets of Roman Catholics, Assyrians, and other Christian groups existed in different parts of the realm. The major ethnic groups were Albanians, Arabs, Armenians, Bulgarians, Greeks, Kurds, Serbs, Turks, and Vlachs.

Despite this ethnic diversity, faith constituted the primary organizing principle of traditional Ottoman society. Thus an ethnic Albanian, for example, could belong to the Muslim, Greek Orthodox, or Roman Catholic community depending on religious affiliation. In certain cases—as in the Muslim areas of Bosnia—religion fused with ethnicity to produce identity. But no ethnic consciousness comparable to modern nationalism existed to an appreciable degree within any of the communities of the empire. In any event, the religious order of society was to crumble over the course of the nineteenth century in the face of the rise of ethnic nationalism. Nationalist leaders would then attempt to sever ties to their larger religious communities and form national religious institutions. Bulgarian nationalists, for example, would struggle against the domination of the Greek Orthodox Patriarchate and form the autocephalous Bulgarian Exarchate.

The political, military, and economic instability of the empire aided the spread of brigandage throughout its domains. The deterioration of the timar system resulted in the release of numerous rural laborers, who became itinerant workers drafted into temporary military service by the state whenever

---

[56] Others who were considered members of the ruling class included freed slaves and concubines of the sultan, freed slaves and concubines of a member of the askerî class and their children, and individuals who could prove descent from the Prophet Muḥammad through his two grandsons. A widow of a member of this class could be considered an askerî only if her father was a member and she had not remarried.

necessary. In times of political and social upheaval, many of these *levend*s resorted to brigandage, and large bands of them terrified populations mainly in Anatolia and Rumelia.[57] The most organized banditry took place during the Mountaineers Revolt of 1791–1808 in Rumelia, when former soldiers and deserters, in league with local notables, subjected large areas to their rapacious rule, sacking major towns and rendering transportation insecure.[58]

The economic and political problems of the empire, as well as the new policies formulated to resolve them, rendered the classical social structure of Ottoman society obsolete. In particular, the non-Muslims gained new power and influence, undermining the traditional ascendancy of the Muslims. The stark division between the Muslim ruling class and the non-Muslim re'aya became increasingly meaningless in a state in which Greek subjects now controlled much of Ottoman naval transportation, with ships sailing under the Russian flag, large numbers of non-Muslims engaged in commerce as "privileged merchants" under foreign protection, and many other non-Muslims obtained tax farms through state auctions. Finally, the emergence of romantic proto-nationalist ideas among the non-Muslim elites of the empire was to render the administration of the non-Muslim subjects more difficult than it had ever been before. But the significance of proto-nationalist ideas in the instigation of early nineteenth-century revolts should not be exaggerated. Neither the new constitution project of Rigas Velestinlis-Pheraios (1797), which envisioned for the subject peoples of European Turkey a Pan-Balkan government based on the principles of the French Revolution, nor the Slavo-Bulgarian history of Paisii Hilandarski (1762), who celebrated the glorious Slavic past of the Bulgarians, can be considered true progenitors of national liberation. Nevertheless, in a time of political, social, and economic upheaval, their ideas could furnish a firm basis from which to launch and legitimize rebellion and separatism, and they were so employed by enterprising rebels. Later nationalist reconstructions turned such thinkers into heroic popular leaders and ideologists of nation-states. In present-day Bulgaria, the image of Hilandarski adorns two-*Leva* banknotes, presenting him as the man who envisioned the modern Bulgarian nation-state, while that of Rigas Velestinlis-Pheraios figures on ten-cent Greek Euro coins.[59] At the time, such recognition would have seemed absurd.

---

[57] Mustafa Cezar, *Osmanlı Tarihinde Levendler* (Istanbul: Güzel Sanatlar Akademisi Yayınları, 1965), pp. 238ff.

[58] Yücel Özkaya, *Osmanlı İmparatorluğunda Dağlı İsyanları, 1791–1808* (Ankara: A. Ü. Dil ve Tarih-Coğrafya Fakültesi Yayınları, 1983), pp. 20ff.

[59] The Bank of Greece justifies its choice thus: "[Rigas Velestinlis-Pheraios] was a fervent defender of the movement for Greece and a martyr of the then-enslaved nation." Bank of Greece, "The Greek Themes on Euro Coins," www.bankofgreece.gr/en/euro/eurocoins.asp.

MATERIAL CULTURE

In a vast area encompassing myriad peoples, traditions, climates, population densities, and economic conditions, material culture was far from uniform. A look at material culture in Istanbul may convey some idea of the situation in the larger urban centers of the empire. Life in rural areas was, of course, very different.

In an attempt to provide a more vivid reconstruction of the physical environment surrounding the residents of Istanbul in the second half of the eighteenth century, I examined the inventories of estates left by members of the askerî class who died between 1751 and 1801.[60] These inventories, found in religious court registers, offer a rare glimpse into the homes of the lower-middle-, middle-, and upper-class in the capital. Overall, they reflect the modest and utilitarian attitudes of their owners. They also reveal that material culture remained remarkably constant during the second half of the eighteenth century. Although various imperial edicts restricting female clothing attest to shifts in fashion,[61] for instance, it is difficult to detect major changes in clothing types or household materials and implements. It was only from the mid-nineteenth century onward that the pace of change began to pick up in the urban centers of the empire, especially after the emergence of press advertisements.

[60] I selected a sample of 204 individuals who died between 1751 and 1801 (four for each year) from among the registers of the *askeri kassam* (distributor of the inheritance shares of the askerî class members) of the city of Istanbul. The data come from the following volumes of records in the İstanbul Müftülük Arşivi, ŞS volumes: 125, 127–48, 150–52, 154, 159, 162, 167, 170, 173, 176, 178–93, 195, 203, 209, 211, 215, 226, 239, 243, 251, 256, 263, 269, 274, 276, 278, 281, 283, 285, 289, 291, 293, 297, 298, 302, 304, 308, 313, 317, 320, 322, 326–7, 329–30, 336, 338–9, 341, 343, 346, 351, 357, 363, 368, 373, 377, 380, 382, 386, 388, 390, 392, 395–6, 403–4, 410, 413, 417, 420, 426, 429, 432, 436, 440, 442, 447, 451–2, 458, 462, 468, 473, 478, 483, 487, 491, 493, 496–98, 501, 504, 507, 511, 514, 516, 523, 527, 531, 536, 540, 544, 549, 551, 556, 558, 560–61, 563, 565, 572, 576–7, 580, 582–3, 586, 590–91, 598, 601, 604, 608, 614–15, 618, 622, 624–5, 628, 631, 635, 639, 643–4, 647–8, 653–4, 660–61, 667, 672, 676, 679, 684, 687, 689, 691, 694, 696, 701, 707, 710, 715–16, 718, 720, 734, 736–8, 740, and 743–4. The sample includes one individual from each of these registers. I selected at random 34 people from each of the following six estate size categories: less than 10,000 akçes; between 10,000 and 50,000 akçes; 50,001 to 100,000 akçes; 100,001 to 140,000 akçes; 140,001 to 300,000 akçes; and more than 300,001 akçes. The aggregate wealth of these 204 individuals was 32,523,871 akçes. The cumulative value of their landed property was 7,838,253 akçes, or 24.1% of their collective net worth. Cash and loans to others totaled 13,334,782 akçes, or 41% of the total, while slaves and concubines accounted for 487,858 akçes, or 1.5% of the total. The physical belongings of the individuals in question (including animals) amounted to 10,862,978 akçes, which is 33.4% of the total value of the estates.

[61] See, for example, an imperial decree dated June 22, 1792 in Ahmet Refik [Altınay], *Hicrî On Üçüncü Asırda Istanbul Hayatı, 1200–1255* (Istanbul: Istanbul Matbaacılık, 1932), p. 4.

Middle-class and lower-middle-class residents of Istanbul tended to own simple clothing, extremely rudimentary furniture, and few personal items. Household contents were simple and easy to move. Sparse furnishings suited not only the traditional lifestyle of the people but also an architectural style that emphasized wooden structures vulnerable to fire. Living-room seating in an average middle-class house included a large cushion for the master of the house and a mattress with cushions and pillows for all other inhabitants and guests. Sleeping arrangements consisted of simple cotton mattresses; these were folded for storage during the day to save space. Coffers and basket boxes served dual purposes as seats and storage containers for garments. Meals were eaten sitting on the floor and required little more than a piece of cloth (or a tray in some upper-class houses) on which to place the pot. With the exception of the upper classes, people ate their meals from the same pot using spoons; dishes were rarely used, obviating the need for cupboards. Chairs were extremely rare and were owned mainly by the more affluent. That most of the objects in the possession of all but the rich were heavily used is attested by the fact that overwhelming numbers of the items in estate inventories were marked as worn out (*köhne*).

Most physical possessions were of domestic origin. Exceptions tended to be luxury items, such as velvet from Iran and India, high-quality furs from Russia, and select British garments. Catalogs of household items demonstrate an impressive flow of trade within the empire, with brand names closely associated with regional expertise: knives, sweaters, and other clothing from Damascus, shawls from North Africa, pillows from Amasya, silk and cushions from Bursa, floor mats from Salonica, face towels from Mosul, and purses from Yambol.

Decorative art was rare in Muslim houses and was generally limited to framed works of calligraphy and miniatures. Upper-class mansions often featured other traditional art forms, such as *ebru*, the Ottoman art of making marbled paper, and decorated tiles. Although non-Muslim houses were not subject to the iconoclastic prohibitions of Islam, as a rule they too contained little art. Upper-class Orthodox households constituted an important exception, in that they often possessed gilded icons. In terms of objects of utility, however, the inventories reveal a surprising degree of uniformity across social strata. The difference in clothing among the various classes, for example, turned on quality, not the type of garment. Apparently, nearly everyone in the capital owned some sort of fur: lower-middle-class people tended to wear robes partially lined with cheap fur (generally white or black cat), while members of the middle-class wore inexpensive fur robes (mostly rabbit and squirrel), and the rich wore higher quality furs such as ermine, fox, pine marten, and sable, depending on their position in high society.

An important determinant of material culture was the combined impact of religion, state regulation, and tradition. In a society organized along strictly religious lines, identity was closely linked to physical markers, especially clothing. The dominant faith, for instance, determined the color codes appropriate for non-Muslims, stipulating which color of robe or shoe a scriptuary was forbidden to wear, such as bright green robes or yellow shoes. As members of a privileged religious class entitled to bear arms, Muslims typically owned various types of weapons, ranging from daggers to rifles. Sartorial regulations also stipulated the type of headgear to be worn by a Muslim male, while imperial decrees reserved certain luxury garments, such as sable and lynx furs, to the imperial family, high-ranking bureaucrats, and ulema. The guidelines changed from time to time, as did the level of enforcement. For example, the Ottoman Muslim religious establishment of the empire forbade the ownership of silver and gold objects by Muslim males. Exploiting this prohibition, many sultans issued decrees ordering subjects to hand over to the imperial mint all silver and gold objects other than women's jewelry. However, estate inventories prove that many Muslim men possessed silver watches, inkstands, plates, and knives in contravention of such directives. Similarly, state restrictions on tobacco use seem to have been ignored, at least in private. On the other hand, Islamic traditions[62] forbidding non-Muslims to ride on a beast or in a horse-drawn carriage past a pedestrian Muslim, although unevenly enforced, did reduce ownership of riding animals and carts by Christians and Jews.

Religion affected material culture in other ways as well. Most Muslims, for instance, owned prayer rugs as well as ewers and bowls for ablution. The strict timetables of Islamic ritual necessitated private means of chronometry, which were in fact ubiquitous. Watches, quadrants, and hourglasses were commonplace, supplementing state-sponsored mechanisms of timekeeping.

The following are lists of the belongings of ten individuals, selected from among different professions, classes, and age groups so as to provide a taste of the material culture of the Ottoman capital (without any pretensions to statistical significance).[63] The inventories of the first five were recorded in Hicrî 1164 (1750–51), while those of the others were registered in Hicrî 1215 (1800–1801). In the Ottoman system, the total worth of a given estate was equal to the aggregated worth of all possessions of the deceased, including physical belongings, property, cash savings, loans to other individuals, and slaves and concubines. This was different from the total

---

[62] Specifically, the Covenant of the Second Caliph 'Umar and the *hadīth* stating "*al-Islām yaʿlū wa-la yuʿlā ʿalayhi*" (Islam overtops, but is not overtopped).

[63] All of the inventories for the year Hicrî 1164 (1750–51) were given in akçes. The inventories for the year Hicrî 1215 (1800–1801) were given either in akçes or in gurushes and paras. For purposes of rough comparison, I converted all these values to 1998 U.S. dollars by using the ratios provided in Pamuk, *İstanbul ve Diğer Kentlerde 500 Yıllık Fiyatlar ve Ücretler*, pp. 28–9 in accordance with the following parities: 1 akçe = 0.15 U.S. dollars in 1750–51; 1 akçe = 0.068 U.S. dollars in 1800–1801; 1 gurush = 5.81 U.S. dollars in 1800–1801.

scheduled for distribution to heirs, which the executor (*askerî kassam*) determined after subtracting funeral expenses (women's funeral expenses were paid by their husbands), outstanding debt, execution fees, and transaction dues. In the case of Janissaries, one-tenth of the estate was given to the Janissary establishment.

Summary Estate Inventories from Hicrî 1164 (1750–51)

1. Sheikh Abdülkerim Efendi, son of Abdullah, resident at the Hüseyin Ağa Medrese. The total worth of the estate is 5,905 akçes [$886]. The estate covered only the funeral expenses, transaction dues, and outstanding debt of the deceased. Recorded on June 6, 1751 (*İstanbul Müftülük Arşivi, ŞS* 130, f. 3a).

> 10 pieces of clothing (one quilted turban, a belt, a shirt, robes, trousers, handkerchiefs, and underwear)
> 3 personal items (one tobacco knife, some tobacco, and a copper inkstand)
> 3 household objects (two small carpets and a piece of a pillow)
> 9 pieces of hardware (one cleaning cup, copper food dishes, one knife, one pickaxe, one hatchet, a candlestick, and rags)

2. Molla Hasan, son of Ahmed, from Niğde in Anatolia, died at the Sofu Mehmed Pasha Medrese while staying there as a guest. The total worth of the estate is 11,587 akçes [$1,738]. Recorded on October 6, 1751 (*İstanbul Müftülük Arşivi, ŞS* 133, f. 10a).

> 7 books on religion, including a collection of verses from the Qur'ān
> 4 pieces of clothing (one fur, two robes, and a handkerchief)
> 8 personal items (one silver case, a watch, three inkstands, rags, a seal, and a saddle bag)
> 1 household item (pillow)
> 1 piece of hardware (a cup)

3. Watch-maker Baltacızâde İbrahim Ağa, son of Mehmed. The total worth of the estate is 50,400 akçes [$7,560]. Recorded on September 4, 1751 (*İstanbul Müftülük Arşivi, ŞS* 132, f. 54a).

> 8 books on religion, history, and a watch-making manual
> 25 pieces of clothing (three furs, one quilted turban, a silk cloak, a shawl, a shirt, trousers, robes, underwear, and handkerchiefs)
> 5 personal items (a quadrant to determine prayer times, a silver inkstand, a haircloth sack, a saddle bag, and a new silver watch)
> 3 pieces of hardware (one clock, a silver knife, and rags)
> 8 household objects and pieces of furniture (quilts, pillows, a mat, and a mattress for sitting on with pillows)

6 pieces of professional materials (four watches, watch-making tools in a coffer, and some copper)

4. Leather manufacturer Elhac Hüseyin, son of Mustafa. The total worth of the estate is 371,607 akçes [$55,741]. Recorded on March 12, 1751 (*İstanbul Müftülük Arşivi, ŞS* 127, f. 30a).

12 books on religion and grammar, including a Qurʾān
24 pieces of clothing (one quilted turban, a turban wrapper, two furs, a belt, a shawl, jackets, trousers, robes, underwear, a pair of boots, and handkerchiefs)
1 personal item (a pair of scissors)
31 household objects (mats, a cotton mattress, mattresses, pillows, five velvet pillows, two large cushions, quilts, quilt covers, a wooden coffer, and a chair)
1 piece of hardware (a candlestick)

5. Teenager Ayşe, daughter of medical doctor Mustafa Efendi. The total worth of the estate is 376,150 akçes [$56,423]. Recorded on August 23, 1751 (*İstanbul Müftülük Arşivi, ŞS* 135, f. 33a).

24 pieces of clothing (six furs, ornamented shirts, ornamented robes, dustcoats, an ornamented drawer band, a scarf, pieces of wool, and handkerchiefs)
13 personal items (pieces of gold, a gold belt, gold bracelets, gold jewelry ornamented with diamonds, pearls, and emeralds, jewels, a small towel, ornamented saddle bags)
9 household items (six wool cushions, one big cushion, a mat, and a quilt)
4 pieces of hardware (a copper tray, a ritual ablution bowl, a ewer, and a copper food dish)

Summary Estate Inventories from Hicrî 1215 (1800–1801)

1. Esseyyid Hasan Ağa, son of Abdullah, former chief inkstand-holder of the qāḍī of Istanbul, Ebubekir Paşazâde Ömer İzzet. The total worth of the estate is 182 gurushes 5 *paras* [$1,061]. Recorded on October 20, 1800 (*İstanbul Müftülük Arşivi, ŞS* 738, f. 13a).

3 books on religion and grammar, including a Qurʾān
35 pieces of clothing (two quilted turbans, two furs, shirts, trousers, handkerchiefs, a pair of light shoes, a pair of shoes, garment belts, and worn-out pieces of clothing)
8 personal items (one silver watch, a garment tobacco pouch, an amber set of worry beads, a pipe, a coffee cup, a comb cover, a saddle bag, and bars of soap)

5 household objects (one basketwork trunk, a mattress, a small prayer
rug, a quilt, and bed sheets)
1 piece of hardware (a knife)

2. Artashir Artoian, son of Yovhannēs, an Armenian syrup producer.
The total worth of the estate is 16,800 akçes [$1,142]. Recorded on March
13, 1801 (*İstanbul Müftülük Arşivi, ŞS* 740, f. 37b).

13 pieces of clothing (one fur, a fur waistcoat, robes, a shirt, a garment
belt, trousers, a fur cap, and worn-out pieces of clothing)
2 personal items (one pinchbeck watch and a gold ring)

3. Opium seller Elhac Ömer, son of Mehmed, son of Abdullah. The
total worth of the estate is 34,412 akçes [$2,340]. Recorded on December
10, 1800 (*İstanbul Müftülük Arşivi, ŞS* 738, f. 50b).

30 pieces of clothing (one quilted turban, six furs, two overcoats, a
shawl, a garment belt, robes, shirts, trousers, handkerchiefs, and a
pair of shoes)
9 household items (cushions, pillows, bed sheets, a small prayer rug, a
box, and coffers)
2 personal items (a rifle and a small sword)
2 pieces of hardware (a big knife and a copper brazier)
1 piece of professional material (some opium)

4. Hafız Hüseyin Efendi, son of İbrahim, a qāḍī who served in Rumelia.
The total worth of the estate is 679 gurushes and 9 paras [$3,950]. Re-
corded on September 5, 1800 (*İstanbul Müftülük Arşivi, ŞS* 738, f. 30a).

8 books, including a Qurʾān and a collection of verses from the Qurʾān,
and miscellaneous papers
30 pieces of clothing (one quilted turban, three furs, robes, trousers, a
pair of boots, light shoes, a garment belt, handkerchiefs, and caps)
23 personal items (one rifle, one rifle with barrel, a powder flask, a gun
powder measurement box, a pair of scissors, a worry bead, a cover,
a small bag for carrying verses from the Qurʾān, a reed pen sharp-
ener, an inkstand, a silver inkstand, a garment saddle and stirrup,
tobacco pouches, a tobacco cup, an ash tray, a quiver, a turban cover,
a turban holder, a leather saddle bag, a horse-hair sack, and a comb)
24 household objects (chairs, small prayer rugs, a fleece, quilts, bed
sheets, big cushions, pillows, mattresses, pillow covers, sacks, bottles,
a rose-bowl, a dessert spoon, a soup bowl, a framed inscription, and
a glass frame)
17 pieces of hardware (one pickaxe, a big knife, lanterns, a candlestick,
copper alloy, a copper brazier, a copper bucket, a coffee grinder, a
coffee cup, a coffee cup cover, ewers, a large bowl, a ladder, and rags)
1 item of material (some lumber)

5. Süleyman Ağa, son of Mehmed son of İsmail, a former Janissary officer, who later served as chief saddler. The total worth of the estate is 132,510 akçes [$9,011]. Recorded on August 28, 1800 (*İstanbul Müftülük Arşivi*, ŞS 744, f. 2b).

2 books (a Qur'ān and a collection of verses from the Qur'ān)
22 pieces of clothing (quilted turbans, two furs, robes, shirts, garment belts, handkerchiefs, waistcoats, garment waist-strings)
6 personal items (one silver watch, a comb, a tobacco case, garment cases, and a saddle bag)
15 household items (pillows, cushions, bed sheets, a chair, and quilts)
21 pieces of hardware (one lamp, coffee cups, copper alloy, a glass lantern, braziers, a dessert spoon, silver coffee cup containers, knives, glass plates, a water-pipe, brass cups, an onion basket, a big wicker box, and candles)
1 item of material (some sand)

THE LANGUAGES OF THE EMPIRE

When in 1911 the Union of All Ottoman Elements, a public affairs committee, published an appeal to all Ottomans to form a united front,[64] it did so in nine languages: Ottoman Turkish, Arabic, Armenian, Bulgarian, Greek, Ladino, Serbian, Syriac (in two different scripts, Nestorian and Serta), and French. This appeal, although it left aside numerous languages in use in the Ottoman lands (such as Albanian, Kurdish, Rumanian, and numerous Caucasian tongues, to name a few of the most significant), gives some idea of the multilingualism of the empire. In such an environment, it is not surprising that bilingualism and trilingualism were common in urban centers. Like other polyethnic empires, the Ottoman state featured a central language of bureaucracy and ceremony based on the language of the founding ethnicity; this in turn was surrounded by a host of other languages, which were widely used although they had no official status. But unlike its counterparts in other empires, Ottoman Turkish was an elaborate language of governance that had evolved so extensively over the centuries that it was in fact no longer the same tongue as the vernacular Turkish spoken by the dominant ethnic group.

The evolution of Anatolian Turkish under Seljuq and Ottoman rule resembled the transformation of Urdu from a North Indian dialect to an imperial language during the Delhi Sultanate and Mughal Empire under the influence of Persian, Arabic, and, to a lesser degree, Turkish. Ottoman

[64] "İttihad-ı Anâsır-ı Osmaniye Hey'eti Tarafından Neşr Edilen Beyânnâmedir," *İttihad-ı Anâsır-ı Osmaniye* [July 23, 1911], pp. [1–4].

Turkish grew out of a dialect belonging to the Oğuz group, one of the major branches of the Turkic languages. It employed a predominantly Turkish syntax, but was heavily influenced by Persian and (initially through Persian) Arabic. It borrowed words not only from the subject peoples of the empire, but also from the languages of its neighbors, such as Italian (especially the Venetian dialect). Incorporation of all these borrowed words and structures from Indo-European and Semitic languages into the syntax of an Altaic tongue produced numerous complexities and problems of standardization. The Ottoman expansion into the Arab Near East and North Africa in the sixteenth century intensified the direct impact of Arabic on the development of Ottoman Turkish. Spanish influence, though never as strong as Italian, also grew, especially after the migration of Iberian Sephardic Jews to the empire in the aftermath of their expulsion from Spain in 1492.

The late eighteenth century marked the start of major borrowing from another European language, French. A memorandum from the significant year 1789 attests to the use of the term *status quo* (istatüko) by bureaucrats; the spelling makes it clear that this Latin phrase had entered Ottoman Turkish from a French source.[65] Thereafter, French words flooded the imperial language: words such as *avance* (avans), *civil* (sivil), *console* (konsol), *journal* (curnal), *manteau* (manto), *physiologique* (fizyolojik/fizyolociaî), and *politique* (politik), became commonplace in Ottoman usage. Admiration for French culture, and not just a shortage of vocabulary, underlay this process of importation; thus the deluge included words that had perfectly acceptable synonyms in Ottoman usage, such as *commission/komisyon* (hey'et), *docteur/doktor* (tabib), *dépôt/depo* (anbar), *dualiste/dualist* (süna'î), *économie/ekonomi* (iktisad), and *police/polis* (zabtiye, inzibat). Much of this borrowing was of course associated with the Ottoman reform movement, which drew upon French legal codes and fiscal regulations, opened the Ottoman market to European materials and techniques of production, and welcomed European advances in the sciences.

The process of linguistic mixing within the empire was a multidirectional one. In the border areas where Kurds and Turks lived side by side, for example, many Kurdish tribes adopted Turkish, while several Turkic tribes made Kurdish their tongue. The non-Turkish languages of the empire, such as Albanian, Bulgarian, and Greek, acquired Turkish loanwords, some of them originally from Arabic and Persian. Ottoman Turkish, in turn, picked up many words from Greek, particularly nautical terms. All the languages of the empire, from Hungarian and Albanian to various Slavic tongues and Armenian, contributed in different ways to the enrichment of the imperial language.

---

[65] [Mehmed] Sa'id, *Gazeteci Lisanı* (Istanbul: Sabah Matbaası, 1327 [1909]), p. 40.

By the nineteenth century, Ottoman Turkish, although not widely spoken, had become one of the richest and most complex languages in the world. Its use was limited to a highly educated portion of the ruling elite, who employed it to conduct affairs of state and to write bureaucratic documents, literary masterpieces, and scholarly works. Ottoman Turkish could be heard at government meetings, in literary conversations, at poetry recitals, and in scholarly conventions; however, even those who mastered the language did not speak it in the market or at home, where it would not have been understood. For Ottoman Turkish was unintelligible to an uneducated native speaker of Turkish. In fact, due to its heavy debt to other languages, Ottoman Turkish was often more comprehensible to non-Turkish intellectuals than to Turks. Only fellow bureaucrats across the empire could follow the stilted language used in the documents of Ottoman officialdom; a seventeenth-century "Turkish" *divan* (a collection of poems composed in rhymes running through the entire alphabet) was more intelligible to a literate Iranian than to a common Turk; an educated native speaker of Arabic would have had a better chance of making sense of a scholarly essay on religion than a simple Turk, while a Greek or Venetian could figure out more words in a naval instruction manual than a Turk who lived far from the sea. In a way, Ottoman resembled Latin as used in medieval or early modern Europe. It supplanted Persian, which had served as the literary language of the cultured upper classes during the first three centuries of the empire. The only exception to this displacement of Persian among the elite was the Kurdish upper class in the autonomous regions, where Persian persisted longer.[66] Those who used the Ottoman language were not necessarily Turks. Rather, they constituted the educated upper classes of a variety of Ottoman groups. Thus, to a certain extent the language formed a transnational link bonding elites together within the empire and alienating them collectively from their respective peoples. Not even all members of the bureaucracy mastered the complexities of the imperial idiom. The gradual expansion of the machinery of government and its concomitant evolution from a tiny elite force to a vast cadre of bureaucrats, beginning in the nineteenth century, exacerbated this problem. One maladroit speaker of the language made it to the position of grand vizier in 1878. Even though he had a fair command of written Arabic and French, his underlings could not resist making fun of his Ottoman Turkish.[67]

[66] For instance, the Kurdish rebel leader Bedirhan Bey did not know any Turkish and in 1846 negotiated the conditions of his surrender in Persian. Since he quoted verses from Khayyām when he later had an audience of the sultan, his mastery of Persian may be considered firm. See *Tarih-i Lûtfî*, 8 (Istanbul: Sabah Matbaası, 1328 [1910]), pp. 143, 503.

[67] İbnülemin Mahmud Kemal İnal, *Osmanlı Devrinde Son Sadrıazamlar*, 6 (Istanbul: Millî Eğitim Basımevi, 1940), p. 939. This grand vizier was Hayreddin Pasha of Tunisia, who served between December 4, 1878 and July 29, 1879.

The Ottoman state never sought to impose Turkish on subject peoples. Even those conquered peoples who adopted Islam did not forsake their traditional languages. For instance, both Serbian Orthodox and Catholic converts continued to speak in Serbo-Croatian in Bosnia. In fact, Pomaks (Bulgarian converts to Islam) employed fewer Turkish words than their brethren who had chosen to remain Christian. Some ethno-religious groups, when outnumbered by Turks, did accept the Turkish vernacular through a gradual process of acculturation. While the Greeks of the Peloponnese, Thessaly, Epirus, Macedonia, Thrace, and the west Anatolian littoral continued to speak and write in Greek, the Greeks of Cappodocia (Karaman) spoke Turkish and wrote Turkish in Greek script. Similarly, a large majority of the Armenians in the empire adopted Turkish as their vernacular and wrote Turkish in Armenian characters, all efforts to the contrary by the Mkhitarist order notwithstanding. The first novels published in the Ottoman Empire in the mid-nineteenth century were by Armenians and Cappodocian Greeks; they wrote them in Turkish, using the Armenian and Greek alphabets.

In areas heavily populated by Turks, vernacular Turkish naturally became the lingua franca even without state-sponsored promotion or imposition. These regions included central, western, and northeastern Anatolia, the eastern parts of Rumelia, and various parts of the provinces of Aleppo, Mosul, and al-Raqqa (Rakka). In the Balkans, the impact of centuries of Byzantine administration was not so easily effaced. As a result, Greek remained both the language of culture among the upper classes—whether Bulgarian, Macedonian, Vlach, Greek, or Orthodox Albanian—and the lingua franca of the major trade centers, coastal regions, and islands, where ethnic Greeks predominated. For instance, two upper-class Bulgarian merchants could have the following exchange in three languages at a café in Varna: "Dobrutro vi, gospodine" (Bulgarian for "Good morning, Sir"), "Ulan, Bulgar burada yok, 'Καλημέρα' desene!" (Turkish for "Hey, fellow, there is no Bulgarian here, say 'Καλημέρα'!" [Greek for "good morning"])[68] A second factor that abetted the retention of Greek was the state-sanctioned authority of the Greek Patriarchate over eastern Orthodoxy. The use of Greek as the liturgical language and the appointment of ethnic Greeks to important positions within the church hierarchy solidified the bond between Orthodoxy and the Greek language, despite occasional protests from Orthodox speakers of Slavic tongues and Arabic. For instance, even in the mid-nineteenth century, the Greek Patriarchate's bishops of Sofia would usually communicate with the Bulgarian laity in Greek. On important occasions, however, bishops would switch to Turkish, addressing their flock

[68] I[van] A[ndraev] Bogorov, *Niakolko dena razkhodka po bŭlgarskite mesta* (Bucharest: K. N. Radulescu, 1868), p. 53.

in this language when seeking to impose heavier church taxes and fees on them.[69]

As the language of the Qur'ān, Arabic was taught in Muslim schools of all levels throughout the empire, though knowledge of the Arabic literary language was of little practical use. In the Arab Near East and North Africa, vernacular Arabic continued to be the lingua franca, although the bureaucracy and the Turco-Mamluk elite in Mamluk Egypt and Iraq spoke the imperial language. As late as the first half of the nineteenth century, official Egyptian documents and even the official state gazette (*Vekayi'-i Mısriyye*, established in 1828) were published both in Ottoman Turkish and in Arabic.[70]

One might say that the empire had one imperial language for the bureaucratic elite (Ottoman Turkish), three major lingua francas (Turkish, Arabic, and Greek), and a host of local languages split into a variety of dialects. The absence of widely read publications perpetuated the linguistic fragmentation of the empire. The persistence of local dialects was especially evident in heavily tribal communities lacking a strong literary culture, where difficulties in communication were most apparent. For instance, a speaker of the mainstream Albanian Tosk dialect (not to mention a speaker of Arvanítika, a subdialect of Tosk spoken by Albanians in the Peloponnese and Epirus) would encounter grave difficulties in conversation with a speaker of Geg, the other major Albanian dialect. The adoption of the Latin, Greek, and Arabic alphabets by Albanians of different faiths only complicated matters further. Similarly, some Kurdish dialects were mutually incomprehensible to such a degree that locals considered them to be independent languages. At the end of the eighteenth century, this linguistic fragmentation corresponded to the general political state of the Ottoman empire.

In the nineteenth century a process of standardization, affecting all Ottoman languages, took place across the empire. Some, which had been all but reduced to the status of defunct ecclesiastical languages, were revitalized and became popular once again. The leveling of language affected Ottoman Turkish as well, although the infiltration of French also continued apace. State-led efforts to standardize and simplify the imperial language, amplified by the emergence of a lively press, the centralization of the bureaucracy, and the adoption of a more inclusive state ideology—Ottomanism—made Ottoman Turkish accessible to more people than ever before. Nevertheless, the language of government did not penetrate below the upper middle classes of society.

---

[69] See Petŭr Dinekov, *Sofiia prez XIX vek do osvobozhdenieto na Bŭlgariia, 9: Materiali za istoriiata na Sofiia* (Sofia: Bŭlgarski arkheologicheski institut, 1937), p. 147.

[70] Ekmeleddin İhsanoğlu, *Mısır'da Türkler ve Kültürel Mirasları* (Istanbul: IRCICA, 2006), pp. 67ff. and 253ff.

INTELLECTUAL LIFE

The end of the eighteenth century and the dawn of the nineteenth witnessed an increasing interest in science, medicine, and geography among the learned elite of the empire. İsmail Gelenbevî (d. 1791), who produced important essays on algebra, logarithms, and other mathematical subjects alongside works on religion, might be considered the last major Ottoman scholar of traditional bent—that is, an ʿālim (scholar) who combined serious religious scholarship with pure science.[71] One of the factors contributing to the intellectual ferment of the age was the decision of the authorities to permit the printing of books dealing with nonreligious subjects in Turkish. A fatwā dated 1727, and an imperial decree based on it, paved the way for the establishment of the first Ottoman printing house to publish such books. The late arrival of the printing house in the empire has often been cited as one of the major causes of the relative decline of Ottoman science and culture in comparison with Europe. It should be noted, however, that the major Ottoman printing houses published a combined total of only 142 books in more than a century of printing between 1727 and 1838.[72] When taken in conjunction with the fact that only a minuscule number of copies of each book were printed, this statistic demonstrates that the introduction of the printing press did not transform Ottoman cultural life until the emergence of vibrant print media in the middle of the nineteenth century.

A comparison of the books registered in the inventories of deceased members of the ruling askerî class for the years 1164 Hicrî (1750–51) and 1215 Hicrî (1800–1801) provides insight into Ottoman cultural life in the capital. In 1164, 82 percent of the 617 books in the possession of 44 individuals were religious:[73]

Religion	494
History	30
Literature	21
Poetry	18
Dictionaries	15
Grammar	9
Law	5

---

[71] Abdülhak Adnan-Adıvar, *Osmanlı Türklerinde İlim* (Istanbul: Maarif Matbaası, 1943), pp. 160ff.

[72] Joseph von Hammer [-Purgstall], *Geschichte des osmanischen Reiches*, 7: *vom Carlowiczer bis zum Belgrader Frieden, 1699–1739* (Pest: Hartleben's Verlage, 1831), pp. 583–95, and idem; *Geschichte der osmanischen Dichtkunst*, 4: *von der Regierung Sultan Suleiman's II bis auf unsere Zeit, 1687–1838* (Pest: Hartleben's Verlag, 1838), pp. 598–603.

[73] İstanbul Müftülük Arşivi: ŞS volumes 125, 126, 128, 129, 130, 131, 132, 133, 134, and 135.

Geography and Cosmography	4
Administration	2
Education	2
Mathematics	2
Military Affairs	2
Encyclopædias	1
Unspecified	12
TOTAL	617

The most popular books seem to be the Qur'ān and collections of verses from the holy book (a combined total of 40 instances), Mehmed ibn Pîr Ali Birgivî's (d. 1573) catechism *Vasiyyet-i Birgivî,* and its commentary by Ahmed el-Kürdî (14); Ibrāhīm ibn Muḥammad al-Ḥalabî's (d. 1549) *Multaqā al-abḥur,* a book on Ḥanafī jurisprudence (13); Çatalcalı Ali Efendi's (d. 1692) *Fetava-yı Ali Efendi,* a collection of legal responsa (9); Musharrif al-Dīn Sa'dī's (d. 1292) *Gulistān,* a classic of Persian literature (9); 'Abd al-Raḥmān Jāmī's (d. 1492) *Nafaḥāt al-uns min ḥaḍarat al-quds,* a treatise on the biographies of Ṣūfīs (8); Muḥammad ibn Sulaymān al-Jazūlī's (d. 1465) *Dalā'il al-Khayrāt,* a common prayer book (10); Birgivî's *Tarikat-i Muhammediye,* a work of puritanical pietism (8); Aḥmad ibn Muḥammad al-Qudūrī's (d. 1037) *Mukhtaṣar al-Qudūrī fī al-fiqh al-Ḥanafī,* on Ḥanafī canonical jurisprudence (8); Hüsrev Molla's (d. 1480) *Dürer el-hükkâm fi şerh-i gürer el-ahkâm,* also on Ḥanafī canonical jurisprudence (8); 'Abd Allāh ibn Yūsuf ibn Hishām al-Miṣrī al-Anṣārī's (d. 1360) *al-i'rāb 'an qawā'id al-i'rāb,* a work on Arabic grammar (5); Musharrif al-Dīn Sa'dī's *Bustān,* another classic of Persian literature (4); Mustafa ibn Abdullah (Kâtib Çelebi/Hacı Halife)'s (d. 1657), *Cihannümâ,* a major Ottoman work of geography and cosmography, which used sources by Western authors like Gerardus Mercator (d. 1594), Giovanni Lorenzo d'Anania (d. 1607), Philippus Cluverius (d. 1622), and Abraham Ortelius (d. 1598) (4); and Mehmed ibn Süleyman Fuzûlî's (d. 1556) *Leyla ve Mecnun,* a romantic poem (4).

By 1215 Hicrî (1800–1801) a half-century later, the situation had not changed dramatically. Similar records of 1,267 books owned by 44 members of the ruling class reveal that 76 percent of the specified books dealt with religious topics:[74]

Religion	928
Poetry	74
Literature	56
History	53
Medical Sciences	25
Dictionaries	14

[74] Ibid., volumes 734, 736, 737, 738, and 744.

Law	14
Grammar	13
Natural Sciences	8
Biographical Works	7
Astronomy	6
Administration	6
Mathematics	6
Geography and Cosmography	5
Maps	4
Calendars	2
Music	1
Astrology	1
Unspecified	44
TOTAL	1,267

Again, the Qur'ān and collections of verses from the holy book came first (a combined total of 64 instances). Among the most popular books were the *Multaqā al-Abḥur* (18), *Dalā'il al-Khayrāt* (15), *Vasiyyet-i Birgivî* with Ahmed el-Kürdî's commentary (15), *Fetava-yı Ali Efendi* (9), *Nafaḥāt al-uns min ḥaḍarat al-quds* (8), and *Dürer el-hükkâm fi ṣerh-i gürer el-ahkâm* (8); these are all works of religious law or piety. Among literary works, ʿAbd al-Raḥmān Jāmī's *Yusuf ile Züleyha* (8), Musharrif al-Dīn Saʿdī's *Gulistān* (8), and *Bustān* (5), and Yusuf Nabî's (d. 1712) *Hayriyye* (5) seemed to be the most popular. Clearly, although a nascent interest in science is apparent, these members of the ruling class still favored religious works by a considerable margin.

The late eighteenth century was a period of turbulence and change in the Ottoman Empire as in all of Europe. In some ways, the imperative of change facing the rulers of the Ottoman Empire was a direct result of the upheavals in Europe, which had unleashed new and dangerous forces. But the growing awareness of the need to evolve or perish stemmed equally from internal weaknesses. To far-sighted contemporaries it was clear that the Ottoman order could survive only if the seepage of power from the center to the periphery were reversed, and if the empire could successfully adjust to new European realities, in particular the military might of the industrializing nation-state. Certainly, a loosely bound association of disparate, semi-independent territories could not expect to survive long in the Napoleonic era. The attempt to establish a new balance between center and periphery was thus an existential imperative. Similarly, the acquisition of new defense capabilities became crucial, and in particular naval power to protect the empire's extended and vulnerable coastline along the eastern Mediterranean and Red Sea against increasingly effective naval competitors. These challenges were so daunting, and so closely bound up with the structural characteristics of the state, that traditional measures of reform were no longer sufficient. To survive, the empire's leaders had to do more than change the state; they had to reinvent it. The story of how they set out to do this, of the environment in which they operated, and of the intended and unintended consequences of their actions, forms both the essential narrative of late Ottoman history and the background to the formation of much of the modern social and political landscape of Southeastern Europe, the Near East, and North Africa.

2

Initial Ottoman Responses to
the Challenge of Modernity

THE CUMULATIVE impact of military, economic, and administrative challenges at the end of the eighteenth century obliged the rulers of the empire to come to terms with the imperative of reform. Their conservative instincts at first produced only superficial changes. But once cosmetic alteration had failed to yield substantial results, a more radical response became inescapable.

Upon conclusion of the Iaşi treaty which ended war with Russia in 1792, Sultan Selim III approached twenty-two prominent men and asked them to pen memoranda on the new order to be implemented in the Ottoman Empire. Those whose opinion was solicited included twenty eminent Ottoman statesmen and ulema, one French military adviser, and Mouradgea d'Ohsson (Muradcan Tosunian), an Armenian intellectual in the service of the Swedish embassy. The resulting papers, which may be likened to the French *Cahiers* of 1789, focused on proposals for military and fiscal reform. There was unanimous agreement among those consulted on the dire need for reorganization. The authors shared the implicit assumption that strengthening the state was the prerequisite for administrative reform and a reorientation of the empire's foreign policy. But their specific proposals for change differed markedly, falling into two distinct categories: those advocating a return to the practices of the golden age of the Ottoman Empire, and those embracing reform through the emulation of contemporary Europe. Among the latter, advocates of the Russian model of reform sponsored by Peter the Great figured prominently.[1] In the words of one proponent, "the Muscovite nation of inconsiderate animals has in thirty years reached the point of posing a danger to states five hundred or a thousand years old." "Since not only the civilized Ottoman but even the ordinary Muslim peasant . . . is

[1] See, for instance, [Rasih Mustafa], *Sefaretnâme-i Rasih Efendi*, IUL, Turkish Mss., no. 3887, ff. 7/b–8/a.

FIGURE 4. A painting (ca. 1791) depicting Sultan Selim III (r) and his Grand Vizier Koca Yusuf Pasha (l) (d. 1800). *Resimli Kitab,* 1/6 (March 1909), p. 526.

more competent than the cleverest European," it was argued, similar reforms could be carried out with ease in the Ottoman context.[2] The admiration for the new Russian army evident throughout the memoranda also attests to the paramount importance contemporaries attributed to the reform of the military.[3]

MILITARY REFORMS

The unavoidable consequence of defeat, military reform had been a priority of the Ottoman state since the early eighteenth century. Awareness of the need to borrow European knowledge was just as old. As an Ottoman officer admitted to his Austrian counterpart in a fictitious dialogue written circa 1718, "although I have spent my life on the battlefield, the Christian

[2] Mehmed Emin Behic, *Sevânih el-Levâyih,* Topkapı Palace Library (hereafter TPL), H. 370, f. 65.

[3] Ahmed Âsım, *Âsım Tarihi,* 1 ([Istanbul]: Ceride-i Havâdis Matbaası, [1867]), p. 266. In 1854, during the later Tanzimat era, a bureaucrat in the Sublime Porte's Translation Bureau— the most important link between the Ottoman administration and the West—composed a History of the Reign of Peter the Great. See İlber Ortaylı, *İmparatorluğun En Uzun Yüzyılı* (Istanbul: Hil Yayın, 1987), p. 202.

skills at manufacturing weaponry and devising superior strategies are beyond my power."[4] Thus the collection of information about European military methods,[5] and especially the translation of major European works on military strategy, became increasingly popular.[6]

By the reign of Sultan Selim III, the entire Ottoman military establishment was in desperate need of reorganization. But, as the proposals he solicited for reform clearly demonstrate, the overhaul of the military was threatened by opposition from the Janissary corps. It was not that the leaders of the Janissaries opposed reform per se; even they recognized that humiliating defeats—such as the rout of more than 120,000 Janissaries at the hands of 8,000 Russian troops on the shores of Danube in 1789—rendered reform inevitable.[7] At the same time, fearing a fate similar to that of the rebellious Strel'tzy at the hands of Peter the Great in 1698, they staunchly opposed the establishment of a new army, or the wholesale transformation of the existing one into a European-style institution.

Initially, therefore, Selim III chose to pursue the policies of his predecessors, but with greater determination. He invited foreign officers to serve as advisers to the Ottoman army[8] and established colleges to teach European military sciences. The Royal College of Naval Engineering had been founded in 1773, but was not functioning effectively. In 1796, Selim III revitalized this school and established another dedicated to Army Engineering. Both institutions were imitations of French academies. They used French as the language of instruction, housed a library imported from France, and employed French instructors—thereby reflecting the Ottoman wish for an officer corps modeled on that of France.[9] Unlike famous predecessors like Baron François de Tott or the Comte de Bonneval (Humbaracı Ahmed Pasha), the new advisers came as formal emissaries of the French government and retained their French ranks and loyalty to France.

Selim III also initiated structural changes in the army. His reformers placed the Artillery and Transportation branches under a single command to enhance the efficacy and mobility of Ottoman firepower. They wrote new regulations for Bombardiers, Sappers, and Miners[10] and introduced

---

[4] *Su'al-i Osmanî ve Cevab-ı Nasranî* (a copy made in 1719), TPL, H. 1634, f. 2.

[5] See, for instance, Ambassador Ebubekir Ratib's *Tuhfet'ül-Sefaret fi Ahvâl-i Asâkir el-Nasara ve'l-İdare* (Submitted to Selim III), TPL, H. 613.

[6] See, for instance, translations by Constantinos Ypsilanti from Vauban and other French military strategists in Vauban, *Darben ve Def'an Muhasara ve Muharese-i Kıla' ve Husun,* TPL, H. 614; and *Tercüme-i Risâle-i Fenn-i Harb,* TPL, H. 615.

[7] *Tarih-i Cevdet,* 6, p. 5.

[8] Ibid., p. 70.

[9] A[ntoine] de Jucherau de Saint-Denys, *Révolutions de Constantinople en 1807 et 1808,* 1 (Paris: Brissot-Thivars, 1819), pp. 75–80.

[10] *Âsım Tarihi,* 1, pp. 34ff.

new battlefield bombing techniques based on those employed by European armies.[11] Similar reforms were launched to make the navy competitive.[12] Yet reform of the technical branches of the military alone, however indispensable, was insufficient as long as the bulk of the army, the infantry and cavalry, remained unchanged. In 1793, a new ministry for Trained Infantry Troops was formed to oversee the reform of the army. Fearing the reaction of the Janissaries, the leaders of the reform persuaded the sultan, who wanted to establish a brand new class of trained infantry, to transform one of the old army formations, the imperial guards, instead. But the sultan insisted that the Janissaries, contrary to their long-standing traditions, drill and train on a regular basis. Though they formally submitted to the order, the Janissaries did everything in their power to obstruct its implementation.

Under the circumstances, the reformists decided to increase the number of new troops by establishing new divisions in the capital and Anatolia. The Janissaries categorically refused to join these divisions, known as "New Order Troops." When the new units were tested in battle against the French expeditionary force at Acre in 1799, their superior performance (in contrast with the regular troops) convinced the reformists to persevere along this path of reform. They did not, however, dare to abolish the Janissary corps—a weakness for which they were to pay dearly in 1807. By the end of 1806, there were 22,865 soldiers and 1,590 officers in the new army, half of which was stationed in Anatolia, while the remainder served in the capital.[13]

ECONOMIC REFORMS

One of the reform memoranda submitted to Selim III focused on the new economic policies to be implemented by the state. The author, Finance Minister Mehmed Şerif Efendi, proposed the gradual abolition of major timars, albeit without dismantling the system as a whole. Mehmed Şerif Efendi recommended a similar approach to the outdated malikâne system. He also suggested that the state liquidate its enormous internal debt in the interest of economic stability.[14] In another memorandum, Tatarcıkzâde

[11] See, for instance, İsmail Çınarî, *Humbara İrtifaʿat ve Mesafât Cedveli*, TPL, H. 640; İbrahim Kâmi, *Humbara Risâlesi*, TPL, H. 619; Mehmed bin Süleyman, *Risâle-i Humbara*, TPL, H. 631.

[12] Ali İhsan Gencer, *Bahriye'de Yapılan Islahât Hareketleri ve Bahriye Nezâreti'nin Kuruluşu, 1789–1867* (Istanbul: Edebiyat Fakültesi Yayınları, 1985), pp. 61ff.

[13] Stanford J. Shaw, *Between Old and New: The Ottoman Empire under Sultan Selim III, 1789–1807* (Cambridge, MA: Harvard University Press, 1971), pp. 132–3.

[14] [Mehmed Şerif], "Sultan Selim Han-ı Sâlis Devrinde Nizâm-ı Devlet Hakkında Mütalâʿat," *Tarih-i Osmanî Encümeni Mecmuası*, 7/38 [June 14, 1916], pp. 75–6.

Abdullah Molla described at length the devastating effects of debasement, and proposed a return to the old monetary practices.[15] All the memoranda underscored the importance of finding fresh sources of revenue to finance the reform of the military.

In order to address these issues, in 1793 the government decided to establish a special treasury named the "New Revenues Treasury." This institution was to finance the new troops and their military campaigns. It was charged with retaining (and not reselling) tax farms and state bonds left by deceased holders, thereby simultaneously liquidating both the malikâne system and the internal debt. In 1801, the new treasury became the sole authority sanctioned to procure state bonds left as inheritance.[16] The new treasury was also to confiscate timars belonging to deceased holders, which were to be converted into tax farms or administered directly by the treasury.[17] The government also granted the new treasury the authority to collect major taxes on commodities such as alcoholic beverages, cotton, wool, and oak apple.[18] By these means the new treasury generated a total of 1,884,803 gurushes in revenue between 1793 and 1797, representing 21 percent of the total expenditure of 8,304,826 gurushes from this treasury during the same period.[19] In 1805, the rising naval expenses compelled the administration to establish an additional treasury, the Arsenal Treasury, which operated along similar lines.[20]

The administration also reinvigorated the monetarization of the economy. A major step in this direction was the gradual adoption of cash salaries in place of the allocation of taxation rights. In 1813, the Imperial Treasury paid 23,140 purses to officials as cash salaries out of a total expenditure of 33,621 purses.[21] One negative consequence of this practice was severe cash shortages. Both the interest expressed by Ottoman statesmen in public lotteries and the admiration professed for European systems of public finance attest to the urgent need for new revenues.[22]

Another concern voiced by the reformists was the need to balance the Ottoman trade deficit. They maintained that the major cause of the deficit was foreign control of Ottoman trade and the consequent flow of trade revenues to foreign countries. Accordingly, they proposed to return control

---

[15] [Abdullah Tatarcıkzâde], *Lâyiha-i Tatarcıkzâde Abdullah Molla Efendi*, Istanbul University Library (hereafter IUL), Turkish Mss., no. 6930 (a copy made in 1813).

[16] Cezar, *Osmanlı Maliyesi*, p. 173.

[17] *Âsım Tarihi*, 1, pp. 355–6.

[18] Cezar, *Osmanlı Maliyesi*, pp. 183–92.

[19] Ibid., p. 178.

[20] *Tarih-i Cevdet*, 7, pp. 286–8.

[21] Cezar, *Osmanlı Maliyesi*, pp. 66–70.

[22] Enver Ziya Karal, *Selim III' ün Hat-tı Hümayunları: Nizam-ı Cedit, 1789–1807* (Ankara: TTK Yayınları, 1946), pp. 134–5.

over foreign trade to Ottoman hands.[23] In the early seventeenth century, the Ottoman government had instituted a preferential 3 percent customs tariff for merchants of Great Britain and the Netherlands. Over time, this privilege was extended to merchants of other foreign powers. Foreign traders thus obtained a considerable advantage over Ottoman non-Muslims, who paid a 5 percent tariff, and Ottoman Muslims, who paid a 4 percent tariff. Furthermore, the system was corrupted by many non-Muslim Ottomans, who abused the privileges granted to Ottoman dragomans and servants in the service of foreign embassies and consulates, becoming merchants under foreign protection. In 1792, for example, instead of six dragomans serving the six consulates in Aleppo, some 1,500 individuals were listed as dragomans, the vast majority of them non-Muslim merchants in disguise.[24] The reformists were determined to end this state of affairs. In 1802, an imperial decree redefined the status of Ottoman merchants engaged in commerce with Europe. Henceforth, all Ottoman merchants, regardless of their religious affiliation, were entitled to the same privileges previously bestowed on aliens. In addition, the government adopted strict controls over the process of enlistment for service in foreign embassies and consulates.[25] Although these were well-considered, astute measures designed to protect Ottoman, and especially non-Muslim, merchants, they did little to solve the main problem confronting the commerce of the empire: the deficiency of Ottoman production. This was a problem that would only grow worse during the age of European industrialization. Selim III enthusiastically supported the creation of military industries, but achieved little in this regard.[26]

THE NEW OTTOMAN DIPLOMACY

Isolationism had been the trademark of Ottoman foreign policy for centuries. By the end of the eighteenth century, it was no longer practicable. The traditional policy of isolation from the "infidels" had proven unworkable in the face of new threats from rising European powers. Averting wars originating in Europe necessitated active Ottoman participation in the European diplomatic arena. The habit of isolationism thus gave way to the principle of engagement, which governed the conduct of Ottoman foreign policy until the collapse of the empire.

[23] *Tarih-i Cevdet*, 6, p. 69.

[24] Ibid., p. 130.

[25] Ali İhsan Bağış, *Osmanlı Ticaretinde Gayrî Müslimler: Kapitülasyonlar, Avrupa Tüccarları, Beratlı Tüccarlar, Hayriye Tüccarları, 1750–1839* (Turhan Kitabevi, 1983), pp. 63–73.

[26] Edward C. Clark, "The Ottoman Industrial Revolution," *IJMES* 5/1 (January 1974), p. 66.

In order to implement the new strategy of engagement, the state needed more detailed information on European powers—their domestic politics, their alliances, their capabilities, and their goals. One obvious prerequisite was the establishment of permanent Ottoman embassies abroad. Information provided by the hospodars of Wallachia and Moldavia was simply not adequate, although these sources continued to supply intelligence even after the establishment of permanent Ottoman embassies in their domains.[27]

The need to counter new and powerful enemies forced Ottoman policy makers to form alliances along the simple lines suggested by the maxim "the enemy of my enemy is my friend." Accordingly, throughout the eighteenth century the Ottoman government would naturally turn to Sweden whenever the Russian threat resurfaced.[28] The Ottomans also communicated on a regular basis with local principalities, some of which were formal Ottoman protectorates, in the Caucasus,[29] sending them instructions for action in the event of a war with Russia.[30] In such alliances the Ottoman state was always the senior partner. However, a series of Ottoman defeats at the hands of Russia, then a weak European power, compelled the Ottomans to join the European game of the balance of power and to seek to manipulate it to their advantage. In return for more meaningful alliances, the Ottomans had to accept junior status. In 1786, while still heir apparent, Selim III sought French help in his famous exchange of letters with Louis XVI. In 1790, the Ottoman Empire for the first time concluded a "defensive and offensive alliance" with a Christian power, Prussia.[31]

Ottoman behavior under Selim III illustrates the strategic premise that a meaningful alliance with a major European power, however unpleasant, was necessary to secure the future of the empire.[32] As Bonaparte's attack on Egypt in 1798 underscored, the Ottoman state, in order to survive, would have to harness European power and turn it against any potential attacker. This premise was a constant of late Ottoman diplomacy throughout the nineteenth and into the twentieth century. When mirrored by a similar strategic design on the part of a European power, an alliance was feasible, although by no means guaranteed; for European governments usually had to navigate an unpredictable obstacle to the conclusion of an alliance with the

---

[27] See, for example, BOA-HH 41024 [June 6, 1814] and 41029 [June 6, 1814].

[28] *Tarih-i Cevdet*, 4, pp. 303–4; 360–62.

[29] Up until the early nineteenth century, the principalities of Abkhazia, Guria, Imeretia, Mingrelia, and Svanetia continued to be Ottoman protectorates. See M. Sadık Bilge, *Osmanlı Devleti ve Kafkasya: Osmanlı Varlığı Döneminde Kafkasya'nın Siyasî-Askerî Tarihi ve İdarî Taksimatı, 1454–1829* (Istanbul: Eren, 2005), pp. 195ff.

[30] See, for example, BOA-HH 21379 [undated].

[31] *Tarih-i Cevdet*, 5, pp. 15 and 294–6.

[32] Enver Ziya Karal, *Selim III.ün Hatt-ı Humayunları* (Ankara: TTK Yayınları, 1942), pp. 10–17.

Ottomans, namely public opinion. When, for instance, the British House of Commons in 1791 debated possible British support for the Ottoman Empire against Russia, Edmund Burke stated that he intensely "dislike[d] this anti-crusade" and opposed "favouring such barbarians and oppressing [C]hristians, to the detriment of civilization and hindrance of human refinement."[33] As the Ottomans quickly learned, the role of public opinion meant that strategic partnership with European powers came with a string attached: the demand for administrative reform, often with the aim of improving the status of the empire's Christian subjects.

Selim III's efforts to secure a European ally produced mixed results. While his efforts to conclude a Franco-Ottoman alliance went up in flames in 1798, Bonaparte's aggression yielded alliances with Russia and Great Britain. Subsequently, a combined Anglo-Ottoman force fought the French in Egypt and a joint Russo-Ottoman flotilla struggled to free the Ionian Islands from French occupation. In 1799, the Ottoman government struck up an alliance with the Kingdom of the Two Sicilies. Further indication of a new Ottoman desire to play by the European rules of the game came in 1807, when the Ottoman government declared war on Russia and, instead of imprisoning the Russian ambassador according to Ottoman custom, allowed him to leave the capital aboard a British vessel.[34]

In 1802, the Ottoman Empire signed a peace treaty with France. Three years later, and only one day before news of the French victory at Austerlitz reached Istanbul, the Ottoman government contracted a defensive alliance with Russia. In both cases, the Ottomans insisted on inserting a mutual guarantee of "territorial integrity" into the treaty.[35] In November 1806, the Russians proved the worthlessness of such guarantees when they attacked their Ottoman allies without an official declaration of war. This aggression triggered a British demonstration of naval force, culminating in the unprecedented appearance of a hostile navy before the Ottoman capital in February 1807. The British fleet returned without achieving anything worthy of mention, but the incident further demonstrated to Ottoman statesmen that even the capital was not safe without the protection of a major power.

Administrative Reform

In 1795, the government launched a major reorganization of Ottoman provincial administration designed to strengthen central control over the

---

[33] *The Parliamentary History of England*, ed. William Cobett, 29 (London: R. Bagshaw, 1817), col. 78.

[34] *Tarih-i Cevdet*, 8, p. 102.

[35] Articles 4 and 5 in the respective treaties, *Muʿahedat Mecmuası* 4 (1298 [1881]), p. 15, and 1 (1294 [1877]), p. 37.

periphery. A new law decreed that there would be twenty-eight provinces in the empire, each to be governed by a vizier. These were: Adana, Aleppo, Anatolia, Baghdad, Basra, Bosnia, Çıldır, Crete, Damascus, Diyar-ı Bekir, Egypt, Erzurum, Jeddah, Karaman, Kars, Marʿaş, the Mediterranean Islands, the Morea, Mosul, Rakka, Rumelia, Sayda, Şehr-i Zor, Silistra, Sivas, Trabzon, Tripoli in Syria, and Van. In practice, however, central control remained weak. The Mamluk governor of Baghdad was also granted control of Basra and Şehr-i Zor, and Adana, Marʿaş, and Kars were deemed not large enough to support a vizier. Nor did the government seek to alter the traditional dispatch of *beylerbeyi*s (governor-generals), instead of viziers, to Mosul and Tripoli in Syria. The number of viziers was thus fixed at twenty-one, although it had the potential to grow if the government were to reestablish central control over detached provinces. The new rules stipulated that governors should serve at least three years and no more than five, in a given province under normal circumstances. The government reserved the right to grant an extension if "the state finds the governor's performance acceptable" and the local "population is satisfied" with his administration. The state also undertook to appoint "intelligent, pious, seasoned, just, moderate, loyal, and honest" governors, and to avoid candidates who "were ignorant of the state apparatus, unqualified, feudal lords, leaders of irregular cavalry, and unknown." Furthermore, the government affirmed, in cases where a governor desired the appointment of a subgovernor unknown to the center, the government would approve the appointee "only after summoning him to Istanbul and getting to know him."[36]

The legislation of 1795 reveals the government's strong desire for centralization. But lacking adequate military and fiscal powers of enforcement, that goal remained an unattainable ideal. Legislation represented only a neat paper solution to the enormous challenges posed by the fragmentation of the empire. The illustrious career of Mehmed Ali illustrates this gap between the ideal and the real. Mehmed Ali volunteered to join the Ottoman force of irregulars sent to Egypt to expel the French in 1798. He advanced swiftly to become administrative director of an Albanian division. In 1801, the French withdrew and the subsequent disengagement of British forces in 1803 left a major power vacuum. A bitter struggle ensued between the Ottoman center and the Mamluks, with the participation of Janissaries and Albanian irregulars. After three years of chaos, serial assassinations, and much intrigue, Mehmed Ali, in May 1805, compelled the notables and religious leaders of Cairo to declare him governor of Egypt. Though dismayed, the sultan nevertheless approved the fait accompli.[37] Mehmed Ali did not fit the gubernatorial profile designated by law. In fact, he possessed many

---

[36] BOA-MM 7584 (Vüzera Kanunnâmesi).

[37] *Tarih-i Cevdet*, 8, pp. 26–8.

characteristics that should have barred him from ever being considered for the position. His boldness underscored the fecklessness of Ottoman administrative reform and demonstrated just how far a provincial governor could go in challenging the imperial center.

But the traditional threats to central control—insubordinate governors, defiant notables, and proliferating local dynasties—were soon to be dwarfed by a new centrifugal force: nationalism.

The Emergence of Nationalism

Ottoman statesmen scoffed at the French revolution.[38] Nevertheless, the revolution had a profound impact on the empire's elites, while the short-lived French occupation of Egypt and the Ionian Islands immeasurably aided the dissemination of revolutionary ideas throughout the empire. In a world of turmoil and inequality, many Ottoman intellectuals succumbed to the charms of nationalism, adopting a romanticized image of the nation rising up from the ruins of a decadent empire. The Ottoman world, and especially its more heavily Christian European provinces, offered fertile ground for such ideas. To be sure, this was a problem shared by all contemporary polyethnic empires, but it was graver in the Ottoman context because of the weakness of central control, the severity of socioeconomic problems, and the structural reality of an empire dominated by Muslims but well-nigh encircled by Christian powers. Under these circumstances, local uprisings, ostensibly indistinguishable from their numerous historical antecedents, took on a deeper significance. All the old grievances—from excessive taxes to maladministration—remained; but they were increasingly supplemented and amplified by new aspirations to equality and self-rule, often nurtured from abroad. Over the course of the nineteenth century, the European powers became much less inclined to dismiss Christian rebellions as instances of reʿaya disobedience best left to the sultan's discretion. Instead they came to regard them as nationalist movements worthy of support. Such movements soon began to pull the empire apart at its ethno-religious seams.

The first revolt to acquire a national character was the Serbian uprising of 1804. The Ottoman authorities had always considered the Serb population particularly difficult to rule.[39] However, the origins of the Serbian national awakening lay in Austria, not in the Ottoman Empire. Beginning in the late seventeenth century, northbound Serbian emigration turned Karlóca (Sremski Karlovci) in the Austrian *Militärgrenze* into the most important

[38] Ibid., 6, pp. 394–401.
[39] Grand vizier to the governor of Vidin [February 18, 1825], BOA-Ayniyat, 611.

center of Serbian culture. The first Serbian *gimnazija* (high school) was
established in Karlóca in 1791. After the closure of the Serbian Patriarchate
in 1776, the town emerged as a major religious center, sporting the second
most important seminary (after the one in Kiev) in Orthodox Christianity.
Moreover, it was Colonel Mihailyevich of Austria, not one of the leaders
from Serbia proper, who boasted that he and his Austrian-backed *Freicorps*
had liberated a substantial portion of "Old Servia" and led the national
struggle against the "Turk."[40] There was of course an old tradition of epic
hajduk (brigand) poetry in which the "Turk" featured as the enemy. But
such sentiments can only be considered a distant precursor to the modern
protonationalist awakening of Serbia.

There were significant socioeconomic reasons for Serbian resentment
which had little to do with Ottoman rule. Chief among them was the emergence of large, illegal, quasi-private *çiftliks* (arable farms) owned by Janissaries. These were different from the traditional small farms run by *sipahi*
(timariot cavalry) families. In the new çiftliks, Serbian sharecroppers, who
for centuries had enjoyed a fair amount of liberty under the sipahis, became
de facto serfs on their own land. Although the introduction of fresh cash
crops by these farms revitalized the local economy, the new system considerably downgraded the status of the peasants. Indeed, one of the initial demands
of the rebels was the abolition of the çiftliks.

Another contributing factor was a local power struggle that became more
acute in the vacuum left by the disappearance of central power. Pazvandoğlu
Osman, who wished to extend the area under his control at the expense of
the Paşalık of Belgrade, challenged Hacı Mustafa Pasha—nicknamed *Srpska
Maika* (Serbian mother) for his just and nonviolent rule. The local Janissaries, who disliked the pasha's strict law enforcement, sided with the challenger. Upon learning that a Serbian delegation had gone to the imperial
capital to beg for the sultan's mercy, the Janissaries killed a number of local
Serb leaders. Their action triggered a Serbian retaliation and a major conflagration ensued. Although later called the Serbian revolt, it was a more
complex affair than the nationalist narrative will allow; for example, a group
of the original Serbian rebels (wearing fur hats donated by Pazvandoğlu
Osman[41]) subsequently changed sides, pledging allegiance to their "August
sovereign" and protesting strenuously that they had neither rebelled against
the Sublime State[42] nor imagined a "Serbian nation." Moreover, as was the
case in all ostensibly nationalist uprisings, old traditions—such as the Serbian representative body, the *Skupština*—were revived and adapted to meet
contemporary needs.

[40] Leopold von Ranke, *Die serbische Revolution: Aus serbischen Papieren und Mittheilungen*
(Berlin: Duncker und Humblot, 1844), p. 79.

[41] BOA-HH 5490 (1220/1805–6).

[42] BOA-HH 16134A (1221/1806–7).

A new and significant aspect of the Serbian revolt of 1804 was outside intervention. Not only did Montenegrin leaders and Serbian clerics in Hungary support the Serbian insurrection; Russia too allied with the Serbs against the Ottoman Empire. Thus, the subsequent Ottoman defeat at the hands of Russia had major implications for the fate of the Serbian cause. The Treaty of Bucharest, signed with Russia in 1812, contained an Ottoman commitment to discuss the demands of the "Serbian community," but did not grant explicit privileges to Serbia.[43] This changed in 1816, when the Ottoman government authorized a measure of Serbian self-rule pertaining to the election of their Chief Knez, the collection of taxes, and judicial administration. These concessions were repeatedly extended until 1838, when an imperial edict to Chief Knez Miloš Obronović created a fully autonomous Serbia, Ottoman only in name.[44]

OBSTACLES TO REFORM

Initial Ottoman responses to the challenges of a new era produced duality in every field: a modern, European-style army alongside a stubbornly conservative corps of Janissaries; an increasingly monetary economy together with the medieval timar system; glimmerings of fiscal responsibility yet multiple budgets; modern academies boasting libraries stuffed with French books along with Ottoman *medrese*s whose curricula had not changed for centuries. It was this inherent tension between the old and the new which issued in the violent rupture of 1807.

The first sign of the coming explosion was the Edirne incident of 1806. On the pretext of sending an expeditionary force against the Serbian rebels, the government dispatched a small army to establish the first headquarters of the New Order Troops in Tekfurdağı in European Turkey. This provoked local notables, Janissaries, and conservatives into an alliance against the new force. As the local qāḍī attempted to read out the imperial decree announcing the establishment of the New Order Troops, the Janissaries lynched him. They then proceeded to rally local armies against the expeditionary force, which beat a hasty retreat back to the capital.

Then, in 1807, Janissary auxiliaries stationed in the Bosporus forts refused to don the European-style uniforms issued to the New Troops, and launched a rebellion. They marched into the capital, where they were joined by the Janissaries themselves. Popular attitudes were mixed. The population of the capital appreciated the security provided by the New Troops, but

[43] *Muʻahedat Mecmuası*, 4, pp. 53–4.
[44] Raşid Belgradî, *Tarih-i Vakʻa-i Hayretnümâ Belgrad ve Sırpistan*, 1 ([Istanbul]: Tatyos Divitçiyan Matbaası, 1291 [1874]), pp. 242–51.

resented the military reforms because of the additional taxes levied to support the Treasury of New Revenues.[45] Moreover, the average person found the "super-Westernization" displayed by the leaders of the reforms utterly distasteful.[46] The ulema openly supported the rebels. Upon receiving their backing, the rebels submitted an ultimatum demanding the abolition of the New Troops and the surrender of twelve prominent statesmen into their hands. Then, finding Selim III's affirmative response insufficient, they demanded his abdication. The sultan yielded and was dethroned, bringing the reform movement to an abrupt end.

The new sultan, Mustafa IV (r. 1807–08), was a well-known supporter of the reactionary movement. For a time, it seemed likely that he would lead a wholesale return to the old policies.

[45] *Tarih-i Cevdet*, 8, pp. 141, 146.
[46] Ibid., pp. 146–8.

The Dawn of the Age of Reform

THE VICTORY of the forces opposing reform was to be short-lived. A communiqué to all foreign and Ottoman ambassadors blamed "unwise ministers, who only wished to acquire more power and property," for "innovating and inventing the regulations named 'New Order,'" and reaffirmed the abolition of all new institutions, including the new army and treasury.[1] As the new sultan and his anti-reform allies soon realized, however, so-called imperial rule extended only to the capital and a number of its surrounding districts; they were powerless to conscript or tax anyone outside this small area.[2]

One way to project imperial power beyond the capital was to bestow imperial favors on powerful notables in the outlying provinces. But doing so necessarily entangled the center in the web of intra-notable rivalries, and could provoke a powerful backlash. For instance, in 1807 Tayyar Mahmud Pasha, leader of the Caniklizâde family—one of the three most powerful Anatolian notable houses—was appointed as acting grand vizier; this pushed the rival Cebbarzâde clan to the verge of all-out rebellion.[3] In the meantime, leading reformists made common cause with notables in European provinces, fleeing to Rumelia to seek refuge in Ruscuk (Ruse) under the protection of the rising notable Alemdar Mustafa Ağa.

Alemdar Mustafa was the primary beneficiary of the erosion of Ottoman power in the European provinces in the wake of the Serbian revolt. The surrender of large areas to Serbian control had considerably diminished the size and importance of Vidin province, once controlled by the famous rebel (turned pasha) Pazvandoğlu Osman. İdris Pasha, governor of Vidin, could muster only 8,000 troops from his truncated lands to face the threat from Alemdar Mustafa, who controlled a vast area between the Danube and the capital, and established an important alliance with Serezli İsmail,

[1] Ahmed Âsım, *Âsım Tarihi*, 2 ([Istanbul]: Ceride-i Havâdis Matbaası, [1867], pp. 56–60.
[2] Ahmed Cevdet, *Tarih-i Cevdet*, 8 (Istanbul: Matbaa-i Osmaniye, 1309 [1891]), p. 277.
[3] Ibid., pp. 274–5.

ruler of modern-day Macedonia. Serezli İsmail was not a warlord in the strict sense of the word. Lacking a substantial military force, he ruled by the consent of his subjects—Muslim and non-Muslim alike. He was especially popular among non-Muslims for the encouragement he afforded them to engage freely in agriculture and commerce. With Serezli İsmail's backing, Alemdar Mustafa emerged as the dominant military power in Eastern Rumelia.[4] As the sultan himself confessed, Alemdar Mustafa's well-trained, well-equipped army of 30,000 men was considered the most powerful force in the empire at the time. And, unlike the other strong men of the periphery—men such as Ali Pasha of Tepelenë in Tosk-inhabited Southern Albania, İbrahim Pasha in Geg-inhabited Northern Albania, or the Bosnian notables and *kapetan*s who ruled Bosnia and Herzegovina—Alemdar Mustafa could threaten the capital.

The sultan and the champions of the conservative establishment feared that Alemdar Mustafa would join the bedraggled imperial army on its return from the Danube front and seize control of the capital with his own forces. Accordingly, they ordered the army to remain in place, despite the relative tranquility at the front and the progress of peace negotiations with Russia. In response, Alemdar Mustafa halted the flow of provisions to the imperial army, whose sustenance depended entirely on his graces. Following protracted negotiations, the two armies marched together toward Istanbul. While en route, a local Rumelian notable, acting on instructions from Alemdar Mustafa, executed the Janissary leader responsible for the deposition of Selim III. Marching into the capital, Alemdar Mustafa's army paraded before the Sublime Porte. The message was clear. At his behest, many Janissaries were executed, many anti-reform leaders banished. On July 28, 1808, Alemdar Mustafa stormed the Sublime Porte, wrenched the imperial seal from the hands of the grand vizier, and declared that "the ulema, the dignitaries of the state, the notables of Rumelia, and the local dynasties of Anatolia had decided in unison to re-enthrone Selim III."[5] The reigning sultan attempted to resist by quickly ordering the execution of Selim III and the heir apparent Mahmud Efendi, who were the sole remaining male members of the royal house. Palace officials managed to slay Selim III, but they failed to murder the heir apparent, who was declared the new sultan, Mahmud II (r. 1808–39), by Alemdar Mustafa. In turn, the grateful young sultan granted Alemdar Mustafa the imperial seal. The assumption of the duties of grand vizier of the Sublime State by an uneducated Rumelian notable marked the heyday of the provincial notables of Anatolia and Rumelia.

[4] Ibid., p. 275.
[5] Ibid., p. 304.

The Deed of Agreement

Alemdar Mustafa was in a unique position to understand that only a new settlement between the notables and the center could save the empire. Accordingly, he invited all local notables and dynastic rulers to a "public consultation" in the capital. Many accepted the invitation and made their way to the capital with their private armies. In October 1808, local leaders and state officials signed the Deed of Agreement, commonly (but mistakenly) referred to as the Ottoman Magna Carta. According to this document, local leaders were to "guarantee and undertake to protect the sultan's imperial person, the sultanate's power, and state order." The local notable houses, notables, ministers, high officials, and dignitaries who participated in the agreement would also "guarantee each other's personal safety and that of their families." As for the imperial center, it would "uphold the position of the leaders of the notable houses as long as they are alive, and support their families afterward."[6]

In addition to conferring official recognition on the notables, the Deed of Agreement also recognized the dependence of the empire on their power: "If a rebellion or conspiracy led by the Janissary units in Istanbul or elsewhere should occur, all local notable houses will hasten to Istanbul; those individuals and Janissary units who dare [to act in this way] will be removed or abolished."[7] The document also charged the notables with overseeing the improvement of administrative practices in the provinces:

> Since it is essential to protect and support the poor and tax-paying subjects, it is necessary that the local notable houses and chief men in the provinces pay attention to public order in the districts under their administration, and that they be moderate in levying taxes on the poor and tax-paying subjects. Therefore, let everyone give serious attention to the continuous implementation of any decision taken by ministers and local notable houses after discussion [between them], with regard to the prevention of oppression and the adjustment of taxes, and let everyone give serious attention to preventing oppression and transgression from taking place in contravention of these decisions. Let local notable houses scrutinize each other and inform the Sublime State if one such house commits oppression and transgression in violation of orders and the sacred sharīʿa, and let all local notable houses work unanimously toward the prevention of such actions.[8]

[6] BOA-HH 35242 [October 1808].
[7] Ibid.
[8] Ibid.

The Deed amounted to recognition of the limits of central control over local notables. As such, it accurately reflected the balance of power at the time. Mahmud II signed the document half-heartedly after his advisers admitted that it "violated his sovereignty, but could not be resisted" under the circumstances.[9]

The Destruction of the Janissaries

Having reset the delicate balance between center and periphery to his satisfaction, Alemdar Mustafa restarted the reforms.[10] He reestablished the new army as an independent corps under a new name;[11] oversaw the formulation of new regulations for the Janissaries; and requested the notables to obey the orders of the central government. Before long, however, the Janissaries revolted once again, and Alemdar Mustafa, who fought bravely to the bitter end, was killed along with hundreds of rebels. Despite the stiff resistance mounted by the new troops, the Janissaries finally prevailed. They lynched many of the leading reformists and, in November 1808, compelled the sultan to abolish the new troops. The abolition of the new troops was a serious setback for the sultan. The elimination of a strong notable who had dominated the political scene, however, was more than a relief; as we will see, it paved the way for the annihilation of the notables' independent power base.

For many years, Mahmud II prudently avoided provoking the Janissaries by establishing a rival army corps. Instead, he strove to control them through the appointment of commanders loyal to him and the cooptation of others. In 1826, the sultan, riding a wave of popular admiration for the modern army of Mehmed Ali following its defeat of the Greek rebels at Missolonghi, finally felt ready to confront the Janissaries. He duly established a new army corps called the *Eşkinciyân* (Mounted Yeomen).[12] Three days after the new force began drilling, the Janissaries took their cauldrons to the *Et Meydanı* in the traditional gesture of rebellion. Turning the tables on his adversaries, who charged that the new army imitated "infidel" practices, the sultan obtained a fatwā that sanctioned the slaughter of the Janissaries. The edict invited "all Muslims to muster under the standard of the Prophet," a flag that was unfurled

[9] *Tarih-i Cevdet*, 9, pp. 7–8.

[10] A[natolii] F[ilippovich] Miller, *Mustafa Pasha Bairaktar: Ottomanskaia imperiia v nachale XIX veka* (Moscow: Izdatel'stvo Akademii Nauk, 1947), pp. 292ff.

[11] Mehmed ʿAtaullah, *Şânizâde Tarihi*, 1 ([Istanbul]: Süleyman Efendi Matbaası, 1290 [1873]), pp. 97–8.

[12] Mehmed Esʿad, *Üss-i Zafer* ([Istanbul]: Matbaa-i Süleyman Efendi, 1293 [1876]), pp. 22–32.

only for holy war.[13] In a bloody engagement that lasted several hours, loyal troops, joined by medrese students and other volunteers, butchered a significant number of the Janissaries, while the remainder fled in panic.

The dramatic downfall of the Janissaries proved a turning point in Ottoman military history and in the wider history of Ottoman reform. Following the "Auspicious Event," as the episode came to be called, the government abolished the Janissary corps (and several others), along with the Bektashi Ṣūfī order with which they were affiliated. The sultan ordered the demolition of major Bektashi lodges, banished leading Bektashis, and forced the remaining members of the order to renounce their beliefs and adopt the mainstream Sunnī dress code.[14] With traditional Janissary opposition to military reform a thing of the past, the government was free to form a new European-style army corps. Named the *Asâkir-i Mansure-i Muhammediye* (Victorious Troops of Muḥammad), the new army was composed of infantry and cavalry.[15] In 1834, a reserve army was established, with units in various Anatolian and Rumelian provinces.[16] In 1838, a Military Council was formed to discuss all military matters pertaining to the empire.[17] Significantly, the provincial armies that had threatened the center in the past were disbanded. As a result of these changes, the Ottoman state now possessed a single military organization under unified command. This was a major accomplishment in centralization.

The destruction of the rebellious Janissary corps and its replacement with a military order wholly subservient to the court destroyed the delicate, centuries-old balance of power within the Ottoman political system. The Janissaries had served as traditional power brokers with the capacity to make or break a sultan. Inclined to align with the ulema against the court and bureaucracy, they formed the linchpin of a front equipped with both the power and the legitimacy to oppose the ruling order and, at times, replace it. With the Janissaries gone, the ulema lost a main source of leverage over the court and the bureaucracy. Shorn of military support, the ulema were compelled to adopt a far more conciliatory stance vis-à-vis the new bureaucracy's pressure for wide-ranging reforms. The collapse of the legitimist opposition strengthened the sultan and his administration immeasurably. Henceforth, until 1908, Ottoman politics was reduced to a game played by two major actors: the bureaucracy of the Sublime Porte and the court of the sultan. In the immediate aftermath of the fall of the Janissaries, it was the court that benefited most. But the ambitious reform program

---

[13] Ibid., pp. 73–4.

[14] *Tarih-i Cevdet*, 12, pp. 166–88.

[15] Ahmed Lûtfî, *Tarih-i Lûtfî*, 1 (Istanbul: Matbaa-i Âmire, 1290 [1873]), pp. 199ff; 258–9.

[16] Mübahat S. Kütükoğlu, "Sultan II. Mahmud Devri Yedek Ordusu: Redîf-i Asâkir-i Mansûre," *Tarih Enstitüsü Dergisi*, 12 (1981–82), pp. 127ff.

[17] *Tarih-i Lûtfî*, 5 (Istanbul: Mahmud Bey Matbaası, 1292 [1875]), p. 70.

initiated by Sultan Mahmud II required the rapid expansion of the bureaucratic machinery for its implementation. Upon his death in 1839, the burgeoning bureaucracy seized the initiative and held it, dominating the Ottoman political scene over and against the resistance of weak sultans for three crucial decades.

Centralization, Westernization, and Administrative Reform

Mahmud II attempted to place as many provinces as he could under central control. On the conclusion of the Treaty of Bucharest with Russia in 1812, the sultan turned to all-out war against rival powers within the empire. Whereas his cousin Selim III had been unable to strengthen central rule because he was preoccupied with successive diplomatic crises and military campaigns, Mahmud II exploited the relative tranquility of the period—up to the outbreak of the Greek revolt and the small-scale war of 1820–23 with Iran—to place centralization at the top of his agenda. His successes in this field were considerable.[18]

The centralization policy worked best in the Ottoman heartland, where the state pursued a two-pronged approach toward the notables, combining rewards and punishment. The rewards for notables who served loyally were very real. Their sons would be allowed to replace their fathers in their local roles on condition that they accepted stricter central control. On the death of İsmail Bey of Serez, for instance, the government permitted his son to replace him.[19] In addition, sons of loyal notables might be given appointments to important positions in the service of the state. In this manner, the state recognized sons of notables as state officials, but no longer as notables. Good examples are governors Cebbarzâde Celâleddin and Karaosmanoğlu Yakub Pashas.[20]

Simultaneously, the state began to employ threats and punishment against dissident notables. The sultan instructed all provincial administrators to suppress them, and threatened those who failed to do so.[21] The provincial administration, in turn, moved against disobedient notables and local dynasties with crushing force. Many prominent notables, such as Tekelioğlu İbrahim and Dağdevirenoğlu Mehmed, were put to death.[22]

---

[18] *Tarih-i Cevdet*, 10, p. 87.

[19] Ibid., p. 117.

[20] Mustafa Nuri, *Netayicü'l-vuku'at*, 4 (Istanbul: Uhuvvet Matbaası, 1327 [1909]), p. 98.

[21] *Tarih-i Cevdet*, 10, pp. 181–2.

[22] *Şânizâde Tarihi*, 2 ([Istanbul]: Süleyman Efendi Matbaası, 1290 [1873]), pp. 304, 349–50, 353.

To break the backbone of local power, the state resettled members of local dynasties in different regions of the empire. Commonly, the government would resettle Anatolian notable families in Rumelia, and vice versa. Thus, for example, the entire Tekelioğlu clan, once dominant in Teke and Antalya, was relocated to Salonica.[23]

By 1820, the center had asserted its control over all of Anatolia and Eastern Rumelia, although occasional clashes with lesser notables persisted for some time. Those notables who adjusted to the new reality of a strong and assertive center continued to wield economic power well into the twentieth century. Those unwilling or unable to adapt disappeared.

The state also seized every opportunity to restore central control over the peripheral regions of the empire. In 1831, it ended Mamluk rule in Baghdad;[24] in 1835, it put an end to the Karamanlı dynasty in Tripoli of Barbary. Many governors who displayed an inclination toward disloyalty and autonomy in smaller provinces were executed. Yet many local leaders continued to exercise considerable influence over decision-making at the regional level.[25] In larger provinces, the state even went to war to unseat independent-minded governors. In such cases, the outcome depended largely on three factors: the recognition accorded the governor by foreign powers, the sophistication of the local bureaucratic apparatus, and the strength of the local army. Ali Pasha of Tepelenë was weak in all but the last, and neither the geographic advantages of Albania nor the ethnic character and extent of the area under his control proved sufficient to save him.[26] Similarly, Husein Kapetan Gradaščević (known as *Zmaj od Bosne*, the Dragon of Bosnia), whose superb army won a military engagement against imperial troops in 1831–32 under the conservative green banner of the crescent and star, was nonetheless unable to exploit his victory in the absence of international support.

In order to bolster central control of the periphery, Mahmud II attempted to institutionalize the link between central and provincial administration. The first step was to amass accurate information about the population of the empire. In 1829, an initial census was carried out in the imperial capital.[27] A special new office was given the task of maintaining population records submitted by provincial authorities.[28] Although the war of 1828–29 with Russia disrupted this work, a general census carried out in 1830–31 provided the government with precise data about its subjects for the first

---

[23] *Tarih-i Cevdet*, 10, p. 148.

[24] *Tarih-i Lûtfî*, 3 (Istanbul: Matbaa-i Âmire, 1292 [1875]), pp. 115–18.

[25] *Tarih-i Cevdet*, 10, pp. 191ff.

[26] *Şânizâde Tarihi*, 3 ([Istanbul]: s.n. 1291 [1874]), pp. 104ff.

[27] *Tarih-i Lûtfî*, 3, pp. 142–5.

[28] Ibid., pp. 145–6.

time in the modern history of the empire.[29] These census results enabled the government to devise a centralized, standardized system of taxation. Relying on accurate records of property holdings, the government could specify in advance the timing and amount of the payments it required.[30] In another move reflecting the strong desire to control the periphery, the state extended the institution of "headmen," originally introduced in the various quarters of the capital, applying it at the local level in other parts of the empire.[31]

Many other developments of this period illustrate the new emphasis on centralization. In 1831, for example, in an attempt to improve the communication of imperial policy throughout the empire, the government launched the publication of the first official Ottoman newspaper, *Takvim-i Vekayi'* (Calendar of Events). In 1838, the state began to issue passports to Ottoman subjects, who had hitherto obtained travel documents from embassies and consulates of countries of destination.[32] The Ministry of the Interior assumed responsibility for issuing internal travel permits. Another sign of the attempt to bind the empire more tightly together was the extensive reform of the Ottoman postal service—which had remained almost unchanged for centuries—starting in 1825.[33] Finally, a symbolic indication of the new stress on central control was the posting of portraits of the sultan in civil and military offices throughout the empire.[34]

The Ottoman central government also underwent a thorough structural reform that produced ministries and councils similar to those in Europe (France was the principal model). The office of the grand vizier became the prime minister's office. New ministries of the interior, foreign affairs, and finance formed the embryonic limbs of a modern bureaucracy.[35] In 1838, the existing ad hoc consultation mechanisms of the executive were institutionalized under two organizations: the Deliberative Council of the Sublime Porte and the Supreme Council of Judicial Ordinances.[36] The burgeoning bureaucracy was reorganized according to a new scheme of ranks and titles for civil, military, and religious personnel.[37] Strict dress codes for

---

[29] 1247 *Senesi'nde Memâlik-i Şâhâne'de Mevcud Nüfûs Defteri*, IUL, Turkish Mss., no. 8867.

[30] *Tarih-i Lûtfî*, 5, pp. 122–3.

[31] Musa Çadırcı, "Türkiye'de Muhtarlık Teşkilâtının Kurulması Üzerine Bir İnceleme," *Belleten* 34/135 (1970), p. 411.

[32] *Tarih-i Lûtfî*, 5, pp. 116–17.

[33] Nesimî Yazıcı, "II. Mahmud Döneminde Menzilhaneler: 'Ref'-i Menzil Bedeli'," *Sultan II. Mahmud ve Reformları Semineri* (Istanbul: Edebiyat Fakültesi Yayınları, 1990), pp. 157–91.

[34] *Tarih-i Lûtfî*, 5, pp. 50–52.

[35] Ibid., pp. 113–14, 147, and 104–5, respectively.

[36] Ibid., pp. 106–7.

[37] Ibid., pp. 26, 102.

state officials distinguished them from the public at large. And new privileges were granted to officialdom, including state protection from confiscation (although the sultan was the first to disregard this assurance).

Mahmud II's administration established new schools or revitalized old ones, such as the Royal Medical Academy, the School for Surgeons, the School for Military Sciences, and the Military School for Engineering. These were designed not to provide college education to the populace but to furnish the administration with educated officials for state service. During Mahmud II's reign, the state also began to send small groups of students to Europe for education, specifically in the military sciences. To limit the dangerous influence of French culture on impressionable young minds, those in charge of the program were instructed to avoid teaching the French language, to enforce the exclusive use of Turkish and Arabic, and to select accommodation outside of Paris. It was emphasized that students were to learn only "sciences," and were then to return to the country without being "unduly influenced by the detrimental values of a foreign culture."[38] But expectations were high. As the Ottoman minister of war instructed those departing: "You belong to a nation long thought incapable of partaking of the science of Europe, and of the advantages that result from them. . . . The sultan, reformer of a system the foundation of which has become decayed, labors incessantly to introduce into his empire the knowledge that may ameliorate the condition of the Ottoman people . . . [O]n your return, it will be your duty to show what civilized Europe can do for our happiness and for our advancement."[39] Clearly, the state aimed to benefit from European scientific knowledge insofar as this could be done without transplanting European culture into the empire.

The institutionalization of Westernization under Mahmud II differed considerably from previous attempts to confront European ideas. For the first time, Westernization appeared as a formal policy linked to extensive bureaucratic reform and implemented with brutal force. The new schools provided the necessary manpower, while a government newspaper supported the effort with appropriate propaganda. These important changes had a lasting effect on the new generation that came of age under Mahmud II, and provided the foundation for the cadres of the later Tanzimat movement. But their effect on mature contemporaries was limited. In 1839/1255, the year in which Mahmud II died after a reign of more than three decades, among the records of hundreds of books in possession of Ottoman officials of approximately the sultan's age group, only one foreign work appears—a map of Europe.[40] Similar holdings of a decade later,

[38] Undated instructions in TSA E. 1518/1.

[39] "Turkish Reform," *Niles' Weekly Register* 7/12 (November 17, 1832), p. 187.

[40] See the estate record of the Director of Finance, Esseyyid İsmail Ferruh Efendi ibn Süleyman, dated June 8, 1839, in İstanbul Müftülük Arşivi, ŞS 1461, f. 54a.

FIGURE 5. Sultan Mahmud II in traditional garb before the destruction of the Janissaries in 1826. *Tanzimat I* (Istanbul: Maarif Vekâleti, 1940), pp. 16–17.

however, contain thousands of books in European languages as well as numerous translations,[41] demonstrating the generational gap in the response to Westernization.

[41] See infra, footnotes 252–5.

FIGURE 6. Sultan Mahmud II in his new uniform after the destruction of the Janissaries. *Tanzimat I* (Istanbul: Maarif Vekâleti, 1940), pp. 16–17.

THE CHALLENGE OF MEHMED ALİ

Mehmed Ali of Egypt presented imperial rule with a domestic challenge of unprecedented magnitude. He not only resisted imperial encroachment with success; he nearly conquered the empire itself. Egypt under the rule of Mehmed Ali produced the most powerful army in the Near East; his efficient bureaucracy outmatched its imperial counterpart; and his negotiations with the French yielded recognition by a great power, though this fell somewhat short of an alliance. Mehmed Ali's suppression of the Wahhābī revolt in Arabia (1811–18) and his decisive intervention on behalf of the sultan in the Greek rebellion (1824–27) indicated that he would prevail in a full-scale conflict with his August Sovereign. Indeed, when war broke out between them in 1832, Mehmed Ali's armies won a series of victories that brought them from Acre on the shores of the southern Mediterranean to Konia in heartland Anatolia. The way to Istanbul lay open.

By this point, however, the empire as a whole, and the Straits connecting the Black Sea with the Mediterranean in particular, had begun to figure prominently in European calculations of the balance of power. Therefore, the Sublime Porte could assume that one of the rival powers, Russia or Great Britain, would come to its rescue to prevent the dangerous blow to the status quo that would result from the conquest of the imperial heartland by an ally of France. Surprisingly, the British Cabinet turned down the desperate Ottoman call for help—Palmerston later wrote "that no British Cabinet at any period of the history of England ever made so great a mistake in regard to foreign affairs."[42] The sultan, reportedly remarking that "a drowning man will clutch at a serpent," then invited the traditional adversary of the empire, Russia, to come to its defense. In late January 1833, the Egyptian army under the command of İbrahim Pasha reached Kütahya, only 223 miles from the capital. But within weeks a Russian fleet anchored before Büyükdere on the Bosporus; in May, Russian troops disembarked on the shores of Asia as allies of the empire. Public opinion at the time swallowed this bitter pill with difficulty; many years later, following the Ottoman entry into the First World War against Russia, the despised stone obelisk erected to commemorate this event was torn down. But the danger to the state was too great for a desperate Sultan Mahmud II to take popular sensibilities into account. To secure Russian intervention, he made an offer that no Russian government could easily decline: a provision regulating the closure of the Dardanelles to "any foreign vessels of war" in the event of armed conflict. Protecting Russia against attack from the south, the Hünkâr İskelesi Treaty of August 1833 represented the peak of Russian diplomatic achievements vis-à-vis the Ottoman Empire up to that point. The accomplishment, however, was short-lived, as British pressure compelled Russia to abandon its privileges at the London Straits Convention in 1841.

In the meantime, Russian intervention obliged Mehmed Ali to negotiate a settlement with the Sublime Porte, which was duly concluded in May 1833. All the same, his gains were considerable: the agreement recognized Mehmed Ali and his sons as the rulers of a small empire covering Egypt,

---

[42] Charles Webster, *The Foreign Policy of Palmerston, 1830–1841: Britain, the Liberal Movement and the Eastern Question*, 1 (London: G. Bell, 1951), p. 284.

Syria, Jeddah, Crete, Adana, and the Sudan—this last a vast land that Mehmed Ali had conquered, ostensibly on behalf of his suzerain, in 1820–21. Both parties seemed dissatisfied with the terms reached, and each was eager to modify them in its own favor. In June 1839, Mehmed Ali's troops once again defeated the imperial army and found themselves in a position to march on to the capital. This time, however, it was Great Britain—which had secured considerable economic privileges from the Ottomans in 1838 and feared the prospect of a new Russian intervention or the aggrandizement of a French ally—which intervened to avert the fall of Istanbul. Sultan Mahmud II's opportune death spared him from hearing of the embarrassing defeat of his armies at the hands of his rebellious governor or of the subsequent surrender of his fleet at Alexandria. Mehmed Ali, reinforced by French support, rejected the terms offered by the other European powers. This resulted in a short war between the Egyptians and a joint task force composed of Ottoman, British, and Austrian naval contingents. In November 1840, Mehmed Ali accepted the reduction of his powers to hereditary rule over Egypt. For the Ottomans, who had entertained the illusion that they might reestablish central control over Egypt, the victory was bittersweet. The deal later forced on Mehmed Ali by the Great Powers served as the basis for contracts subsequently negotiated with local leaders such as Imām Yaḥyā Ḥamīd al-Dīn and ʿAbd al-ʿAzīz ibn Saʿūd in the Arabian Peninsula.

In the 1840s, Mehmed Ali resumed his challenge to the imperial center in Africa. In 1846, the Sublime Porte responded to his attempts to annex the remnants of the old Ottoman province of Ethopia (roughly, the coastal parts of modern Eritrea) with an offer of the Eritrean customs dues (fixed at 625,000 French francs per year) for life. Upon the death of Mehmed Ali in 1849, the Ottoman administration sought to wrench Eritrea away from Egyptian control by returning the rump province to the authority of the Province of Jeddah. But in 1865, Ismaʿīl Pasha managed to restore Egypt's rights to Eritrean tax revenues. Finally, in 1866, the Ottoman government all but ceded Eritrea to Egypt in return for an annual payment.[43] Though the Ottomans thereby lost access to two strategic ports, they retained formal sovereignty over them and, for the time being, thwarted their takeover by a hostile European power.

EUROPEAN THREATS TO THE INTEGRITY OF THE EMPIRE

In the early nineteenth century, Ottoman efforts to re-assert control over the periphery began to encounter a new form of resistance. Although the illegitimacy of Muslim rule over Christians was a common theme in

---

[43] Rauf Ahmed and Ragıb Raif, *Mısır Mes'elesi* (Istanbul: Matbaa-i Âmire, 1334 [1918]), pp. 8, 35–7.

FIGURE 7. Ottoman provinces and autonomous principalities in Europe in 1833.

premodern Europe, European governments in the modern age had generally considered Ottoman rule over its Christian subjects an internal affair of the Ottoman state. When, for instance, Russia had supported the Serbian rebels during the Russo-Ottoman War of 1806–12, European policy makers and public opinion refrained from making a moral issue of the "Serbian Question." Russian demands for protective rights over the Orthodox subjects of the

Ottoman Empire, however, had revitalized this issue. The Greek rebellion may be considered a watershed event in this regard. In fact, it was largely because of international support for the insurgents that the Ottomans failed to put down the Greek revolt, as they had done with countless other uprisings in the past. To be sure, European sentiment in favor of the Greeks was a some- what special case; still, from this point onward, European public opinion began to express sympathy for other anti-Ottoman uprisings launched by Christians. These sympathies tended to override strategic concerns or interstate rivalries. The Greek rebellion, and the independent Greek kingdom that arose in its wake, represented glaring violations of the conservative spirit of the Vienna Congress of 1815 (an event in which the Ottoman administration did not participate). Yet European concern for the status quo was never fully extended to the Ottoman domains. The Greeks set a precedent for the other Christian peoples of the empire, who observed that internationalization of local grievances provided an effective new lever for the dilution or termination of Ottoman rule.

The internal threat posed by separatism paralleled an increase in the threat of partition from without. Bonaparte's invasion of Egypt in 1798 had demonstrated that a European power could conquer a major Ottoman territory—and one overwhelmingly inhabited by Muslims—with impunity. Previous Ottoman losses in the East and West had been limited to areas inhabited by Christian majorities which were lost to Russia and Austria. But the French and British occupations of Perim, a strategic island situated at the mouth of the Red Sea, in 1738 and 1799, respectively, displayed the sever- ity of the danger to the Ottoman periphery.[44] This threat was underscored by the French occupation of Algeria in 1830, against which the Ottoman administration could do no more than lodge an official protest.

ECONOMIC REFORM

The trend toward centralization also extended to Ottoman economic policies. The financial institutions of the empire became more centralized, especially after 1826. In 1813, the central government decided to grant local tax farms only to local administrators. In theory, the measure would prevent tax farmers from overtaxing the people; it would also place more assets at the disposal of local administrators, who had lost their traditional sources of revenue. Although on paper the new practice seemed to help the local administrators, in reality it turned them into salaried officials who remitted local revenues to the center.[45] Furthermore, in 1838 the state allocated cash

[44] BOA-HR.SYS. 102/3 [1799].

[45] Yavuz Cezar, *Osmanlı Maliyesinde Bunalım ve Değişim Dönemi: XVIII. yy dan Tanzimat'a Mali Tarih* (Istanbul: Alan Yayıncılık, 1986), pp. 242–3.

salaries to all officials; henceforth, all other sources of income, including the collection of transaction fees, were shut down.[46] This was a major step toward creating a centralized, monetary economy; it also bolstered the status and image of officialdom. The state further introduced new, standard gold and silver coins at fixed value and banned the circulation of foreign coins, which were to be surrendered to the mint office at prices set by the state. Like other attempts to regulate the economy by decree, however, this effort proved ineffective in the long run.[47]

In a transparent bid to emulate Mehmed Ali's successful policies, the state increased the number of agricultural products, such as opium, silk, and cotton, that were purchased, sold, and exported through monopolies. As a result, however, production sharply decreased, while smuggling increased. Annual production of opium, for example, fell from 75 million pounds before the introduction of the monopolies to 35 million pounds shortly afterward.[48] The Ottoman authorities also underestimated the losses they would incur from reductions in tariffs on foreign goods. According to Ottoman practice at the time, goods derived their taxable status from the nationality of the merchant, not from the place of production. Thus, imported Russian grain was charged a third of the duty imposed on Ottoman domestic grain; American tobacco could be purchased at a better price in Alexandria; and Swiss silk was cheapest in Lebanon.[49] Such concerns induced the Ottoman government to sign the Anglo-Ottoman commercial treaty of 1838, which resulted in greatly lowered tariffs and also the abolition of the monopolies and other restrictions on trade. According to the treaty, British merchants could purchase all goods and products produced in the Ottoman Empire; they would pay a customs tariff equal to that paid by domestic merchants; and the Ottoman administration would lift all prohibitions on exports. In practice, a 3 percent tariff was levied on British goods entering the Ottoman market, whereas Ottoman exports were taxed at a rate of 60 percent.[50] The Ottoman authorities hoped that the benefits of increased trade and production would compensate for the losses stemming from the abolition of the monopolies and the lower tariffs. However, just as in Egypt, which had paid a heavy price for abolishing her monopolies, this treaty and its gradual extension to other powers had a negative impact on Ottoman manufacturing and on the economy as a whole.

[46] *Tarih-i Lûtfî*, 5, pp. 132, 180–81.

[47] *Şânizâde Tarihi*, 2, pp. 160–61.

[48] Mübahat S. Kütükoğlu, *Osmanlı-İngiliz İktisâdî Münâsebetleri*, 1 (*1580–1838*) (Ankara: TKAE Yayınları, 1974), p. 87.

[49] David Urquhart, *How Russia Tries to Get into Her Hands the Supply of Corn of the Whole Europe: The English Turkish Treaty of 1838* (London: R. Hardwicke, 1859), pp. 358–9.

[50] Kütükoğlu, *Osmanlı-İngiliz İktisadî Münâsebetleri*, 1, pp. 109–10.

Three decades after the heyday of the provincial notables, the imperial administration had managed to transform the empire into a relatively centralized state. In fact, despite major territorial losses, such as Greece and Algeria, and the grant of extensive autonomy to Serbia, Egypt, and the island of Samos (Sisam), the state actually expanded the area under its direct administration. The apparatus of government acquired more information on its subjects, became more visible, and penetrated more deeply into the fabric of daily life throughout the empire. But the strengthening of the state rested mostly on expanding recruitment for the army and collecting more taxes. Neither measure decreased social discontent.

The Tanzimat Era

ON NOVEMBER 3, 1839, Foreign Minister Mustafa Reşid Pasha read an imperial decree before Sultan Abdülmecid and an assembled audience of state dignitaries, religious leaders, prominent bureaucrats, foreign diplomats, and nobles, including Prince de Joinville, the third son of King Louis Philippe. Although it conformed in form and tone to the long tradition of edicts promising administrative fairness in the name of the sultan,[1] this proclamation, soon to gain fame as the Rose Chamber Edict, was like nothing seen before in Ottoman history. At the ceremonial level, the singular importance attached to the edict was underscored by a solemn oath taken by the sultan, witnessed by the assembled ulema and invited dignitaries, including foreign ambassadors, in the palace chamber in which the Prophet Muḥammad's mantle was preserved. But the real novelty of the decree lay in its content. Following a preamble citing neglect of the Qurʾān and the sharīʿa as the causes of Ottoman troubles over the last century and a half, the edict promised new laws guaranteeing life and property rights, prohibiting bribery, and regulating the levying of taxes and the conscription and tenure of soldiers. It promised the enactment of legislation that would outlaw execution without trial, confiscation of property, and violations of personal chastity and honor. In addition, it heralded the abolition of the odious system of tax farming and the establishment of an equitable draft system. Like the prospective penal code under consideration at the time, these laws were to be drafted by the Supreme Council of Judicial Ordinances and the Military Council.[2] Most significantly, they would apply to all Ottoman subjects, Muslim and non-Muslim alike.

The declaratory value of the Rose Chamber Edict clearly outweighed its legal significance. Although it did not constitute a piece of legislation, the edict was an important statement of Ottoman intentions. Its intended

[1] Halil İnalcık, "Sened-i İttifak ve Gülhane Hatt-ı Hümâyûnu," *Belleten* 28/112 (1964), p. 611.

[2] Ahmed Lûtfî, *Tarih-i Lûtfî*, 6 (Istanbul: Mahmud Bey Matbaası, 1302 [1885]), pp. 61–4.

audience has been a matter of some debate. To an extent, the edict was directed at European ears. Its architect, Mustafa Reşid Pasha, was well known to be the foremost proponent of Ottoman accession to the European concert.[3] In a sense, the document served as an assurance to the Great Powers that demanded domestic reforms in return for future recognition of the Ottoman Empire as a member of the concert of Europe. Thus, for instance, many issues and formulations were clear allusions to the 6th, 7th, 13th, and 17th articles of the French *Déclaration des droits de l'homme et du citoyen*. At the same time, the striking similarities between the section discussing the responsibilities of the government and the Virginia Bill of Rights of 1776[4] indicate that the appeasement of European powers was not the only reason behind the incorporation of foreign ideas into the proclamation. Indeed, it seems clear that those Ottoman bureaucrats who drafted the document sincerely believed in the modernization of the Ottoman conception of government based in part on concepts borrowed from abroad. Thus, the edict was directed both inward and outward, at once a serious commitment to reform out of self-interest and an appeasing gesture directed at Europe. The religious trappings of the edict itself and the ceremony surrounding its proclamation are misleading; an early draft of the decree contained far fewer references to Islamic concepts than the final version, indicating that Islamic citations in the final text were cosmetic changes added as a sop to the ulema in order to shield the government from the criticism that it was imitating infidel practice.[5]

The role of the Ottoman bureaucracy in drafting, codifying, and implementing the administrative reform was unprecedented, and it signaled a decisive shift in the internal balance of power within the empire. Above all, the reform was associated with three men: Mustafa Reşid Pasha, Mehmed Emin Âlî Pasha, and Keçecizâde Mehmed Fu'ad Pasha. These prominent statesmen adopted Metternich as their role model and his oppressive bureaucracy as their source of inspiration for top-down conservative reform. These leaders of the Sublime Porte—which under Mahmud II came to refer to a central bureaucratic institution, not merely the residence of the grand vizier—took charge of the next three and a half decades of reform, generally referred to as the Tanzimat era. Under their firm leadership, the bureaucratic cadres of the Sublime Porte oversaw the entire administration of the state, ruling the empire until 1871 with only trivial interference from the imperial palace or the ulema.

The edict noted the universal applicability of the new laws. This not only revealed the wish to establish a single legal system for all subjects; it indicated

[3] Ibid., p. 59.
[4] Yavuz Abadan, "Tanzimat Fermanının Tahlili," *Tanzimat I* (Istanbul: Maarif Vekâleti, 1940), p. 52.
[5] Ibid., pp. 48ff.

a change in the official ideology of the state. Not long before, Mahmud II had hinted at such a change when he stated: "From now on I do not wish to recognize Muslims outside the mosque, Christians outside the church, or Jews outside the synagogue."[6] The formulation of this vision of an imperial administration based on universal laws in the context of the imperial edict was a significant first step toward the transformation of hitherto Muslim, Christian, and Jewish subjects into *Ottomans*.

Indeed, one effect of the reform movement as a whole was to undermine the traditional Ottoman legal categories of Muslim, dhimmī, and non-Muslim foreigner. The reforms introduced a new category of *ecnebî* (foreigner), which referred to all foreign nationals regardless of religious affiliation (although the phrase occasionally referred more specifically to non-Muslim foreigners). A second new legal term, that of "Ottoman," replaced the old distinction between Muslims and dhimmīs. Finally, the important designation of dhimmī was replaced by "non-Muslim Ottoman." The Ottoman Law of Nationality of 1869 formalized these concepts.[7]

The reconciliation of this new, nondenominational ideological basis of the state with Islam's traditional centrality in the legitimizing framework of the empire remained the most delicate and challenging issue for the administration until the end of the Ottoman era. In this regard, the Tanzimat epoch exemplified a general inclination toward a more secular conception of the state. But this was not always sustained. For instance, the new penal codes of 1840 and 1851 explicitly invoked the sharī'a and attempted to reconcile it with the principles laid out in the Rose Chamber Edict and with modern European concepts of law. And although the third penal code of 1858 was firmly based on the French penal code of 1810, pushing Islamic principles into the background, the sharī'a courts were not dismantled until after the collapse of the empire (although they steadily lost ground to the civil court system).

Finally, the *Majalla*—a comprehensive compendium of Ḥanafī fiqh to be administered in the new civil (*Nizamiye*) courts—prevailed over an adaptation of the French civil code of 1804. The Majalla was a monumental work that has since served as the civil code in a number of successor states (e.g., in Iraq until 1951, and in Jordan until 1952), and as a major source for the composition of a civil code in others (e.g., by the renowned jurist ʿAbd al-Razzāq Aḥmad al-Sanhūrī in Egypt in 1949, in Syria in 1949, and in Iraq in 1951, as well as in Israel, where several of its statutes are still in effect). It has even inspired the civil codes of several nonsuccessor states, such as Afghanistan and Malaysia. The French civil code, despite its roots in Justinian's *Institutes*, was favored by many Tanzimat statesmen, who thought it a eulogy to "common sense" better suited to the goal of unifying the

---

[6] Éd[ouard] Engelhardt, *La Turquie et le Tanzimat; ou Histoire des réformes dans l'Empire ottoman depuis 1826 jusqu'à nos jours*, 1 (Paris: A. Cotillon, 1882), p. 33.

[7] *Düstûr*, I/1 (Istanbul: Matbaa-i Âmire, 1289 [1872]) pp. 16–18.

empire's subjects, but their view failed to carry the day.[8] The secular tendencies of the official ideology of the state became more pronounced in the later decades of the Tanzimat era, but never to the point of removing Islam as a pillar of the empire-caliphate.

The ulema were not the only religious figures threatened by the ascendance of the new ideology; non-Muslim clerics likewise viewed the new policies as a threat to their positions in the established order. The reform edict of 1856, which granted equality to non-Muslims in all aspects of life, provided a more solid legal basis for the promotion of the new official ideology—much to the dismay of conservative Muslims, who reacted to its promulgation with anguish: "For Muslims this is a day to weep and mourn."[9] The edict also weakened the privileged status of the Greek Patriarchate vis-à-vis the other non-Muslim religious institutions. A typical Greek reaction to the reform edict was: "the state has made us equal with the Jews. We were satisfied with Muslim superiority."[10] Particularly revealing was the insistence of *all* Ottoman religious communities that the relationship between each community and the center remain a bilateral one; *millet* leaders insisted that any new privileges must be conferred on them as a distinct community, not as Ottomans. Thus, far from encouraging the dissolution of barriers between the various communities, millet representatives fought for their preservation. This pattern persisted in later years, as national groups began to draw on the model of Austro-Hungarian dual monarchy to voice comparable demands. In 1870, the Bulgarians petitioned the sultan to "strengthen forever the ties that attach us Bulgarians to your throne, by proclaiming our religious and political autonomy, based on a free Constitution, and by adding the title 'Tsar of the Bulgarians' to your [present] title 'Sultan of the Ottomans.'"[11] Later certain Greek intellectuals entertained similar ideas,[12] just as Arab visionaries would later dream of a Turco-Arabian Empire on the same model.[13]

In the course of the Tanzimat era, the official boundaries between religion and ethnicity became increasingly blurred. On the one hand, religion still served as the principal organizational and ideological focus of the millets, and was so treated by the authorities. As late as 1870 the Bulgarians appealed

[8] Ebül'ulâ Mardin, *Medenî Hukuk Cephesinden Ahmet Cevdet Paşa* (Istanbul: Hukuk Fakültesi Yayınları, 1946), pp. 63ff.

[9] Cevdet Paşa, *Tezâkir*, 1, ed. Cavid Baysun (Ankara: Türk Tarih Kurumu Yayınları, 1953), p. 68.

[10] Ibid.

[11] *Khristomatiia po istoriia na Bŭlgariia*, 2, eds. Khristo A. Khristov and Nikolai Genchev (Sofia: Nauka i izkustvo, 1969), pp. 324–32.

[12] A. J. Panayotopoulos, "The 'Great Idea' and the Vision of Eastern Federation: A Propos of Views of I. Dragoumis and A. Souliotis-Nicolaïdis," *Balkan Studies* 21/2 (1980), pp. 331ff.

[13] [Ahmed Cemal], *Cemal Paşa Hâtıratı, 1913–1922* (Istanbul: Ahmed İhsan ve Şürekâsı, 1339 [1922]), p. 48.

to the state for recognition not as ethnic Bulgars, but as a distinct religious community in the traditional mode, to be headed by an ethnarch in Istanbul. The state, in turn, continued to recognize the religious foundation of the millets, drafting organic laws governing the self-administration of the three major non-Muslim communities: the Greek Orthodox (1862), the Armenians of the Apostolic Church (1863), and the Jews (1865).[14] Yet at the same time, certain reforms launched by the state tended to subvert the religious nature of the millets. The state came to stand for Ottomanism, an inherently secular ideology. It began to appoint non-Muslims to important bureaucratic positions. Likewise, it undermined the traditionally dominant position of the clergy within the various communities by organizing representative assemblies to manage community affairs; in these a new balance between laymen and clergy was established.

By increasing the representation of all communities as Ottomans in the state bureaucracy, courts, and local assemblies, the state signaled its commitment to Ottomanism and simultaneously bolstered support for the new doctrine within the establishment. Mixed commercial courts permitted non-Muslim representation as early as 1847. The Law for Provincial Administration of 1864, which established provincial executive councils, stipulated that two Muslim and two non-Muslim representatives, chosen from the local populace, would serve on each of these bodies alongside state bureaucrats.[15] It should be noted that representation, as conceived by the statesmen of the Tanzimat, had little to do with democracy. Rather, it was a policy designed to co-opt different ethno-religious groups into the administration by soliciting advice and intelligence from their loyal and respected leaders without actually allowing them to participate in political decision-making. Such, for instance, was the purpose behind the government's invitation, in 1845, to two Muslim notables and two non-Muslim headmen from each province to the capital to provide information on local problems and propose additional reforms.[16] The leaders of the Tanzimat feared, with good reason, that their polyethnic, multi-faith empire would not survive the introduction of a truly representative system of government.[17]

DIPLOMACY, WAR, AND REFORM

The Tanzimat leaders were undoubtedly sincere in their desire to reinvigorate the empire through reform. But the reforms served another principal

---

[14] *Düstûr*, I/2 (Istanbul: Matbaa-i Âmire, 1289 [1872]), pp. 902–75.

[15] Article 13, *Düstûr*, I/1 (Istanbul, 1289 [1872]), p. 610.

[16] *Tarih-i Lûtfî*, 8 (Istanbul: Sabah Matbaası, 1328 [1910]), pp. 15–17.

[17] Un Impartial [Mehmed Emin Âlî], *Réponse à son altesse Moustapha Fazil Pacha au sujet de sa lettre au Sultan* ([Paris]: Imprimerie Jouaust, 1867), pp. 24ff.

goal for them: acquiring the international respectability required for membership in the European concert. The dual purpose of the reforms was especially evident in those innovations aimed at achieving equality before the law: advancing such equality promoted the cohesiveness of a fractious multinational empire, and at the same time it placated European public opinion, which was increasingly sensitive to the inequality of the empire's Christians. When, in 1849, failed revolutionaries fled from Poland and Hungary to seek safe haven in the Ottoman Empire, the Sublime Porte rejected Austrian and Russian demands that it surrender the fugitives, thereby bolstering the image of the empire as progressive and reformist in liberal circles in Europe. Winning over public opinion in Europe was not merely a question of popularity; it was crucial for the defense of the empire. When, in 1853, Russia attempted once more to intervene in Ottoman politics on behalf of the Orthodox subjects of the empire, it faced strong British and French opposition. To be sure, strategic considerations were paramount in the Anglo-French resistance to the Russian attempt to reinterpret its vague protective rights over the Orthodox population of the empire. But for the first time, considerations of interest were reinforced by the pro-Ottoman pressure of public opinion. In this sense, the Crimean War (see below), ostensibly fought over a dispute regarding the Holy Places in Jerusalem, was a great victory for Ottoman public diplomacy.

The cornerstone of Tanzimat foreign policy was the informal alliance with Great Britain.[18] This alliance rested on a set of shared interests and above all on the existence of a common enemy: Russia. Fu'ad Pasha's political testament, written shortly before his death in 1869 in the form of advice to the sultan, offers perhaps the best explanation of the basic precepts of Ottoman foreign policy during this period. No one, he wrote, should be surprised by Russian expansionism. "Had I been a Russian statesman," he confessed, "I too would have turned the world upside down to capture Istanbul."[19] The inevitability of Russian hostility meant that the Ottoman government was duty-bound to strengthen the defense of the empire against this perennial threat and guarantee its integrity by means of formal alliances. To gain internal strength and external legitimacy (in the eyes of France, symbol of progress), the empire must modernize itself. To acquire allies, it must turn to the British. As he put it, "the English people . . . will always be the first to have our alliance and we will hold fast to that alliance to the last." Fu'ad Pasha considered the importance of British support against Russia so vital that it "appeared preferable that . . . we should relinquish

[18] Mustafa Reşid Pasha had attempted to forge an Anglo-Ottoman alliance even before the Tanzimat. See Reşat Kaynar, *Mustafa Reşit Paşa ve Tanzimat* (Ankara: Türk Tarih Kurumu Yayınları, 1954), pp. 148–51.

[19] Mehmed Galib, "Tarihden Bir Sahife: Âlî ve Fu'ad Paşaların Vasiyetnâmeleri," *Tarih-i Osmanî Encümeni Mecmuası* 1/2 [June 14, 1910], p. 79.

several of our provinces rather than see England abandon us."[20] As for Austria, its decline made it a less valuable ally, although it retained a vested interest in sustaining Ottoman rule in the Balkans. With regard to France, the Ottoman government should take care to maintain cordial relations with this powerful nation, not in the illusory hope of receiving its protection, but in order to prevent it from joining a hostile coalition.[21]

The Ottoman preference for a British alliance derived from several factors, including the Russophobia that prevailed in the British press from the 1830s onward, the Anglo-Russian "Cold War" in Europe and across the great plains of Central Asia, the rise in British economic and strategic interest in the Levant, and Britain's naval supremacy. As seen from London, the Russian threat to the Ottoman Empire, and particularly Russia's designs on the Bosporus and the Dardanelles in pursuit of its long-standing goal of acquiring warm-water access for the Russian navy, threatened British naval supremacy and the balance of power in Europe. Accordingly, preservation of the Ottoman Empire as a bulwark against Russian expansion (and, more generally, denying the empire's strategic assets to any hostile power) became a British defense priority from the mid-1830s until the 1880s.

But British commitment to the defense of the Ottoman Empire was inherently limited. As Palmerston noted of the Crimean crisis, the primary British aim was "to curb the aggressive ambition of Russia. We went to war not so much to keep the Sultan and his Mussulmans in Turkey as to keep the Russians out of Turkey."[22] The British sought one thing only: to check the expansion of Russia. Their commitment did not extend beyond defense against Russian encroachments. Nor did they have an interest in building up the Ottoman Empire as a major actor on the international scene, or in supporting Ottoman policy in a broad sense. Thus, not unlike U.S. support for Turkey during the Cold War, the cooperation between Great Britain and the Ottoman Empire rested above all on the persistence of Anglo-Russian rivalry. Accordingly, any signs of a reduction in the British preoccupation with the Russian threat, whether in Europe or in Asia, were greeted with alarm in Istanbul.[23]

The international crisis over the Holy Places, which erupted in May 1850, put British commitment to the test. The crisis began with a French demand for Roman Catholic guardianship over Christian sites in the Holy Land. Based on a liberal reinterpretation of the 13th article of the Ottoman-French Treaty of 1740, the French asked that the Ottomans revoke the row of privileges since granted by successive Ottoman sultans to the Greek Orthodox

---

[20] Ibid., p. 78.

[21] Ibid., p. 79.

[22] W. E. Mosse, *The Rise and Fall of the Crimean System, 1855–71: The Story of a Peace Settlement* (London: MacMillan, 1963), p. 1.

[23] Mehmed Galib, "Tarihden Bir Sahife: Âlî ve Fu'ad Paşaların Vasiyetnâmeleri," p. 80.

and Armenian Apostolic churches. The Ottoman government responded to this explosive demand with an attempt to appease all relevant parties. The overthrow of the French republic in December 1851 provided a short breathing space. But when Charles-Louis Napoleon renewed French pressure with extraordinary vigor in the course of 1852, the Ottoman government felt compelled to work out a solution favoring the Roman Catholic Church.

Not surprisingly, Russia, self-anointed protector of Orthodox Christianity, reacted strongly. The Russians were also uneasy about the rapprochement between the Ottoman Empire and Great Britain and France, and were especially irked by the Ottoman refusal to return Polish and Hungarian political refugees who had fled to Ottoman territory in the aftermath of the 1848 revolutions. When the Ottoman governor of Bosnia occupied Montenegro and revoked its autonomous status in the fall of 1852, Tsar Nicholas I seized on the opportunity to rally British and Austrian support for Russia's claim to rights of protection over the Ottoman Empire's Orthodox subjects. In doing so, he miscalculated the position of all relevant parties.

Apparently sensing that the time was right to strike a deal with Great Britain over the future of the Ottoman Empire, the Tsar broached the delicate subject of partition. In conversation with Sir Hamilton Seymour, the British ambassador to St. Petersburg, on January 9, 1853, he famously characterized the empire as the "Sick man of Europe," and indicated that Russia and Great Britain should prepare for its peaceful partition in the near future. But the British, ever wary of Russian intentions, declined to discuss the matter further, even when the Russians sweetened their proposal with the offer to award Egypt and Crete to Great Britain, and thereby secure the sea route to India.

Still more grievous was the Russians' misreading of the Austrian and Ottoman positions: failing to understand that Austria much preferred the Ottoman-supported status quo to Russian domination of the Balkans, they overestimated the extent of Austrian support; misjudging the extent of Ottoman opposition to the grant of any rights of protection over Ottoman subjects to a foreign power, they underestimated Ottoman resistance. When, in February 1853, the Ottoman government made a timely concession to Austria, restoring the status quo ante in Montenegro, Austrian support for Russia's position evaporated. Having effectively split the dangerous liaison between Austria and Russia, Ottoman statesmen were in a much better position to deal with the demands of the Tsar's extraordinary envoy, Kniaz Admiral Alexander Sergeyevich Menshikov, who arrived in Istanbul aboard a Russian man-of-war in late February 1853.

On March 22, 1853, Kniaz Menshikov presented his bold demands to the Ottoman government. He asked for a treaty that would redefine Russia's hitherto vague protective rights over the Orthodox Christian subjects of the Ottoman Empire (as stipulated in the 7th, 8th, 14th, and 16th articles of the Küçük Kaynarca Treaty) and went so far as to submit a draft for approval by the sultan. Although it was presented as a purely religious matter, this was in fact a political demand with potentially far-reaching consequences. The Russians requested that the Greek Orthodox Patriarchs of Istanbul, Antioch, Alexandria, and Jerusalem receive life-term appointments from the Ottoman government. But the emergence of patriarchs independent of Istanbul and beholden to St. Petersburg would significantly reduce Ottoman control over the Greek Orthodox population of the empire, which encompassed millions of Albanians, Arabs, Bulgarians, Macedonians, and Vlachs, as well as ethnic Greeks.[24] Moreover, the Russians sought rights of legal and political intervention for Russian diplomats, in cooperation with the Orthodox clerical establishment, on behalf of Greek Orthodox subjects throughout the empire. Implementation of the treaty would have resulted in a significant measure of Russian control over one-third of the Ottoman population.[25] Clearly this was a request to which no Ottoman government could accede.

The Ottoman government responded with delaying tactics designed to gain time for the acquisition of British and French support. The British Ambassador Stratford Canning returned to the Ottoman capital at the height of the crisis and, overstepping his instructions from London, urged his Ottoman friends to resist Russia's demands or face the destruction of their empire.[26] Policy makers back in London, however, were more cautious; they decided not to dispatch the Royal Navy despite the formal request of their chargé d'affaires in Istanbul. Catholic France, enraged by the latest challenge from Orthodoxy, adopted the dubious role of protector of the Ottomans. Louis Napoleon (now Emperor Napoleon III), in a combative mood, ordered the fleet to set sail for the Aegean on March 25. Their resolve stiffened by the appearance of new allies, the Ottoman government turned down Russia's request for a treaty on May 10.

Menshikov, who had expected the Ottoman government to yield quickly to the brutality of his approach, and who had already committed his country's prestige beyond the point of no return, now began to lower the bar for an agreement. He employed a series of threatening ultimata attached to strict deadlines, but to no avail. The Ottoman government turned them all down, including the last, which abandoned the reference to the Treaty of Küçük Kaynarca as well as the demand for a new convention or treaty, and merely requested a diplomatic note assuring Russia that the Greek Orthodox Church would enjoy all the privileges previously granted it by the Ottoman authorities or guaranteed by existing treaties between the Ottoman government and Russia. Though this last approach was much more

---

[24] Ali Fuat Türkgeldi, *Mesâil-i Mühimme-i Siyâsiyye*, 1, ed. Bekir Sıtkı Baykal (Ankara: Türk Tarih Kurumu Yayınları, 1960), pp. 253–4.

[25] Ibid., p. 255.

[26] Harold Temperley, *England and the Near East: The Crimea* (London: Longmans [1936]), p. 318.

conciliatory both in form and substance than the previous Russian ultimata, the Ottomans felt that to issue a binding document to a foreign power
concerning its own subjects was an undesirable risk. Accordingly, they rejected the demand, supported by the diplomatic community in Istanbul,
who believed that Ottoman acquiescence would entail an unacceptable disruption of the status quo in Russia's favor. Having failed utterly in his mission, Menshikov sailed away on May 21, accompanied by the entire Russian
diplomatic staff. On June 4, the Ottomans similarly rejected a subsequent
Russian ultimatum issued by Count Karl Robert Nesselrode, the Russian Foreign Minister. This final snub prompted the Russians to invade and occupy
Wallachia and Moldavia on July 3, 1853.

The failure of diplomacy over the following three months resulted in the
Ottoman declaration of war on October 4. Diplomatic efforts to contain the
war and reestablish the status quo ante continued until the Russian destruction of the Ottoman fleet at the Black Sea harbor of Sinop on November 24.
The growing threat to the balance of power represented by Russian expansion eventually trumped Anglo-French concerns about the transformation
of a local conflict into a major European war. On January 3, 1854, the French
and British fleets entered the Black Sea to protect Ottoman transports. On
February 27, the British and the French delivered an ultimatum to the Russian Empire, requesting the withdrawal of Russian troops from Wallachia
and Moldavia. St. Petersburg rejected the ultimatum, and Britain and
France declared war on Russia on May 28. What for eight months had been
almost purely a Russo-Ottoman confrontation now turned into a major
European struggle—the first since Russia and Great Britain had joined
forces at the beginning of the century to destroy the Napoleonic threat.

In the ensuing war, which lasted a little more than a year and a half, the
British and French led the hostilities against Russia in the Black Sea basin
and the Baltic Sea, while the Ottoman armies fought in supporting roles on
land. Although the Russian army had occupied Wallachia and Moldavia,
the major theater of war was in the Crimea. The projection of Russian
power in the Black Sea basin rested on the fort and naval base of Sevas-
topol. The British admiralty felt that without its destruction, Istanbul would
never be secure. In October 1854, British, French, and Ottoman expeditionary forces laid siege to the key port city, which fell in September 1855. In
a desperate attempt to prevent Austria from entering the war, Russia evacu-
ated Wallachia and Moldavia in the summer of 1854, allowing the Austrians
to occupy them until the termination of hostilities. But in 1856, with Austria threatening to enter the war on the side of the emerging victors, the
Tsar yielded to the superior power of the front arrayed against him. Russia
accepted preliminary peace terms in early February 1856.

Although the military victory over Russia was a major achievement, it
was clearly inconceivable without Austrian neutrality and Anglo-French

Crimean War.

support. When on the defensive, Ottoman troops performed well, especially against Russian attacks in Wallachia during the early days of the war; but they played only a secondary role in the major offensives of the war and their contribution to the ultimate victory was marginal. Thus, the greatest Ottoman achievement in the Crimean War was a diplomatic one of strategic magnitude. The Ottoman statesmen had managed to maneuver successfully between the two nonliberal powers of Europe who threatened the borders of the empire, astutely manipulating the differences between Austria and Russia and sundering the alliance between them. They had then succeeded in aligning the Ottoman Empire with the principal liberal powers of Europe and orchestrating the formation of the first coalition in which the Ottoman army fought shoulder-to-shoulder with European armies. The balance of forces engineered by the diplomats at the outset of the war all but guaranteed victory on the battlefield. Finally, the Ottomans had succeeded in gaining admission, however qualified, to the European club of powers. The Paris Treaty of 1856, which provided an unprecedented guarantee of the territorial integrity of the Ottoman state, made the empire, in effect, a member of the European concert. From the Ottoman perspective, this was a more important result than the Russian surrender of southern Bessarabia or even the neutralization of the Black Sea, which the British, Austrians, and French all viewed as the major achievement of the war and a vital check against the expansion of Russian power.

But the very success of Ottoman diplomacy in the Crimean War undermined its long-term viability, for the victory over Russia brought about a reduction in the British perception of Russia as a threat. Despite a temporary revival of Russophobia in 1871, when Russia denounced the Black Sea clauses of the Paris Treaty of 1856, it never again reached the peak of 1853. Once fear of Russia diminished, anti-Ottoman attitudes—long buried under sentiments of unity against a common foe—gradually resurfaced. As George Villiers (4th Earl of Clarendon), one of the architects of the Crimean system, noted in 1866, the British public drastically changed its mind about the Ottomans in the aftermath of the war, "as people [came to] know more about the united ignorance and stupidity of the Mahomedans who squat in some of the fairest regions of the world in order to prevent their being productive."[27] Such sentiments reflected the popular aversion in Great Britain to fighting another war ostensibly to protect the Ottomans from the Russians. Often expressed in the form of stronger public pressure for privileges for British trade or reforms favoring Ottoman Christians, they complicated continued strategic cooperation between Great Britain and the Ottoman Empire.

Strategic cooperation with Great Britain was not undermined only by the perceived diminution of the Russian threat to British interests; it also

---

[27] Mosse, *The Rise and Fall of the Crimean System*, p. 3.

went against the reality of increasing competition between the Ottoman Empire and Great Britain in the Arabian Peninsula. The Ottoman effort to reconquer portions of Yemen and reestablish suzerainty along the perimeter of the Persian Gulf during the last years of the Tanzimat constituted a direct challenge to British hegemony in the region and thus fundamentally altered the nature of Anglo-Ottoman relations. Active rivalry between the two powers and their clients over Arabia replaced the uneasy status quo and continued up until the eve of the Great War.

However, as Ottoman diplomats were to discover time and again until the collapse of the empire, there was no reliable substitute for British friendship. Ottoman diplomacy leaned toward France after 1856, but France was both unwilling and unable to provide a comparable measure of security against Russian advances. Nor were the Ottomans alone in this predicament: Austria too paid a heavy price for its support of the liberal powers during the Crimean War, and was reduced to second-tier status in Europe. There was no getting around the fact that Great Britain was the only power capable of holding the Russians at bay. This contradiction between the impossibility of replacing British protection and the diminishing basis for strategic cooperation with Great Britain continued to plague Ottoman decision makers until the Great War, though Ottoman-German rapprochement was to provide a temporary remedy in the post-Bismarckian era.

One new and remarkable feature of Ottoman diplomacy during the Tanzimat was the extraordinary power wielded by foreign ambassadors in the Ottoman capital. As the strategic importance of the empire rose in European estimates, the scene of the Great Power struggle for influence over its policies and dominions shifted to Istanbul. But the battle was not restricted to the foreign diplomatic community; it penetrated the Ottoman bureaucracy itself, fueling rivalry between domestic factions associated with particular foreign powers. The principal axis of rivalry, naturally, lay between the pro-British and pro-Russian factions in the Palace and Sublime Porte, who exploited the conflict between the two powers to bolster their own positions within the Ottoman political system. The Crimean War brought the French into play as well, setting the stage for a bitter three-way contest between Russia, Great Britain, and France, and between the Ottoman parties supporting them.

The pro-British faction generally held the upper hand, thanks to Britain's status as protector of the Ottoman Empire and the extraordinary character of her ambassador, Viscount Stratford Canning. Nicknamed "Little Sultan" by Ottoman statesmen and the Ottoman public, Canning (who represented Great Britain in Istanbul for almost twenty years, intermittently, between 1810 and 1858) came to dominate the Ottoman political scene, eventually acquiring more influence than the grand viziers and foreign ministers with whom he dealt. In fact, he could have them hired or fired almost at will. Canning was also in a position to influence crucial Christian clerical appointments, including that of the Patriarch of the Greek Orthodox Church. Fu'ad Pasha is said to have remarked on the appointment of Tanzimat architect Mustafa Reşid Pasha's son, Ali Galib Pasha, as foreign minister on Canning's recommendation in 1856: "We too have the Holy Trinity. Reşid Pasha is the Father, Ali Galib Pasha is the Son, and Lord Stratford [Canning] is the Holy Ghost."[28] In November 1856, Canning intervened more bluntly, appealing to the sultan to replace Grand Vizier Âlî Pasha and Foreign Minister Fu'ad Pasha (because of their alleged inclination to a pro-French policy) with "personalities who would not be affected by French policies and would lean toward Great Britain."[29] The sultan duly dismissed the cabinet and appointed Mustafa Reşid Pasha grand vizier.

By contrast, the pro-Russian faction was crippled by the patent weakness of its case; after all, the fundamental aim of Russian policy was territorial aggrandizement at the expense of the Ottoman Empire. Accordingly, the Russians and their Ottoman supporters fought an uphill battle for influence, succeeding only at moments when the uncertainty of British support coincided with flagging Ottoman spirits in the face of Russian threats. The heyday of the pro-Russian party came in 1871 and 1875, at times when the leading pro-Russian statesman, Mahmud Nedim Pasha, briefly became grand vizier. Nicknamed "Nedimov" by the Muslim population, who viewed him as a tool in the hands of the Pan-Slavist Russian ambassador, Count Nikolai Pavlovich Ignatiev, he did not survive long in power.

The domestic dimensions of the factional struggle occasionally caused Ottoman politicians to change sides in opportunistic fashion. Thus, Mustafa Reşid Pasha, leader of the pro-British faction, availed himself of Russian support on the eve of the Crimean War to become foreign minister in May 1853. However, he soon returned to his traditional support of the British line in a timely switch that earned him the grand viziership in November 1854.[30]

It should be remembered that, to a certain extent, the Tanzimat reforms owed much of their existence to the encouragement of liberal Europe, and especially Great Britain. But in the eyes of the Ottomans support for gradual reform was one thing; pressure for immediate change was another entirely. British statesmen found the Ottoman pace slow. They never fully comprehended the dilemma confronted by the Ottoman reformers, caught between liberal public opinion abroad and stubborn resistance by the Muslim masses at home. As their frustration grew, and the tide of public

---

[28] İbnülemin Mahmud Kemal İnal, *Osmanlı Devrinde Son Sadrıazamlar*, 2 (Istanbul: Millî Eğitim Basımevi, 1940), p. 188.

[29] Ibid., 1, pp. 15, 159.

[30] Temperley, *The Crimea*, pp. 324ff.

opinion behind them shifted, the British role in the Ottoman reform program began to take on the negative form of pressure, and was accordingly resented by ever-larger portions of the Ottoman elite.

The linkage between the need for international recognition and domestic reform was most evident at the conclusion of the Crimean War. It is no coincidence that the Reform Edict of February 1856 was issued scarcely one month before the conclusion of the Paris treaty, which made the Ottoman Empire a member of European concert and placed its territorial integrity under the collective guarantee of the Great Powers of Europe. The postwar settlement of 1856 was a landmark in the history of Ottoman-European relations. To be sure, it had many shortcomings—the most important being the differences of interpretation to which it gave rise, particularly with regard to the territorial integrity of the empire. In contemporary terms, one could portray the difference of opinion on this issue as similar to that between Ṣaddām Ḥusayn and the U.S. government, when each referred to the "territorial integrity of Iraq" following the First Gulf War. The Great Powers of Europe envisioned an Ottoman entity made up of many autonomous provinces, governed by representative assemblies that embodied self-rule for non-Muslims. Such a vision, epigrammatically described by a leading Tanzimat statesman as the *États Désunis de Turquie*, was particularly undesirable from the perspective of the Ottoman leadership.[31] They wished to see a strong, unified state, secured from without by a collective guarantee of territorial integrity and from within by a centralized, efficient administration guided by enlightened laws applicable to all. However, Muslim resentment made the immediate and full implementation of the Reform Edict of 1856 impossible. To cite just one revealing example, Christian demands for permission to ring metal church bells in place of the dull wooden ones traditionally allowed were denied in many places to avoid provoking public disorder.[32]

After 1856, the quest for centralization clashed with the reality of progressive dissolution. Several regions, provinces, and principalities remained nominally within the Ottoman world, but increasingly loosened their ties to the center. Serbia and Montenegro were now Ottoman in name only. Ottoman influence over Wallachia and Moldavia diminished sharply after 1858, when new organic regulations came into effect there; the unification of the two principalities, followed by Ottoman recognition of the fait accompli in 1861, reduced Ottoman leverage to nil. In Mount Lebanon, massacres and counter-massacres between the Druzes and Maronites, followed by attacks on Christians in Damascus, triggered foreign intervention.

[31] Roderic H. Davison, *Reform in the Ottoman Empire, 1856–76* (Princeton: Princeton University Press, 1963), p. 235. Keçecizâde Mehmed Fu'ad Pasha made this sarcastic comment.

[32] Grand vizier to the Ministry of Justice [September 10, 1891], BOA-Ayniyat 1406.

The Beyoğlu protocol of 1861 granted Mount Lebanon an organic law.[33] In Crete, a revolt of the local Christians resulted in the conferral of a special administrative status on the island in 1868.[34]

PROVINCIAL GOVERNMENT

Having achieved a reasonable degree of centralization in the heartlands of the empire, the Tanzimat statesmen set their sights on reforming provincial government beginning in 1853. Their major project was the preparation of new regulations that would make local administration uniform throughout the empire. Although this standardization of provincial government carried the centralization project one step further, and thus could be expected to engender further resistance from the periphery, it was balanced by an attempt to broaden participation in local governance. Thus, while on the one hand stripping the provinces of their special privileges and exemptions, the central government held out the prospect of participatory rule through representative councils on the other. A key provision of the new regulations was the establishment of municipalities, inspired by the French system of the *Préfecture de la ville*, and modeled on the municipal organization of Istanbul as it had been since 1854.[35] To test the new Regulations for Provinces, the government decided in the first instance to apply their major principles in a single province, the newly created Province of Danube, in 1864. Ahmed Şefik Midhat Pasha, one of the reform movement's most brilliant practitioners, led the implementation of the necessary reforms in this province under special authority. In 1865, similar regulations were issued for Bosnia.[36] By 1867, all provinces had been placed under the new regime.[37] In 1871, the government issued a new set of provincial regulations[38] which enhanced the powers of the governor, as representative of the central government, and applied equally to all the provinces of the empire, with the exception of Danube and Bosnia.

A central theme of the Tanzimat era was the attempt to enhance control over those parts of the Muslim periphery which resisted the reforms. In areas heavily populated by Albanians and Kurds the state crushed any

---

[33] *Düstûr*, I/4 (Istanbul, 1295 [1880]), pp. 695–701.

[34] *Düstûr*, I/1, pp. 652–87.

[35] İlber Ortaylı, *Tanzimattan Sonra Mahalli İdareler, 1840–1878* (Ankara: TODAİE, 1974), pp. 116ff.

[36] Ibid., p. 40.

[37] *Düstûr*, I/1, pp. 608–24.

[38] Ibid., pp. 625–51.

resistance. Elsewhere, it was generally more lenient. In some regions, once it had stamped out local opposition, the state asserted its authority by carving out new provinces;[39] in others, it retained existing administrative units but exiled their chieftains and notables, replacing them with new ones who owed their privileged status solely to the state.[40] In the Arabian Peninsula, the state tended to recognize local leaders as Ottoman officials and furnish them allowances. For instance, in 1870 Sheikh ʿAbd Allāh Āl Ṣabāḥ accepted a contract as district-director of Kuwait in Basra Province, with assurances of self-rule and exemption from taxes. In return for such tangible benefits, the state always insisted on maintaining the symbolic trappings of Ottoman rule. A typical demand was that local sailboats traversing the Red Sea sail only under the Ottoman flag.[41] In the Persian Gulf, as a result of the agreement with Istanbul, more than two thousand Kuwaiti vessels which had hitherto sailed under British and Dutch colors began to fly the Ottoman flag.[42] But when such symbolic arrangements proved unsatisfactory, the Ottoman government did not hesitate to intervene directly. For example, a succession struggle between two members of the House of Saʿūd served as a pretext for the dispatch of Ottoman troops to al-Ḥasā in 1870.[43] Ottoman expeditionary forces reconquered Yemen and ʿAsīr, which were fused into a new province in 1871.[44] Although Ottoman rule was generally limited to the coastal plains of Yemen, and local dynasts never ceased to challenge Ottoman authority,[45] the center did establish nominal control over much of the country.

The resistance to the centralization of power and the standardization of law was naturally shared by the empire's nomadic populations. Classical Ottoman high culture sang the praises of *temeddün* (from the Arabic *tamaddun*—to become civilized, leave nomadic life, and settle in towns).[46] In the pre-reform era, the state had launched extensive settlement programs designed to encourage the process.[47] Despite the indignant interpretations of later Turkish nationalists, derogatory references by members of the Ottoman

---

[39] *Tarih-i Lûtfî*, 8, p. 175.

[40] Ibid., 7 (Istanbul: Mahmud Bey Matbaası, 1306 [1889]), p. 89, and 8, pp. 142–4.

[41] Grand vizier to the governors of Yemen and the Ḥijāz [April 18, 1875], BOA-Ayniyat, 876.

[42] *Midhat Paşa: Hayat-ı Siyasiyesi, Hidemâtı, Menfa Hayatı*, 1: *Tabsıra-i İbret*, ed. Ali Haydar Midhat (Istanbul: Hilâl Matbaası, 1325 [1909]), pp. 102–4.

[43] BOA-İrade-Dahiliye, no. 44930 [1870].

[44] BOA-İrade-Meclis-i Mahsus, no. 1705 [1871].

[45] BOA-Y.Mtv. 8/52 [1882].

[46] See, for example, *Risâle der Beyân-ı Lüzûm-i Temeddün ve İctimaʿ-i Beni Âdem*, Süleymaniye Library, Halet Efendi Mss., no. 765/13 [1815–16], especially pp. 1–3.

[47] Cengiz Orhonlu, *Osmanlı İmparatorluğunda Aşiretleri İskân Teşebbüsü, 1691–1696* (Istanbul: Edebiyat Fakültesi Yayınları, 1963), passim.

ruling class to unsettled Turks in the pre-reform era were not insults directed at a specific ethnic group. Similar attitudes toward nomads—and
tribesmen in general—persisted in the reform era. Thus, post-reform de-
scriptions of Druzes or Maronites in Mount Lebanon, of Kurds in Mosul
province, of Albanian highlanders, or of Arab Bedouins as warlike savages,
did not reflect nationalist stereotypes or "Orientalist" attitudes in Ottoman
official circles. Rather, they were primarily manifestations of Ottoman frustration at these groups' stubborn refusal to abandon local practices and accept central administration and the standardization of law. For instance,
the insistence of the Albanians on preserving the *Kanuni i Lekë Dukagjini*—
a northern Albanian code of customary law dating from the fifteenth
century—in defiance of the new penal code[48] made them appear refractory
to the reform-minded center, which in the pre-reform era had not just tolerated but encouraged the preservation of local traditions in a variety of
codifications. Similarly, while the state viewed the typical Damascene as a
member of the *kavm-i necîb-i Arab* (the noble Arab people), it regarded a
Syrian Bedouin or a highland Arab of Mount Lebanon as a *vahşi* (savage).
Arab (Arab) and *Urban* (Bedouin) were used in antithesis.

Resistance to the reforms took on different characteristics in the Christian periphery. For instance, uprisings in Nish and Vidin in 1841 and
1849–50, respectively, revealed the stiff resistance of Christian leaders to
the economic reforms proposed by the Tanzimat leaders;[49] these were not
so heavily opposed by the Muslim inhabitants of those areas. They also
exposed the readiness of Austria and Russia to intervene in response to
radical changes affecting the Christian population of the empire.[50] A fundamental factor in areas heavily populated by Christians was the attempt of
Christian leaders, particularly in the Balkans, to portray the reforms as a
broad assault on the nationalist cause. In order to widen the base of the opposition, they too cast their arguments against reform in economic terms,
hoping that shared opposition to the oppressive Muslim landlords would
unite bourgeoisie, intellectuals, and peasantry against the government.[51]
Muslim landlords, in turn, united to oppose the new tax collection methods
on economic grounds, forcing the government to rescind them two years
later.[52] The tax collectors were replaced by provincial governors, leading to
the gradual reinstatement of tax farming in the provinces.

[48] "Suret-i Fermân-ı Âlî," *Ruznâme-i Ceride-i Havâdis* [March 16, 1874].

[49] H[alil] İnalcık, "Application of the Tanzimat and Its Social Effects," *Archivum Ottomanum* 5 (1973), pp. 115ff.

[50] Ahmet Uzun, *Tanzimat ve Sosyal Direnişler: Niş İsyanı Üzerine Ayrıntılı Bir İnceleme*
(Istanbul: Eren, 2002), pp. 87–94.

[51] İnalcık, "Application of the Tanzimat and Its Social Effects," p. 127.

[52] *Tarih-i Lûtfî,* 7, pp. 34–6.

THE ECONOMY

The Tanzimat heralded substantial changes in the economic realm. The Rose Chamber Edict expressed the desire to reestablish economic relations on a more equitable basis. Subsequent legislation sought to realize this vision, with mixed results. One of the most ambitious reforms aimed to redefine the relationship between landowners and peasants through the abolition of the exploitative *corvée*—a widespread phenomenon on arable farms throughout the empire. But despite changes to the law, the practice persisted in various forms.

Regulation of taxation was another major area of reform. Several months after the promulgation of the Rose Chamber Edict, the government issued a decree announcing the appointment of state tax collectors who, with the help of local councils, would assume sole authority over direct tax collection throughout the empire.[53] The practice of farming customs revenues had already been discontinued when the decree was announced, but the complete abandonment of the old tax system constituted a revolution. The new collectors were given the task of surveying property values and revenue potentials and determining fair tax rates in the regions under their control. They were forbidden to collect any additional fees alongside state taxes.[54] The move to a rational system of taxation based on individual capital and actual income was not only more equitable than the old system of collecting excise taxes based on landholding; it was progressive as well, since in principle it benefited the lower classes at the expense of landowners, and rural people at the expense of city dwellers. But the reality was often more complicated. The standardization of taxes on agricultural production affords a good example. Prior to the reforms, Ottoman farmers paid "tithes" ranging from one-tenth to one-half of their crop, depending on the region. New regulations fixed a universal rate of one-tenth.[55] Although fair in theory, the reform actually created significant inequalities, because it ignored the varying productivity of land.[56] By contrast, the introduction of modern cadastral surveys conducted by engineers was an unqualified success. Such a survey was first carried out in Bursa in 1859, providing a fair basis for taxation while increasing state revenues.[57]

[53] Abdurrahman Vefik, *Tekâlif Kavâidi*, 2 (Istanbul: Kanaat Kütübhanesi, 1330 [1912]), pp. 7–38.

[54] *Tarih-i Lûtfî*, 6, pp. 154–5.

[55] Abdurrahman Vefik, *Tekâlif Kavâidi*, 2, pp. 45–7.

[56] Ömer Lûtfî Barkan, "Türk Toprak Hukuku Tarihinde Tanzimat ve 1274 (1858) Tarihli Arazi Kanunnamesi," *Tanzimat I*, p. 357.

[57] Abdurrahman Vefik, *Tekâlif Kavâidi*, 2, pp. 72ff.

But attempts to rationalize the tax system met with vigorous resistance from the propertied class, who opposed the invasive surveys aimed at uncovering hidden assets and revenue sources. As a result, overall tax revenues actually declined, forcing the government to abandon the new system and reinstate tax farming in 1841–42. Despite repeated initiatives to introduce reforms during the Tanzimat and Hamidian eras, tax farming remained the principal method of taxation employed in the empire.[58] Tax reform exemplified a more general pattern of Tanzimat-era economic reform: ambitious attempts to abolish the old system, regardless of any intrinsic merits it might possess, followed by varying degrees of failure and retreat.

Other tax reforms, while simplifying the complex assortment of dues traditionally collected from non-Muslims, stopped short of abolishing religiously based tax discrimination. The state replaced a number of customary taxes owed by non-Muslims with a single tax, collected and remitted to the treasury by religious leaders.[59] The poll tax (*jizya*) remained, but was transformed in 1856 into a payment for exemption from military service.[60] Despite the fact that non-Muslims continued to pay the same amount under a different name, that a Muslim administration should replace the Islamic basis of taxation with a secular one was unprecedented and symbolically significant.[61]

In an attempt to further monetarize the economy, the state declared in 1840 that payments of tax in kind would no longer be acceptable; all tax payments were to be in cash.[62] Furthermore, all state officials, including the sultan and members of the royal house, began to receive monthly salaries directly from the imperial treasury. These changes, taken together, signified the removal of the last remaining vestiges of the archaic timar system. This was formalized in a series of regulations and finally in the Land Law of 1858, which reorganized land ownership, inheritance law, and the issuance of deeds. Henceforth, private ownership of property acquired de jure status.[63]

A number of new measures addressed the fiscal and monetary aspects of centralization. In 1840, the state abolished its multiple treasuries and announced a return to the principle of "one budget and one treasury."[64] Beginning in 1841–42, the treasury prepared detailed budgets listing all

---

[58] See, for instance, *Düstûr*, I/1, p. 244; I/2, pp. 4–5; 29; 42–6; 49; and I/3 (Istanbul: Matbaa-i Âmire, 1289 [1872]), p. 242.

[59] Abdurrahman Vefik, *Tekâlif Kavâidi*, 2, pp. 20–21.

[60] Ibid., pp. 197–9.

[61] Ibid., p. 194. An excepion was the abolition of jizya in the Mughal Indian Empire between 1562 and 1679.

[62] Abdurrahman Vefik, *Tekâlif Kavâidi*, pp. 49–50.

[63] Barkan, "Türk Toprak Hukuku," pp. 351ff.

[64] Yavuz Cezar, *Osmanlı Maliyesinde Bunalım ve Değişim Dönemi: XVIII. yy dan Tanzimat'a Mali Tarih* (Istanbul: Alan Yayıncılık, 1986), p. 290.

state income and expenditure.[65] To increase state control and further monetarize the Ottoman economy, the government promoted the establishment of banks to replace traditional money lenders. In 1845–46, the government and two local bankers established the short-lived Banque de Constantinople, the first Ottoman bank. In 1856, the Ottoman Bank was established in London, with British capital, to fund commerce with the Ottoman Empire. In November 1862, French shareholders joined the British founders of the bank, turning it into an international syndicate, named Banque Impériale Ottomane, which was subsequently recognized by the sultan as the most important financial institution of the empire. By 1875, the bank played such a central role in Ottoman debt management that the sultan granted it the right to control the budget and expenditures of the state, thus in effect making a foreign syndicate treasurer of the empire.[66] By the end of the Tanzimat period, the bank had branches throughout the empire, including Alexandria, Damascus, Beirut, Isparta, İzmir, Larnaca, Port-Said, Ruse, and Salonica, as well as in London and Paris. Other foreign-owned banks, such as the Société Générale de l'Empire Ottomane (1864) and the Banque Austro-Ottomane (1872), likewise assisted government efforts to revitalize the economy. The Constantinople Stock Exchange was founded in 1873, and dealt mainly with the exchange of treasury bonds, private equity, and foreign currency; its volume of trade, however, was negligible when compared to its European counterparts.[67] The first state-backed agricultural credit union was established in Ruscuk (Ruse) in 1864 to provide low-interest loans to agricultural producers, hitherto forced to borrow money from usurers at exorbitant interest rates. Many similar credit unions soon emerged throughout the empire, and their conduct was regulated by a series of government regulations in 1867.[68]

In 1840, the government tried to introduce paper money in the form of treasury bonds bearing 8 percent interest. A decade later, the state issued zero-interest banknotes resembling European currency. But paper money never caught on as an acceptable financial medium outside the major cities. A rash of counterfeiting followed by a market crash on December 13, 1861, eroded consumer confidence,[69] forcing the treasury to withdraw the notes

---

[65] *Düstûr*, I/2, pp. 70–73.

[66] Adrien Biliotti, *La Banque Impériale Ottomane* (Paris: Henri Jouve, 1909), pp. 12ff; *Düstûr*, I/2, pp. 976–83. The Banque Impériale Ottomane served as the state bank of the empire and subsequently of the Turkish Republic until the establishment of the Turkish Central Bank in 1931. See André Autheman, *La Banque Impériale Ottomane* (Paris: Ministère de l'économie et des finances, 1996), pp. 266–7.

[67] *Düstûr*, I/3, pp. 484–97.

[68] *Düstûr*, I/2, pp. 387–98.

[69] Süleyman Sûdî, *Usûl-i Meskûkât-ı Osmaniye ve Ecnebiye* (Istanbul: A. Asadoryan, 1311 [1893]), pp. 119ff.

in 1862.[70] The treasury had resorted to debasement of the Ottoman coinage in 1840 and 1844. Subsequently, it sought to fix the values and types of coins.[71] On the one hand, this represented a significant step toward establishing a monetary economy under central control; at the same time, it increased pressure on the government to borrow money. Soaring budget deficits compounded the problem. They rose from 4,163,000 gurushes in 1841–42, representing a mere 0.7 percent of total revenues, to 172,223,384 gurushes in 1861–62, constituting 14.1 percent of total revenues.[72] Consequently, the internal debt continued to grow, and in 1854 the Ottoman Empire began to borrow from European governments and banks by means of long-term bonds. By 1874, the state had borrowed a total of Lt (Lire turque/Ottoman lira) 238,773,272, but had received less than Lt 127,120,220 in revenue, after the deduction of commissions.[73] Out of this amount, the government invested a mere 17 percent in infrastructure, such as irrigation projects, and spent the rest on budget deficits and projects of dubious benefit, such as the construction of imperial palaces.[74]

In October 1875, the desperate Ottoman government decided to default unilaterally on interest payments on its foreign debt. This decision provoked an outcry on European stock markets and tarnished the Ottoman image abroad. A contemporary observer remarked that European creditors had no problem with imperfect government in Istanbul "when it paid them seven percent, but discovered all its iniquities when the rate [was] reduced to three."[75] More ominously, the Ottoman default raised doubts about the future viability of the empire and reduced British commitment to its integrity. Shareholders insulted Ottoman ambassadors; articles in the British and French press accused the Ottoman government of foolishly squandering European investments; and some even questioned the desirability of "continued Ottoman existence in Europe"—a backdrop of negative public opinion that severely constricted the freedom of action of Ottoman diplomats during the major international crisis over the Balkans then beginning to unfold.[76]

---

[70] Hasan Ferid, *Nakd ve İ'tibar-ı Malî*, 2: *Evrak-ı Nakdiye* (Istanbul: Matbaa-i Âmire, 1334 [1918]), p. 245.

[71] Ibid., p. 211.

[72] Tevfik Güran, "Tanzimat Dönemi'nde Osmanlı Maliyesi: Bütçeler ve Hazine Hesapları, 1841–1861," *Belgeler* 13/17 (1988), pp. 213ff.

[73] İ. Hakkı Yeniay, *Yeni Osmanlı Borçları Tarihi* (Istanbul: İktisat Fakültesi Yayınları, 1964), p. 51.

[74] Refii-Şükrü Suvla, "Tanzimat Devrinde İstikrazlar," *Tanzimat I*, p. 287.

[75] Donald C. Blaisdell, *European Financial Control in the Ottoman Empire: A Study of the Establishment, Activities, and Significance of the Administration of the Ottoman Public Debt* (New York: Columbia University Press, 1929), p. 81.

[76] İnal, *Osmanlı Devrinde Son Sadrıazamlar*, 2, p. 207.

Another important field of Tanzimat economic activity was industrialization. Much of the early investment in industry went to projects begun under Selim III and Mahmud II. But the scale of production was larger than ever before. An industrial park was established on the outskirts of Istanbul, the Grande Fabrique in Zeytinburnu, where new factories produced garments, ammunition, paper, shoes, and silk. British engineers and skilled laborers (as well as a handful of Germans) operated expensive machinery imported mainly from Great Britain, producing penknives, razors, calicoes, cotton stockings, cannon, ploughshares, iron railings, iron pipes, castings, swords, and padlocks. Their motto was: "Everything must be done at home, *sur la place!*"[77] A small factory complex in Makriköy (modern-day Bakırköy in Istanbul) contained a calico manufacturing facility, a small steamship assembly line, several tanneries, an iron and copper foundry, and a workshop for the production of coarse woollen cloth.[78] Clearly, encouraging local industry on the one hand, while lowering customs tariffs and opening the domestic market to European goods on the other, amounted to an incoherent economic policy. Without long-term state protection, the new industries stood little chance of withstanding the competition from Europe; in fact, relatively few survived and prospered, and only with the help of heavy subsidies. The Ottoman authorities eventually took steps to protect local industry, increasing customs tariffs to 8 percent in 1861[79] and granting the new factories a fifteen-year customs exemption on imported capital goods in 1873.[80] Although these measures proved insufficient, they marked a significant transition during the last decade of the Tanzimat from a policy of laissez-faire to one of protectionism, which, by and large, became the standard approach to trade and the economy until the collapse of the empire. As a consequence of these new economic policies and other international factors, such as the shift in Europe from the production of consumer goods to capital equipment, a minor Ottoman industrial revival began in the 1870s.[81] It did not, however, lead to a major economic transformation. The overall contribution of manufacturing to the Ottoman economy remained at a level far below that of the world's industrialized economies.

[77] Charles MacFarlane, *Turkey and Its Destiny: The Result of Journeys Made in 1847 and 1848 to Examine into the State of That Country*, 2 (London: John Murray, 1850), pp. 603–11.

[78] Clark, "The Ottoman Industrial Revolution," *IJMES*, pp. 67–9.

[79] Süleyman Sûdî, *Defter-i Muktesid*, 3 (Istanbul: Mahmud Bey Matbaası, 1307 [1889]), pp. 83ff.

[80] *Düstûr*, I/3, p. 398.

[81] Donald Quataert, *Ottoman Manufacturing in the Age of the Industrial Revolution* (Cambridge: Cambridge University Press, 1993), pp. 167ff.

CULTURAL AND INTELLECTUAL CHANGES

The Tanzimat era of reform marks a watershed in Ottoman intellectual and cultural life, and one in which the Young Ottomans played a vital role. Until the Tanzimat, the Ottoman press, such as it was, published only the official state gazette, first in Turkish and French, and later in various Ottoman languages. The press was merely a one-way communication channel between government and subjects for the express purpose of disseminating information and positive commentary on official policies. The Tanzimat witnessed the birth of provincial gazettes, published by governors for the same purpose. Nonofficial journals in languages other than Turkish had existed long before the Tanzimat, but these had always been community papers of limited reach; even the French press of the pre-Tanzimat era focused on issues of concern to foreigners and Levantines.[82] During the reform era, new newspapers, such as *Ceride-i Havâdis* (1840), and especially *Tercüman-ı Ahvâl* (1860) and *Tasvir-i Efkâr* (1862), appeared. These fostered debate on hitherto unheard of subjects, such as the rights of man, regime types, and economic problems. They also provided information concerning developments abroad. Between 1862 and 1867, the journal of the Ottoman Scientific Society, *Mecmua-i Fünûn*, introduced popularized European scientism to the empire. In its persistent focus on the superiority of modern science, it always took care to disguise criticism of religion as an assault on superstition.[83]

Journals such as *Diyojen* and *Hayâl* satirized political and social issues in cartoons. Such satirical publications were immensely influential and contributed greatly to the remolding of Ottoman public opinion, hitherto shaped in coffeehouses, salons, and unofficial ulema discussion groups at both popular and elite levels.[84] The circulation figures for some newspapers—as much as 20,000 for *Tasvir-i Efkâr*[85]—were amazingly high, given the low rate of literacy in the empire. The number of people they reached was higher still, since such newspapers were often read aloud in coffeehouses to the illiterate. The lively debate in the press also stimulated the evolution of Ottoman Turkish from a flowery language of poets and a stilted idiom of bureaucrats to a dynamic medium for the exchange of new ideas among a wider public.[86]

---

[82] G[érard] Groc, "La presse en français à l'époque ottomane," *La presse française de Turquie de 1795 à nos jours: Histoire et catalogue*, eds. G. Groc and İ. Çağlar (Istanbul: Isis Press, 1985), pp. 5ff.

[83] See, for instance, Münif, "Muvâzene-i İlm ü Cehl," *Mecmua-i Fünûn*, no. 1 [June–July 1862], pp. 29–30.

[84] *Tarih-i Lûtfî*, 1, pp. 168–9.

[85] V[ladimir] A[leksandrovich] Gordlevskii, *Izbrannye sochineniia*, 2 (Moscow: Izdatel'stvo Vostochnoi Literaturi, 1961), p. 354.

[86] [Mehmed] Sa'id, *Gazeteci Lisanı* (Istanbul: Sabah Matbaası, 1327 [1909]), pp. 5ff.

The demand for printed news underscored the importance of public opinion, which journalists presumed to represent.[87] This stance placed the press on a collision course with the Tanzimat administration, which did not aspire to see the press leveling criticism at the government on behalf of the public. As a result, in 1864 the government issued a series of statutes to regulate journalistic activity and set up the means to punish "dangerous" publications.[88] As one Tanzimat leader put it, "conveying the shortcomings of the state to the nation could not be considered patriotism."[89] A more restrictive decree of 1867 intensified government scrutiny of the press.

The growing fascination of the bureaucratic elite with Western culture marked a sea-change in the intellectual climate of the empire. One of the manifestations of this transformation was the new status of European languages in Ottoman officialdom. When Mahmud Raif Efendi had written his *Tableau des nouveaux règlements de l'Empire ottoman* in 1798, it was the first serious essay written by a Muslim Ottoman bureaucrat in a Western language; even in 1821, when the government decided to replace Greek Phanariot dragomans with Muslim translators, it managed to locate only a single convert to perform translation services.[90] But by the second half of the century, the Ottoman Foreign Ministry was corresponding with its own representatives abroad in French, knowledge of which had become essential for advancement in government service.[91] When, in 1864, *Mecmua-i Fünûn* invited its readers to contribute books toward the establishment of a new library, many high-ranking statesmen rose to the occasion. Among the 126 volumes donated—including works of Bacon, La Fontaine, Helvétius, Montesquieu, and Adam Smith—only two were non-European: a volume of the Ottoman legal code and the *Muqaddimah* of Ibn Khaldūn.[92]

Such examples provide interesting insights into the Westernizing proclivities of the Ottoman elite. They do not, of course, reflect any parallel tendency at the popular level. Still, beginning in the third decade of the Tanzimat, translations of European works began to reach less educated audiences as well. Yusuf Kâmil Pasha's Turkish rendition of Fénelon's *Aventures de Télémaque*, published in 1862, marked the first translation of a European literary work in modern times. It contained a subtle criticism of absolutist rule. His work was followed by translations of Defoe, Hugo,

---

[87] "Efkâr-ı Umumiye," *İbret*, no. 40 [October 28, 1872].

[88] *Düstûr*, I/2, pp. 220–27.

[89] Server İskit, *Türkiyede Matbuat İdareleri ve Politikaları* (Istanbul: Başvekâlet Basın Yayın Umum Müdürlüğü, 1943), p. 24.

[90] BOA-HH 21304 [1825].

[91] Bernard Lewis, *The Muslim Discovery of Europe* (New York: W.W. Norton, 1982), p. 88.

[92] "Bazı Zevât Tarafından Cemiyete Verilen Hedaya," *Mecmua-i Fünûn*, no. 22 [March–April 1864], pp. 432–6.

Lesage, Molière, Bernardin de Saint-Pierre, Anne Radcliffe, and others.[93] İbrahim Şinasi's *Tercüme-i Manzûme* (Translations of Poetry), published in 1859 in prose form alongside the original French, was the first publication of European poetry in Turkish. It included translations from La Fontaine, Gilbert, and Racine.[94]

The records of books owned by members of the Ottoman ruling class in the mid-nineteenth century demonstrate that low-ranking officials continued to read classical catechisms, such as the *Vasiyyet-i Birgivî*, major popular books of Hanafī jurisprudence, such as the *Multaqā al-abhur*, and Sūfī prayer books, such as the *Dalā 'il al-Khayrāt*—all texts that had been equally popular a century beforehand. In the libraries of higher-ranking officials, however, books about Europe began to appear. For instance, the library of an Ottoman governor (*mir-i mirân*) included a three-volume set entitled *İtalya ve Katerina ve Diğer Nizâma Dâir Risâle* (A Treatise on Italy and Catherine and Other Regimes).[95] Officials began to record books in "Frankish letters,"[96] "books in French," and "illustrated books in French."[97] In 1852, the clerk who registered Marshal Mehmed Emin Pasha's 339 volumes in English and 468 volumes in French knew both these languages well enough to describe the books in detail, using constructions uncommon in Ottoman Turkish, such as "Book about Administration and Rights of the People in French."[98]

As these examples illustrate, Westernization remained primarily a class-oriented phenomenon even into the late nineteenth century. But as the nineteenth century wore on, European manners and ideas became more widespread. Accordingly, the taste for things European began to be associated with generational attributes and urban living, rather than strictly with class orientation. By the end of the century, young ladies in upper-class mansions and houses could be found leafing through *Hanımlara Mahsus Gazete* (Ladies' Gazette), while their male counterparts perused the illustrated literary journal *Servet-i Fünûn* (Wealth of Sciences); their elders, meanwhile, read "old books printed on yellow paper that nobody [else] could read."[99]

---

[93] Ahmet Hamdi Tanpınar, *19 uncu Asır Türk Edebiyatı Tarihi* (Istanbul: Çağlayan Kitabevi, 1982), pp. 285–6.

[94] [İbrahim] Şinasi, *Fransız Lisanından Nazmen Tercüme Eylediğim Bâzı Eş'ar* (Istanbul: Press d'Orient, 1859), passim.

[95] See the record of Governor Mehmed Haydar Pasha ibn Abdullah's estate, made on September 12, 1849. İstanbul Müftülük Arşivi, ŞS 1642, f. 121a.

[96] See, for instance, the record of the estate of Esseyyid Mehmed Muhyiddin Nüzhet Efendi ibn Mehmed, a clerk at the Imperial Mint, made on May 2, 1851, ibid., ŞS 1658, f. 46b.

[97] See, for instance, the record of Kazasker Esseyyid Mehmed 'Ataullah ibn Esseyyid Mehmed Raşid's estate made on April 21, 1852, ibid., ŞS 1664, f. 35a.

[98] See the record of the estate dated March 23, 1852, ibid., ŞS 1664, f. 50a ff.

[99] Abdülhak Şinasi Hisar, *Boğaziçi Yalıları, Geçmiş Zaman Köşkleri* (Istanbul: Bağlam Yayınları, 1997), p. 43.

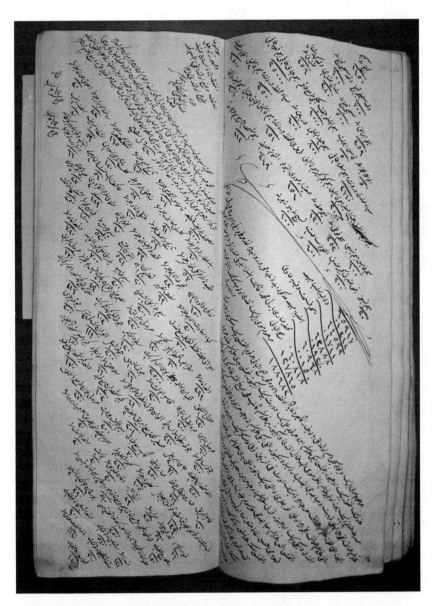

FIGURE 8. The record of Governor Mehmed Haydar Pasha ibn Abdullah's estate
(1849) marshaling his books including *İtalya ve Katerina ve Diğer Nizâma Dâir
Risâle* (A Treatise on Italy and Catherine and Other Regimes, at the end of the
third row of titles) and other possessions. İstanbul Müftülük Arşivi, ŞS
1642, f. 121a.

The writing and conception of history also underwent major changes. Ahmed Cevdet Pasha's monumental history of the Ottoman Empire, begun in 1854 and completed in 1884, marks the watershed between classical historiography and post-Tanzimat writing of history. When the Academy of Sciences, a product of the reform era, decided to commission a new work of history to complete Joseph von Hammer's *Geschichte des osmanischen Reiches*, and cover the crucial period between 1774 and 1826, it bestowed the honor upon this medrese-educated pasha, one of the most prominent conservative statesman-scholars of the age. The selection itself speaks volumes about the change in Ottoman conceptions of history. There existed histories of the period by distinguished historians, such as Ahmed Âsım, Ahmed Vâsıf, Edib Mehmed Efendi, Halil Nuri, Şânizâde Mehmed ʿAtaullah, and Trabzonî Sadullah Enverî. But clearly the Academy sought a history that would contextualize documents, historicize developments, and analyze events in the mode of von Hammer. Ahmed Cevdet Pasha must have studied the works of Buckle, von Hammer, Macaulay, and Taine.[100] The resulting work—with its historiosophical introduction, its situation of Ottoman history in the context of European and world history, its attempts to fashion analytical frameworks for developments that transcended mere chronology, and its overall critical approach—leaves no doubt that Ahmed Cevdet Pasha was a historian in an entirely new mode, however much the form of his work might resemble those of his predecessors.

During the Tanzimat era, Ottoman authors also started to write in European literary genres, such as the novel or play. The first Ottoman novels appeared in Turkish written in Armenian script, since both authors and readers were Armenians. Yovsep Vardanean's *Akabi Hikâyesi* (The Story of Akabi/Agape), published in 1851, was the first example of this new genre. It was an Armenian *Romeo and Juliet*, depicting a love affair between two Armenians of different denominations—Armenian Apostolic and Catholic—and touching upon the sensitive question of sectarianism in the Armenian community.[101] In the same year, Yovhannēs Hisarean authored the first novel in modern Western Armenian, *Hosrov ew Makʿruhi*. In Istanbul a decade later, in 1861, Vasil Drumev wrote the first Bulgarian novelette, *Neshtastna familiia* (The Unfortunate Family). In the 1870s, Ottoman Greeks, inspired by their brethren in Greece and abroad, began to write literature in Karamanlı, a central Anatolian Turkish dialect written in Greek script. In 1872, Evangelinos Missailidis published his *Temaşa-i Dünya ve Cefakâr ü Cefakeş* (Observing the World and the Tormentor and Sufferer), the first novel in Karamanlı, which was adapted from an earlier Greek novel published in Athens. In Arabic literature, classical

---

[100] Tanpınar, *19 uncu Asır Türk Edebiyatı Tarihi*, p. 172.

[101] Vartan Paşa [Yovsep Vardanean], *Akabi Hikyayesi: İlk Türkçe Roman (1851)*, ed. A. Tietze (Istanbul: Eren, 1991).

forms persisted into the twentieth century, although Arab authors were not immune to the general trend toward analysis and criticism of society.[102] For instance, Aḥmad Fāris al-Shidyāq's *al-Sāq ʿalā al-sāq fīmā huwa al-Fāryāq* (Leg over Leg Concerning "Faryāq," a play on the author's name), published in Paris in 1855, was a four-part treatise, modeled on the *maqāmah* tradition in Arabic literature, in which the hero of the story takes the narrator on a trip around the Mediterranean Sea and Europe. The book contains criticism of Christian clergy, an analysis of British and French customs and social conditions, and discussion of philosophical, linguistic, and literary matters. The first novel ever penned by a Muslim Ottoman, *Taaşşuk-ı Talât ve Fitnat* (The Romance of Talât and Fitnat), written by Şemseddin Sami Frashëri in 1875, was an open and provocative treatment of gender issues in the Muslim community. It represented an enormous leap from pre-Tanzimat works such as *Muhayyelât-ı Aziz Efendi* (Imaginations of Aziz Efendi, 1769), composed in the form of the *Thousand and One Nights* and designed purely for entertainment.

The novel was a powerful new tool for highlighting social problems, popular primarily because it was easy to understand. The Ottoman novel remained deeply rooted in realism, a proclivity reinforced by the surging popularity of naturalism and materialism in intellectual circles. This approach to the novel peaked in 1885 with the radical proposal of Beşir Fu'ad, the first Ottoman naturalist and a disciple of Ludwig Büchner, that Ottoman authors abandon all literary activity save the production of novels in the mode established by Émile Zola in the mid-1880s.[103] A similar trend may be observed in several of the Ottoman communities: Grigor Zōhrab published the first realist Armenian novel, *Anhetatsatz serund mě* (A Vanished Generation), in 1887; the Egyptian author Muḥammad Luṭfī Jumʿah defended realistic fiction in *Fī buyūt al-nās* (In People's Houses, 1904); and Aleks Stavre Drenova (the future author of the Albanian national anthem) in the early twentieth century composed Albanian poetry which reflected a shift from romanticism to realism. All three were influenced by Zola.

One of the more important effects of the Tanzimat on literature was the increase in literary exchanges between the various Ottoman communities. This was due in large part to the increasing acceptance of Ottoman Turkish as a spoken medium, to the ideological bond formed by the new official ideology of Ottomanism, and to the emergence of French as a new literary language of the elites. Figures such as Ahmed Midhat Efendi, Şemseddin Sami Frashëri, Naim Frashëri, Vaso Pasha, Yovsep Vardanean, Theodor Kasab, Nikolaki Soullides, Louis Ṣābūnjī, and Aḥmad Fāris al-Shidyāq

---

[102] Muḥammad Ḥusayn Haykal's *Zaynab*, published in Egypt in 1913, is generally considered the first Arabic novel.

[103] See Beşir Fu'ad, *Victor Hugo* (Istanbul: Ceb Kütübhanesi, 1302 [1885]), pp. 181ff.

served as key agents of literary exchange. Beginning in this period, Ottoman communities began to read works of authors from other communities on an unprecedented scale. They also began to read major Turkish journals.[104]

Drama too flourished under the Tanzimat. In 1839, there were four theater buildings in the capital—two of which hosted foreign circus shows. Thereafter, local theaters proliferated throughout the empire. Early theater produced mainly translations of European plays. İbrahim Şinasi's play, *Şair Evlenmesi* (The Marriage of the Poet), written in 1859 as a criticism of the match-making tradition, was the first original play in Turkish. During the early years, Armenian actors, and especially actresses, dominated the Ottoman theatrical scene. For a Muslim woman to become an actress was out of the question during the Tanzimat era. But the audiences of the time were microcosms of the Ottoman elite, representing the high society of the empire in all its ethnic and religious diversity.

The key concept of *Alla Franca* was closely linked to the notion of progress. It was a catchword of the Tanzimat era, and one that symbolized European supremacy. Originally a term used by the elite of the eighteenth and early nineteenth centuries to refer to European objects such as toilets or furniture, during the Tanzimat it began to denote a way of life associated with a particular type of Westernized individual. As such it had a negative connotation until roughly mid-century when, in accordance with the changing intellectual climate, it came to connote superiority, the natural marker of progress in the eyes of the upper classes. The term gradually became a household word.[105] It carried prodigious power, and could confer instant worth or legitimacy on an object or habit. As such, it was often the target of ridicule by sophisticates: "Oh! It is Alla Franca! Who can still disapprove of it?" exclaimed the sarcastic Ahmed Midhat Efendi, the most popular Ottoman author of the late nineteenth century. He wrote the first book on European good manners to show his compatriots that it was wrong to accept "all scandalous things [just] because they [were] Alla Franca."[106] A cartoon in a satirical journal of 1874 featured an Alla Franca lady rebuking an Alla Turca lady who dared to question her dress: "You are the one who should be ashamed of her dress in this century of progress!"[107] As late as 1910, the founders of a new satirical journal went so far as to name it *Alla Franca*, because the phrase signified "observing good manners and excessive efforts toward being elegant."[108]

---

[104] Johann Strauss, "Who Read What in the Ottoman Empire (19th–20th Centuries)?" *Arabic Middle Eastern Literatures* 6/1 (2003), pp. 53ff.

[105] Ahmed Midhat, *Avrupa Âdâb-ı Muaşereti yahud Alafranga* (Istanbul: İkdam Matbaası, 1312 [1894]), passim.

[106] Ibid., pp. 2, 11.

[107] *Hayâl*, no. 157 [June 17, 1875], p. 4.

[108] "Arz-ı Maksad," *Alafranga*, no. 1 [December 13, 1910], p. 1.

FIGURE 9. An Ottoman cartoon depicting a conversation between a traditional and a modern lady. (For a discussion of the cartoon's caption, see p. 100.) *Hayâl*, no. 157 [June 17, 1874], p. 4.

A related, and crucially important, cultural development of the Tanzimat era was the wide audience given to European materialist ideas in Ottoman intellectual circles. Foreign visitors were often stunned by the extent to which works of nineteenth-century French materialism, such as d'Holbach's *Système de la Nature*, held sway over the Ottoman educated class. One observed that every graduate of the new imperial schools seemed to emerge "a materialist, and generally a libertine and a rogue."[109] The rise of an educated class reared on popular materialist ideas created the conditions for an explosion of Ottoman materialist activity in the last two decades of the nineteenth century, which in turn would exert a profound influence over both the intellectual progenitors of the Young Turk Revolution and the founders of modern Turkey.

[109] See MacFarlane, *Turkey and Its Destiny*, 2, p. 271.

EDUCATION

The Ottoman educational system underwent significant change during the Tanzimat era. First, the reformers attempted to centralize and standardize the system of education. In 1845, a Council of Education was founded, followed by a Ministry of Education in 1857. In 1869, the administration issued detailed regulations standardizing education.[110] The new Regulations for Education, issued under the inspiration of Jean-Victor Duruy's secular reform program in France, laid out a blueprint for a new educational system featuring preparatory, middle and high schools, as well as colleges with modern curricula, including European languages. They also instituted a chain of military schools at middle school, high school, and college levels. In addition, the law permitted communities and individuals to establish their own schools. Having revised the schooling system, the reformers sought to use it to inculcate the new state ideology. They made elementary education compulsory and enrolled students from different ethnic and religious groups in the new schools as Ottomans. They failed in this due to low enrollment numbers, a dearth of competent educators, and the privileges that had been granted to foreign and community schools. The Tanzimat reformers also invigorated the educational system for training civil servants. The establishment of the School of Administration in 1859 was a major step toward creating an educated bureaucratic elite.[111] Unlike their predecessors, who still clung to the illusion that the medreses could be transformed into modern institutions of learning, the Tanzimat statesmen founded scientific societies and a university. In 1851, the sultan attended the opening ceremonies of the Academy of Science with twenty-two Muslim and eleven non-Muslim permanent members. However, this institution, modeled on the Académie Française, did not live up to the great expectations of the Tanzimat statesmen.[112] The Dârülfünûn (University), which opened in 1870 and accepted students the following year, fared no better; it was closed in 1871, due to a combination of financial difficulties and controversy sparked by Jamāl al-Dīn al-Afghānī's comments on the art of prophecy at a university lecture.[113] In education as in all other fields, the grand ideals could not be fully realized at once; at the same time, the success

[110] *Düstûr*, I/2, pp. 184–219.

[111] Mücellidoğlu Ali Çankaya, *Son Asır Türk Tarihinin Önemli Olayları ile Birlikde Yeni Mülkiye Tarihi ve Mülkiyeliler, 1: Mülkiye Tarihi, 1859–1968* (Ankara: Mars Matbaası, 1968–1969), pp. 51–3.

[112] Ekmeleddin İhsanoğlu, "Cemiyet-i İlmiye-i Osmaniye'nin Kuruluş ve Faaliyetleri," *Osmanlı İlmî ve Meslekî Cemiyetleri* (Istanbul: IRCICA, 1987), pp. 198–200.

[113] Osman Ergin, *Türkiye Maarif Tarihi, 2: Tanzimat Devri Mektepleri* (Istanbul: Osmanbey Matbaası, 1940), pp. 453–68.

of the Tanzimat in equipping the new elites with a modern education cannot be overemphasized.

THE YOUNG OTTOMANS

The most resonant political voice of opposition to the Tanzimat policies
was that of the Young Ottomans. This was a loose coalition of intellectuals
and former bureaucrats who coalesced around a shared hostility toward
the reforms and their exponents. They formed a secret society in 1865, and
began to express dissent within the limits of official censorship in Istanbul.
Young Ottoman publications in the Ottoman press caused a stir in public
opinion, provoking an official backlash that ended in the closure of their
newspapers and the banishment of their leading figures to remote corners
of the realm. After 1867, the Young Ottomans in exile articulated their opposition with greater freedom. They acted under the financial sponsorship
of Mustafa Fâzıl (Muṣṭafā Fāḍil) Pasha, the former Egyptian heir apparent
who had lost his status to his brother, the Khedive Ismāʿīl, in a deal bro-
kered by Fu'ad Pasha. Abroad, the Young Ottomans published the first
uncensored Ottoman opposition journals in London, Geneva, Paris, Lyon,
and Marseille. All but one of the most eminent Young Ottomans returned
to the empire following the general amnesty declared after Âlî Pasha's
death in 1871.

Although they shared many ideas and a common cause, the Young Ottomans were hardly monolithic. While some marginal Young Ottoman journals promoted revolutionary ideas,[114] the radical line was rejected by mainstream figures. Young Ottoman leaders strongly criticized the Tanzimat as
a capitulation to European dictates.[115] The adoption of European laws at
the expense of the sharīʿa, they contended, had resulted in "tyranny."[116] As
to the economic reforms of the Tanzimat, they were ruinous acts of irre-
sponsibility which could lead only to the destruction of Ottoman industry[117] and the debilitating accumulation of debt.[118] While their benefactor
Mustafa Fâzıl Pasha appealed to the sultan in an open letter (authored
in fact by a Polish intellectual) calling for the institution of liberal secular

[114] M. Kaya Bilgegil, *Yakın Çağ Türk Kültür ve Edebiyatı Üzerinde Araştırmalar, 1: Yeni
Osmanlılar* (Ankara: Atatürk Üniversitesi Yayınları, 1976), pp. 138ff.

[115] [Namık Kemal], "Tanzimat," *İbret*, no. 46 [November 17, 1872], p. 1.

[116] "Mülâhazat," *Hürriyet*, no. 23 (November 30, 1868), p. 4.

[117] "Yeni Osmanlılardan Bir Zât Tarafından Matbaamıza Gönderilüb Gazetemize Derc
Edilmekde Olan Hâtıraların Mabaʿdıdır," *Hürriyet*, no. 42 (April 12, 1869), p. 8.

[118] "İstikraz-ı Cedîde Üzerine Yeni Osmanlılar Cemiyeti'nin Mütalâʿatı," *Hürriyet*, no. 22
(November 23, 1868), pp. 1–2.

administration and representative government,[119] the Young Ottomans espoused a form of constitutionalism based on such Islamic notions as *al-amr bi'l ma'rūf wa'l nahy 'an al-munkar* (commanding right and forbidding wrong)[120] and *mashwarah* (consultation).[121] Such principles, they believed, ought to replace the "enlightened" absolutism of Âlî and Fu'ad Pashas. The Young Ottomans attempted to reconcile Islamic concepts of government with the ideas of Montesquieu, Danton, Rousseau, and contemporary European scholars and statesmen, such as Constantin-François de Chasseboeuf Volney and Félix Esquirou de Parieu.[122] Confessing that "[the Ottoman] position in comparison to France is like that of an uneducated child beside an accomplished scholar," they nevertheless insisted that Ottoman importation from Europe be limited to "scientific and industrial progress,"[123] and that Ottoman constitutionalism be based on Muslim fiqh, even as it mimicked the representative institutions of Europe.

Although Abdülhamid II found little of use in the Islamic constitutionalism of the Young Ottomans, as will be seen their ideas dominated Ottoman intellectual life for decades. Theirs was an original response to the challenges of Western modernity that was to inspire future Muslim constitutional movements, such as that of Iran. But subsequent generations of the secular intelligentsia tended to ignore the Islamic content of Young Ottoman thought, choosing to focus instead on the patriotic Ottomanism of Namık Kemal—who coined Turkish versions of key terms like "freedom" and "fatherland"—and on the courage and nascent Turkist sentiments of Ali Suâvî.

The Ambiguous Legacy of Reform

The challenge of modernization coupled with the urge to preserve Ottoman and Islamic traditions reinforced a tense dualism evident in every field touched by the Tanzimat. The ideal of an overarching Ottoman identity clashed with the increasing autonomy of religious communities within the empire; bureaucratic centralization conflicted with political fragmentation;

---

[119] "Lettre adressé à sa Majesté le Sultan par S.A. Le Prince Moustapha-Fazil Pacha," *La Liberté*, March 24, 1867.

[120] "Şahsiyyat," *Muhbir*, no. 28 (March 23, 1868), pp. 1–2.

[121] Namık Kemal, "Wa-shāwirhum fi'l-amr," *Hürriyet*, no. 4 [July 20, 1868], pp. 1–4; "Usûl-i Meşveret," *Muhbir*, no. 27 [March 14, 1868], p. 1.

[122] Şerif Mardin, *The Genesis of Young Ottoman Thought* (Princeton: Princeton University Press, 1962), pp. 315–26; [Ali Suavi], "Demokrasi: Hükûmet-i Halk, Müsâvat," *Ulûm Gazetesi*, no. 18 (May 17, 1870), pp. 1093–4.

[123] Reşad, "Frenklerde Bir Telaş," *İbret*, no. 10 [June 26, 1872], p. 1.

the ideal of participation came up against the principle of top-down reform; the conservative spirit that gave rise to the Majalla contradicted the progressive drive to emulate the French penal code; new civil courts coexisted uneasily side by side with the traditional sharī'a courts; a modern university with old medreses; an academy of modern sciences with the ulema gatherings of the past; European theater with the time-honored shadow puppet show; and the novel with Divan poetry. Although the old persisted alongside the new, the Tanzimat backed the "new" in almost every field.

The major blind spot of the reformers consisted in their assumption that the "old," being unable to compete with the "new," would gradually disappear from the scene. But Tanzimat culture (as opposed to the more structural aspects of reform) did not penetrate very deeply. The differential pace of modernization broadened the gap between elite and mass cultures immeasurably. Mutual alienation was the inevitable result. While European music stars such as Parish Alvars, Leopold de Meyer, and Franz Liszt might perform to enthusiastic applause in Istanbul (and find appreciation in the European quarters of such cosmopolitan towns as Beirut or Salonica), the Ottoman masses, on the whole, not only disliked Western music but despised it. The people similarly tended to loathe the Tanzimat elite's bizarre taste for the European avant-garde—exemplified in an extreme fashion by Ottoman diplomat Halil Şerif Pasha's commissioning of an extraordinary work of nudism, the infamous *L'origine du Monde*, from Gustave Courbet in 1868.

The greatest impact of the Tanzimat was on the city. The foremost Ottoman historian of the late nineteenth century, for example, comments that in the capital "women-lovers proliferated while boy-lovers disappeared, as if the people of Sodom and Gomorrah had perished all over again."[124] Apparently, this factor was partly responsible for a shift in sexual behavior among men of the elite, from the traditional preoccupation with boys to an increasing interest in women. The new visibility of women led to new forms of flirtation; one method employed by Istanbul's pedestrians was to try to grab the attention of women in passing coaches by waving or passing notes to them.[125] Another important factor in this regard was the intrusion of European sexual mores into Ottoman society, and the consequent stigmatization of homosexuality. The same historian recounts: "Renowned upper-class boy-lovers, such as Kâmil and Âlî Pashas, vanished along with their entourages. In fact, Âlî Pasha tried to conceal his interest in boys out of fear of the criticism of foreigners."[126] Material culture changed along with behavior. In living and dining rooms, for instance, chairs replaced

---

[124] Ahmed Cevdet, *Ma'rûzât*, ed. Yusuf Halaçoğlu (Istanbul: Çağrı Yayınları, 1980), p. 9.

[125] Ibid.

[126] Ibid.

cushions, couches substituted for divans, and tables took the place of the cloths hitherto spread on the floor for meals.[127] The estates left by members of the askerî class attest to the vast change in the material culture of the empire. Items such as large sofas, tables, chairs, *konsols* (from the French *console*, which became a generic term for all kinds of cupboards, chests, drawers, and chifonniers), heavy curtains, large mirrors, elaborate china sets, and enormous European-style mats became popular among the urban upper and middle classes. Suggestive of the social breadth of this cultural transformation is the fact that such objects are found not only in the estates of bureaucrats and palace officials who had regular contact with the West, but in those of many ulema as well.[128] Askerî estates also attest a considerable increase in the number of personal effects in the possession of members of the lower-middle to upper-middle classes, and point to a decisive break with the utilitarian attitudes that had characterized the same classes in the pre-Tanzimat era. European products and their domestic imitations, such as English-style (*İngilizkârî*)[129] or French-style (*Fransızkârî*)[130] dress accessories, now flooded upper- and middle-class households, as did new gadgets such as field glasses.[131]

The supranational ideology of Ottomanism, perhaps the Tanzimat's most significant contribution to the empire, presupposed a rapid embrace of rational ideas and the abandonment of religious obscurantism. The Tanzimat statesmen failed to understand that the major rivals of the Ottomanist orientation were no longer religious identities, but nationalist ones.

---

[127] Ibid., p. 10.

[128] For interesting examples, see the estates of the chief tent maker of the sultan, Esseyyid Mehmed Sa'di Efendi ibn Esseyyid İbrahim (dated January 24, 1851), İstanbul Müftülük Arşivi, ŞS 1657, f. 57bff; a valet of the sultan, Mehmed Sabit ibn Mustafa (dated January 31, 1855), ibid., ŞS 1706 f. 53aff; the under-secretary of the Ottoman Foreign Office, Esseyyid Mustafa Nureddin Bey ibn Hasan (dated January 20, 1859), ibid., ŞS 1735, f. 53bff; a control officer at the Tobacco Customs, Elhac Mehmed Emin Efendi ibn Osman (dated July 31, 1870), ibid., ŞS 1819, f. 79aff; a religious scholar, Esseyyid Mehmed Faiz Efendi ibn İbrahim (dated August 8, 1870), ibid., ŞS 1819 f. 18aff; and a musician, Elhac Mustafa Haydar Ağa ibn Elhac Abdullah (dated January 17, 1871), ibid., ŞS 1819, f. 95aff.

[129] See, for instance, the estate of a merchant, Elhac Mehmed Ağa ibn Yahya, dated August 12, 1859, ibid., ŞS 1743, f. 46b.

[130] See, for example, the estate of Mustafa Şakir Efendi ibn Elhac Mehmed, a clerk at the Pious Foundations Directorate, dated January 1, 1840, ibid., ŞS 1478, f. 1b.

[131] Some of these field glasses were "English-style" (see the estate of a medrese professor, Esseyyid Mehmed Âşir Efendi ibn Halil Fevzi Efendi [dated December 26, 1854, ibid., ŞS 1706, f. 50b]), while many others were of unspecified designs. See, for example, the estates of a clerk at the Imperial Pious Foundations Ministry, Ahmed Ra'if Bey ibn Esseyyid Mehmed Şakir (dated June 3, 1853, ibid., ŞS 1677, f. 34b), a merchant, Ömer Efendi ibn Hüseyin Ağa (dated May 2, 1854, ibid., ŞS 1698, f. 85b), and the former chief coffeemaker of the sultan, Elhac Mehmed Ağa ibn Abdullah (dated September 19, 1863, ibid., ŞS 1785 f. 20b).

The new-fangled official ideology fared well in social strata already benefiting from the Pax Ottomana. Greek Phanariots, members of the Armenian Amira class, Bulgarian merchants who imported garments from Manchester and sold them in Aleppo—these were the typical enthusiastic consumers of an ideology that promised to remove the social disabilities afflicting non-Muslims. Wider swaths of the Ottoman population, such as Bulgarian peasants who continued to chafe under their *Gospodars*, or Christian Bosnian and Herzegovinian peasants serving Muslim landowners, derived little benefit from the new ideology. This helps to explain why nationalist movements during and after the Tanzimat often carried strong socialist undertones, the best examples being the Bulgarian, Macedonian, and Armenian nationalist movements. The lack of a centralized primary school system that could socialize young children as Ottomans, the high rates of illiteracy which limited the effects of the trumpeting of the new ideology in the press, and finally the view from the periphery which saw Ottomanism and centralization as policies of Turkification[132]—all these resulted in the very partial success of reform.

Paradoxically, the very reforms designed to create a more coherent society unified by a common ideology, and a more centralized polity founded on universal, standardized laws, had the effect of exposing and deepening the fissures within the Ottoman state and society. Local resistance to the center's determined attempts to penetrate the periphery accentuated the fragmentation of identity throughout the empire. The unprecedented attempt to unify multiple religious, ethnic, and regional groups only served to strengthen their splintered identities in defiance of central policies. The ambition to universalize law and practice necessarily trampled on local traditions everywhere, thereby raising the consciousness of difference and instilling a group-based sense of grievance. Any innovation was bound to be seen by someone in the empire as offensive. Such was the dilemma of the reformer. Whereas in Istanbul (and in many of the Anatolian and European provinces) religious scholars piously presided over elaborate new ceremonies in which the sultan's portrait was mounted in government offices, the same practice provoked a passionate outcry from ulema in the Arab provinces, who considered it an idolatrous, un-Islamic innovation.[133] When, in 1855, the government decided to ban slavery in order to appease liberal public opinion in Europe (in reality the practice persisted in different forms until 1909),[134] it faced no opposition from ulema or from the general public in the capital and central provinces. In Najd and the Ḥijāz, however, the measure prompted uprisings, while in the Caucasus many

[132] [Ismail Qemali], *The Memoirs of Ismail Kemal Bey*, ed. Sommerville Story (London: Constable, 1920), pp. 11–12.

[133] *Tarih-i Lûtfî*, 5, pp. 51–2.

[134] *Düstûr*, II/1 (Istanbul: Matbaa-i Osmaniye, 1329 [1911]), pp. 831–2.

tribes that made a living from the slave trade severed their ties with Istanbul.[135] Thus it was that the abandonment of the old order—with all its irrational nuances, messy compromises, and respect for local practice—in favor of a more modern, unitary system, ended up abetting the very process of fragmentation that the reforms were designed to reverse.

The Rose Chamber Edict and the Tanzimat era that followed it reflected the visions of the reforming statesmen for the future. Their ideal resembled a Rechtsstaat as later described by Rudolph von Gneist, which is why they placed a premium on legal reform. The reformers sincerely wished to promote both fiscal justice and equality before the law. Undoubtedly, they underestimated both the complications of implementation and the scale of opposition from social classes who stood to lose ground because of the reforms. In many areas, new laws remained valid on paper while old practices continued. Still, the codification of new thinking created a body of law that could no longer be ignored. In June 1908, a maltreated dissident was able to challenge the authorities in court on the grounds that "non-legal administrative decisions and torture had been prohibited by the Rose Chamber Edict, which [was] a document safeguarding the existence and well-being of the state."[136] As late as 1917, the Ministry of the Interior was reminding all prison authorities that "cruel treatment of inmates and torturing them" had been banned by the Rose Chamber Edict.[137]

[135] Cevdet Paşa, *Tezâkir*, 1, pp. 101–52.
[136] BOA-BEO/ file 249177 [June 4, 1908].
[137] DH. MB. HPS, 58/48 [March 1, 1917].

The Twilight of the Tanzimat and
the Hamidian Regime

THE ACCESSION to the throne of heir apparent Abdülaziz (r. 1861–76), after Sultan Abdülmecid's long-expected death in 1861, marked one of the smoothest successions in late Ottoman history. This owed much to the progressive seepage of power from the royal court to the Sublime Porte, which continued to predominate throughout the 1860s. But as Sultan Abdülaziz matured, he began to challenge the status quo. The contest for political power between the palace and the bureaucracy intensified after the death of Âlî Pasha, the last great reforming statesman of the Tanzimat, in 1871. The Tanzimat reformers, who had labored to construct a Weberian administrative structure founded on rational-legal authority independent of the throne, now saw the realization of their ambition threatened. An uneasy equilibrium between court and Porte prevailed until the deposition of the sultan in 1876 and the accession of Abdülhamid II to the throne. This event, however, heralded a bitter struggle between the sultan and the Sublime Porte, which the former won decisively. In 1895, the Sublime Porte made its last gambit for power, demanding a return to responsible government and the restoration of authority to the bureaucracy. The failure of this attempt resulted in the absolute domination of the political system by the palace until the Young Turk Revolution of 1908.

The favored statesman of Sultan Abdülaziz, Mahmud Nedim Pasha, professed the belief that "happiness and peace in the affairs of state derive from loyalty."[1] Labeled "Old Turkey" by foreign diplomats, the statesmen loyal to Abdülaziz were not hostile to the reforms as such, but questioned the undue influence of British and French advice over Ottoman policy. This line of criticism had become fashionable even in the ranks of the bureaucracy, as the negative aspects of the Tanzimat policies became apparent. A particular source of grievance was the failure of the Great Powers to keep their

[1] [Mahmud Nedim], *Sadr-ı âzâm Mahmud Nedim Paşa'nın Âyine-i Devlete Dair Kitabı*, Fatih Millet Library Mss., no. Trh. 1022, p. 7.

promises (e.g., on keeping Wallachia and Moldavia separate) even as they stepped up the pressure for more extensive reforms (e.g., the French diplomatic note of 1867). Many felt that the reforms had exacerbated the economic crisis of the empire, fostered Ottoman dependency on European loans, failed to stifle ethnic and religious separatism encouraged by Great Britain and France, and provoked unrest among Muslims. These last perceived the reforms as a capitulation to European dictates that conferred benefits upon non-Muslims at their expense. In 1859, a group of ulema and low-ranking bureaucrats conspired to exploit Muslim resentment and launch a rebellion, but their movement was swiftly suppressed.[2] In a dramatic turn of events in 1871, the sultan backed a number of marginalized statesmen in a bid to undermine the independence of the Sublime Porte. The reforming statesman, Midhat Pasha, at the helm of the Young Turkey Party, fought back to preserve the Sublime Porte's political domination at home and the pro-British orientation abroad. The sultan, yielding to reformist pressure, appointed Midhat Pasha grand vizier in 1872, but then quickly dismissed him.

The Constitutional Moment and the
Russo-Ottoman War of 1877–1878

This internal struggle for power took place against the backdrop of the reopening of the Eastern question in Europe and the rise of separatist pressures in the Balkans. Since the end of the Crimean War, the Great Powers had sought to avert conflict among themselves by upholding formal Ottoman territorial integrity. They managed the challenge of change by allowing cosmetic alterations to the territorial status quo, in accordance with the principle that any degree of autonomy was acceptable, as long as the region in question remained de jure within the Ottoman fold. Several factors, however, served to alter both the balance of power in Europe and European strategic interests in the Near East. First, in 1871 the rising power of Germany took the place of Prussia in Central Europe. Second, in the same year Russia nullified the Black Sea clauses of the Paris Treaty of 1856, shaking off the restrictions imposed by the victors of the Crimean War. Third, the Suez Canal was inaugurated in 1869, creating a vital trade and military link between East and West.

However, it was the conjunction of the renewed threat from Russia with increasing instability in the Balkans that posed the gravest menace to the empire. Traditional Pan-Slavic sentiments represented by such thinkers as

---

[2] Uluğ İğdemir, *Kuleli Vak'ası Hakkında Bir Araştırma* (Ankara: Türk Tarih Kurumu Yayınları, 1937), p. 38.

František Palacký were being transformed into a Russian doctrine of Slav liberation from Ottoman and Austrian rule at the hands of such Russian pundits as Nikolai Danilevskii and Rostislav Fadeyev. This transformation inevitably linked Russian expansionism to Balkan nationalism. Even those Russian leaders who opposed an ideological foreign policy, such as Foreign Minister Prince Alexandr Mikhailovitch Gorchakov, found their hands tied by the new pro-Slav fervor in Russia. When Slav peasants revolted against their Muslim landowners in Herzegovina in July 1875, the post-Crimean status quo crumbled. The old mixture of cosmetic reform and enhanced self-government no longer supplied the formula for stability. Ottoman public opinion reacted strongly against the idea of granting further autonomy to a region heavily populated by Muslims; Russia, as the champion of Pan-Slavism, could no longer be satisfied with superficial change; and Serbia and Montenegro—ostensibly Ottoman territories with an enormous stake in any future Balkan settlement—refused to look on passively while Ottoman troops suppressed the rebellion. Count Gyula Andrássy, Austria-Hungary's foreign minister, spared no effort in the attempt to sketch out a compromise that would uphold the status quo. But the situation deteriorated nonetheless. A fresh rebellion broke out in Bulgaria in April 1876. It was put down with a heavy hand, prompting the notorious moral crusade of British Liberal Party leader William Gladstone against the "Turkish race," which he labeled "the one great anti-human specimen of humanity."[3] The replacement, in the British imagination, of the post-1849 image of liberal Ottomans with one of bloodthirsty Muslim tyrants brutally oppressing defenseless Christians, made a repetition of Britain's earlier displays of support for its beleaguered Ottoman ally all but impossible.

The deteriorating situation in the Balkans and mounting disorder in the capital resulted in the dismissal of Mahmud Nedim Pasha, leader of the Old Turkey Party, in May 1876. The same month, pro-reform bureaucrats led a coup d'état and deposed Sultan Abdülaziz, who committed suicide or was murdered (accounts vary) within a few days of his dethronement. In July 1876, Serbia and Montenegro declared war on their supposed sovereign. The new sultan, Murad V, was known as a staunch supporter of the reformist party in the Sublime Porte, but his already weak mental condition worsened following the coup and the subsequent death of his uncle, and resulted in his deposition by fatwā after a reign of only three months. Murad V's younger brother, Abdülhamid II (r. 1876–1909), came to power promising to promulgate a constitution.

The idea of a constitution first emerged in the Ottoman context in the political vacuum that opened up following the destruction of the Janissaries

---

[3] W[illiam] E[wart] Gladstone, *Bulgarian Horrors and the Question of the East* (London: John Murray, 1876), p. 13.

in 1826. The obliteration of the traditional balance of power within the Ottoman system made possible the rise of the bureaucracy to power, thereby enabling the reform movement as a whole to flourish. The centralizing enterprise of the bureaucrats necessarily weakened political participation at all levels of government. By the second decade of the Tanzimat, demands for a check on central power were being voiced throughout the empire, most coherently by the Young Ottomans. In 1868, the state responded to these concerns by forming the State Council, an appointed body charged with monitoring official conduct and its conformity with the law. The opposition, led by the Young Ottomans, found this measure insufficient, as this body was not founded on the representative principle and thus did not reflect popular opinion.[4] Partly as a matter of principle, and partly in an attempt to subvert the hegemony of the Sublime Porte, they claimed that "the rule of law was preferable to the administration of talented bureaucrats" and that only the people could legislate on the basis of the real needs of society.[5] Legislation "adapted from European laws and regulations, without taking national morals and traditions into consideration," should be rejected.[6]

The proposed alternative to rule by officialdom was constitutional government, under which a constitution would restrict the arbitrary power of the bureaucrats,[7] while an assembly would make the voice of the Muslim masses heard, making "public opinion in effect the sovereign [governing] through the people's representatives."[8] While the constitutionalist movement was primarily a Muslim phenomenon, similar calls for greater representation issued from the non-Muslim elites of the empire. For, although the government-sponsored formation of assemblies of laymen in the three major non-Muslim religious communities between 1862 and 1865 dramatically increased political participation in these groups, these assemblies served mainly as a tool in the hands of the Tanzimat statesmen to weaken the clergy, and in any case empowered only a narrow secular elite that remained deaf to the appeals of the community at large. Reform of communitarian governance also gave rise to a widespread Muslim grievance against the state for having opened a gap between the level of political representation afforded to non-Muslims and Muslims. Thus, at the popular level, Ottoman constitutionalism was fundamentally a reaction to the dictatorship of the bureaucracy coupled with resentment against the preferential treatment granted to non-Muslims.

---

[4] See "al-Ḥaqq yaʿlū wa lā yuʿlā ʿalayhi," *Hürriyet*, no. 1 (June 29, 1868), pp. 2–3.

[5] "Efkâr-ı Âmme ve Erbâb-ı Kabiliyet," *Terakki*, no. 197 (August 7, 1869), pp. 3–4.

[6] See "Acele Etmeyelim," *Vakit*, June 6, 1876, and "Halimizi Bir Kere Düşünelim," *İstikbâl*, August 9, 1875.

[7] See "Me'murlar Mes'ul Olmalıdır," *İstikbâl*, July 4, 1876.

[8] "Efkâr-ı Âmme ve Erbâb-ı Kabiliyet," *Terakki*, no. 197, p. 4.

Significantly, the rhetorical basis for the constitutionalist critique of bureaucratic centralism in the Ottoman Empire was essentially conservative and Islamic, and became more so with time. This was not surprising, for the constitutionalists sought allies and legitimacy from among those elites that had lost most from the ascendancy of the Sublime Porte, elites of which the ulema formed a prominent component. The ulema viewed constitutionalism principally as a means of regaining political power. Symbolic of the growing influence of the ulema on the movement as a whole was the shift from the initial secular depiction of a *nizâm-ı serbestâne* (free order)[9] to the more Islamic *usûl-i meşveret* (system of consultation), paying tribute to the Islamic concept of *mashwarah* (consultation). The idea of a representative assembly was at first referred to in the press as *Şûra-yı Ümmet*,[10] again a reference to the Islamic value of consultation. The traditional duality of the Ottoman legal system (with sultanic law coexisting alongside the sharī'a) made it easier for proponents to claim that constitutionalism was not a forbidden innovation and was in complete accordance with Islam. It was no coincidence that advocates of the movement referred to the proposed Ottoman Constitution as a *Kanun-i Esasî* (Basic Law), stressing the continuity of the new legislation with the sultanic laws of old.

At the same time, a constitution and a parliament continued to be regarded by the secular elite as symbols of modernization and progress, without which the Ottoman Empire risked extinction. A common line of thought ran like this: "Is there any absolutist government [left in Europe] except the Russian state? . . . Since European public opinion is like a tidal wave flooding in that [liberal] direction, and the Sublime State is regarded as a European state, it will be impossible for us to survive if we set ourselves against the entire [Western] world."[11] It was impossible to overlook the fact that constitutional regimes and representative bodies emerged in all the regions that gained autonomy or semi-independence from the empire in the nineteenth century: Serbia reintroduced its *Skupština* in 1805, Rumania formed a bicameral legislature in 1866, Mount Lebanon established a mixed assembly in 1864, and Crete was endowed with a general assembly in 1868 by imperial edict. This pattern was not limited to the Christian-dominated regions of the periphery. Tunis, which formally remained an Ottoman province until 1881, proclaimed the first constitution in the Muslim world in 1861, while Khedive Ismā'īl set up his *Majlis Shūrā al-Nuwwāb* in Egypt

[9] Mustafa Fâzıl, *Paris'den Bir Mektub: Sultan Abdülaziz Han'a Cemiyet-i Ahrar Re'isi Mısırlı Mustafa Fâzıl Paşa Merhum Tarafından Gönderilen Mektubun Tercümesidir* (Istanbul: Artin Asadoryan Matbaası, 1326 [1908]), pp. 17–18.

[10] See, for example, "Varaka: Birinci Fıkra," *Vakit*, June 15, 1876.

[11] [Abdülhamid Ziyaüddin], *Ziya Paşa'nın Rüyanâmesi*, IUL, İbnülemin Mahmud Kemal İnal Mss., no. 2461, f. 2.

in 1866. Constitutionalists were often heard to argue: "Montenegro, Serbia, and Egypt each have [representative] councils . . . Are we at a lower level of culture than even the savages of Montenegro?"[12] Similarly: "Even Greece has a [constitution] and parliament."[13] By comparison, it was argued, the Ottoman administration that had emerged since the early nineteenth century was a "Bedouin government in the heart of Europe, exercising a form of absolutism fit only for tribes."[14]

Although the constitutional movement originally grew out of opposition to the iron rule of the bureaucracy, the reassertion of sultanic power beginning in the 1870s prepared the way for the joining of forces between the bureaucrats and their erstwhile critics. The reemergence of the court as a center of power threatened the bureaucrats' position, driving them to make common cause with the constitutionalists against the possibility of a sultanic absolutism devoid of reformist content and uninhibited by legal restraints. As an Ottoman statesman later reflected, "the Constitution of 93 [1876] was in fact an undertaking by the very bureaucrats of the despotic regime, who intended to curtail the absolute dominance of the sultan and establish a counter-balancing jurisdiction to match his authority."[15]

A final consideration fueling the constitutionalist movement in the late Tanzimat era was the desire to stave off European pressures for pro-Christian reform. A constitutional regime, it was argued, would turn all Ottoman subjects into equal citizens, thereby ending all community-specific privileges within the empire and removing the logical basis for European criticism.

Thus, Ottoman constitutionalism emerged over a half-century out of a complex set of impulses, bringing together conservatives and liberals, ulema and secularists, Muslims and non-Muslims, bureaucrats and their opponents under the wing of one broad movement with the stated aim of instituting constitutional government in the Ottoman Empire. Not surprisingly, the first Ottoman experience with a constitution reflected these tensions and contradictions.

On the programmatic level, the proponents of a constitution faced two major dilemmas. One was the familiar conundrum of how to broaden representation without encouraging nationalist separatism; the other was the enormous doctrinal challenge of reconciling constitutional rule with the religion of Islam and the institution of the Caliphate. No amount of casuistry could gloss over the fundamental incompatibility between the doctrinal supremacy of the sharīʿa and the political conception of a man-made constitution embodying the supreme law in the land. A constitution could be defended from an Islamic viewpoint only insofar as it was ultimately

[12] "Wa-shāwirhum fī'l-amr," *Hürriyet*, no. 1, pp. 3–4; see also *Sabah*, May 28, 1876.
[13] "Kavânin-i Esasîye," *Vakit*, June 8, 1876.
[14] "Mütaläʿa," *Vakit*, June 5, 1876.
[15] Saʿid Halim, *Buhranlarımız: Meşrutiyet* (Istanbul: Şems Matbaası, 1335 [1919]), p.3.

subordinated to the sharī'a and did not contradict it. Fashioning a legal order in complete harmony with divine law was a tall order in any society, and one which neither the French constitutionalists nor their American counterparts had to face. In the context of a highly legalistic religion like Islam (which in this respect resembles Judaism), it was well-nigh impossible. The second challenge confronting the Ottoman constitutionalists was the set of problems likely to result from genuine representation in a polyethnic, multidenominational empire. For instance, bona fide representation would entail non-Muslim participation in the legislative process. To assuage Muslim concerns, the constitutionalists underscored the "consultative" character of the parliament[16] and dismissed as alarmist claims that non-Muslims would attempt to draft laws (contrary to the sharī'a) or even request "the abandonment of the sharī'a."[17] Similarly, they maintained that the parliament would not be in a position to issue a civil code, which only a council of ulema could prepare.[18] As these examples indicate, Ottoman constitutionalists had limited room for doctrinal maneuver: on the one hand, they faced the danger of stripping the constitution of its meaning through surrender to the primacy of Islamic law; on the other, they risked the potentially devastating loss of conservative support for the constitutionalist project.

But Muslim scholars were not the only opponents of full constitutionalism. Even the most fervent supporters of a constitution from within the bureaucracy did not envision the sort of constitutional government that would seriously curtail their authority and transfer some of it to a body of elected representatives. That, they believed, would mean the end of top-down reform, which necessitated a strong government willing to implement change, if necessary against the will of the masses. Moreover, a genuinely liberal constitution and a truly representative government would promote separatism.

One school of thought within the bureaucracy carried such arguments to their logical conclusion, and rejected the very notion of a constitution. Instead, they suggested various measures of administrative reform to enhance local participation in politics and increase state supervision of government agents.[19] A bolder proposal called for the establishment of a partly elected, partly appointed consultative body with quotas for the representation of the various religious communities.[20] Like the Slavophile revival of the *Zemsky Sobor*, the sixteenth-century Russian advisory council to the Tsar, many reformist statesmen supported the reestablishment of an adapted version of

---

[16] "Şûra-yı Ümmet," *İstikbâl*, May 17, 1876.

[17] See *Sabah*, May 29, 1876.

[18] "Meşrutiyet İdare: Beyân-ı Haki[ka]t," *Vakit*, October 27, 1876.

[19] See, for example, "Devlet-i Aliyye'nin Tamamiyet-i Mülkiyesi ve Ânın Medâr-ı Vikâyesi," *Terakki*, no. 149 (July 20, 1869), p. 3.

[20] "Tavassutun Reddi—Meclis-i Umumî'nin Te'sisi," *Vakit*, September 28, 1876.

the old Ottoman consultative assemblies that used to advise the sultan in times of crisis. They proposed the formation of a largely appointed council that would proffer advice to the sultan on behalf of the people and monitor the fair application of the law. Variants of this proposal continued to inspire opponents of an elected parliament, including prominent Young Turks, well into the 1890s.[21]

The dethronement of Abdülaziz paved the way for an open discussion of reform in the Ottoman press. In an edict marking his accession to the throne, Murad V accentuated the necessity for "basing the administration of the state upon a strong principle."[22] This was a reference to a constitution. A leading conservative statesman countered: "we should be glad that we have not adopted a constitution by way of imitation. What we need is not a constitution, but institutions."[23] The ulema participated in the debate, maintaining that, although consultation was indeed enjoined in two Qur'ānic verses, the reference was only to consultation *among Muslims.* Consequently, a constitutional regime that led to a parliament with non-Muslim deputies would violate Islamic principles.[24] The constitutionalists, headed by Midhat Pasha, rejected these views. They maintained that the only way to block the imposition of pro-Christian reforms by the Great Powers was to promulgate a constitution that would turn all subjects into citizens, equal before the law.[25] Rebuffing the Islamist critique, they asserted that both the constitution and the parliament would be in full accordance with Islam.[26]

Having gained the upper hand, the pro-reform group assembled a constitutional commission made up of twenty-eight eminent statesmen and ulema, including Midhat Pasha and several Young Ottomans. Their attempt to draft a constitution triggered a major showdown between liberal constitutionalists and the assertive young sultan. The sultan insisted on protecting his sovereign rights, compelling the liberals to make significant concessions. The most important of which was a clause reminiscent of the French *lois des suspects* of 1793: it stipulated that the sultan could exile, without trial, individuals who endangered public safety. Many liberals believed that ceding such a whimsical power to the sultan would imperil

---

[21] [Mehmed] Mourad, *Le palais de la Yildiz et la Sublime Porte: Le véritable mal d'Orient* (Paris: Imprimerie Centrale, 1895), pp. 43ff.

[22] See *Sabah,* May 27, 1876 and "İstibşâr," *Vakit,* June 4, 1876.

[23] İbnülemin Mahmud Kemal İnal, *Osmanlı Devrinde Son Sadrıazamlar,* 4 (Istanbul: Millî Eğitim Basımevi, 1940), p. 635.

[24] Ahmed Midhat, *Üss-i İnkılâb,* 2 (Istanbul: Takvim-i Vekayi' Matbaası, 1295 [1878]), pp. 316ff.

[25] Mahmud Celâleddin, *Mir'at-ı Hakikat,* 1 (Istanbul: Matbaa-i Osmaniye, 1326 [1908]), p. 190.

[26] See, for example, H., "Meşrutiyet İdare: Beyân-ı Haki[ka]t," *Vakit,* October 27, 1876; and *Sabah,* May 29, 1876.

the successful implementation of the constitution. The exigencies of the international crisis, however, compelled them to concede. Its major deficiencies notwithstanding, the 119-article constitution represented a major step toward the limitation of the power of the sultan and his government. Moreover, it showed the potential for bridging the gap between constitutional government and Islamic law: although in subsequent years some ulema vehemently opposed the legislative rights granted to the parliament by the constitution,[27] many others approved them as compatible with Islam.[28]

The constitution was modeled on the liberal Belgian Constitution of 1831,[29] which served as a basis for many constitutions adopted in former Ottoman dominions (e.g., Bulgaria, Serbia, and Egypt), but it was adapted to suit Ottoman conditions. For instance, the document recognized Islam as the religion of the state (art. 11) and underscored the sultan's duties as the "protector of the Muslim faith" (art. 4). But in the editorial process, the Belgian source was also stripped of much of its liberal content. As a consequence, the executive branch of government was heavily privileged over the legislative—legislative authority was limited to pre-defined areas of competence while the crucial principle of ministerial responsibility to the parliament was eliminated—and basic rights found no expression in the constitution, including the right to form political parties or assemble peacefully.

The international crisis reached its peak while work on the constitution was still under way. Although Ottoman armies won noteworthy military victories against the Serbians in August and September 1876, a Russian ultimatum prevented them from reaping the fruits of their battlefield accomplishments. The British, fearing Russian military intervention, proposed an international conference to discuss the Eastern Question. The Ottoman authorities accepted the proposal at gunpoint when Lord Derby informed them that the alternative was war with Russia with no prospect of British intervention. A few days before the conference convened in the Ottoman capital on December 23, 1876, the sultan, in a series of well-coordinated moves evidently intended to appease his European guests, appointed Midhat Pasha as grand vizier and then promulgated the constitution on the opening day of the meeting. Neither of these initiatives impressed the representatives of the Great Powers or the leaders of the anti-Ottoman campaign in Europe. In Britain, "public opinion was . . . formed and guided by men animated by a blind hatred of everything Turkish, who represented the new constitution

---

[27] See, for example, Mustafa Sabri, "Edeb-i Tahrir," *Beyan'ül-Hak*, no. 15 [January 11, 1909], pp. 326–8.

[28] Manastırlı İsmail Hakkı, "Kuvve-i Teşri'iye," *Beyan'ül-Hak*, no. 17 [January 25, 1909], pp. 381–2.

[29] Both the French constitution of 1848 and the Prussian one of 1851 were used in the preparation of the document, but the Belgian Constitution served as the main model.

as a sham or 'paper' constitution."[30] Gladstone made a sarcastic entry in his diary, which read: "Turkish Constitution!!!"[31]

The conference participants suggested exceptionally harsh terms for ending the crisis. They proposed to establish three large provinces—Eastern Bulgaria, Western Bulgaria, and Bosnia-Herzegovina—which would be administered by Christian governors, appointed to five-year terms with the consent of the Great Powers. Even Midhat Pasha, characterized by some as one who "always wished to follow English advice,"[32] described these terms as the realization of the "Russian dream of establishing small autonomic States" on Ottoman territory.[33] European and Ottoman interpretations of the empire's territorial integrity had never been further apart. The Marquis of Salisbury remarked wryly that "earlier concessions on the part of Sultan Mahmoud would probably have preserved Greece as an integral part of the Turkish Empire."[34] Midhat Pasha responded that "he resigned himself to the will of God, if it was decreed that the Empire should fall, but no Turk would yield" to the terms being imposed by the Great Powers.[35] In a final, desperate move, he sent an Armenian confidant to Lord Derby with an offer to place implementation of the Ottoman Constitution under European supervision. The emissary returned empty-handed.[36] When, on January 18, 1877, an Ottoman Grand Council rejected the terms proposed by the conference, the stage was set for a new Russo-Ottoman war, which began on April 24, 1877.

Throughout this crisis a hurried election campaign—the first in the history of the empire—was under way to select deputies for the first Ottoman parliament. The elections, held between January and March 1877, were an imperfect affair. No elections were held in autonomous regions that had their own representative institutions. Thus, Egypt, Montenegro, Rumania, Samos, Serbia, and Tunisia were not represented in the Ottoman parliament; the local council in Mount Lebanon decided not to send deputies to Istanbul; while in Crete, the Muslim community elected one deputy, but the Greek Orthodox community, in an act of defiance, declined to send a representative. Instead of overcoming sectarian divisions through

---

[30] Henry Elliot, "The Death of Abdul Aziz and of Turkish Reform," *The Nineteenth Century and After* 23/132 (February 1888), p. 276.

[31] *The Gladstone Diaries with Cabinet Minutes and Prime-Ministerial Correspondence*, 9 (January 1875–December 1880), ed. H.C.G. Matthew (Oxford: Clarendon Press, 1986), p. 183.

[32] Elliot to Derby, Constantinople, December 19, 1876 (telegraphic), PRO/F.O. 424/46.

[33] Elliot to Derby, Pera, December 28, 1876 (telegraphic), PRO/F.O. 424/37.

[34] Salisbury to Derby, Pera, January 1, 1877/no. 78 (Confidential), PRO/F.O. 424/37.

[35] Ibid.

[36] Bekir Sıtkı Baykal, "Midhat Paşa'nın Gizli Bir Siyasî Teşebbüsü," *III. Türk Tarih Kongresi* (Ankara: Türk Tarih Kurumu Yayınları, 1948), pp. 473–4.

the institution of universal representation, the elections reinforced the communitarian basis of society by allotting quotas to the various religious communities based on projections of population figures derived from the census of 1844; Istanbul, for example, was to be represented by five Muslims and five non-Muslims (two Greeks, two Armenians, and a Jew). In order to appease the European powers, the Ottoman administration drafted an exceedingly uneven representational scheme that favored the European provinces by an average 2:1 ratio. As a result, the Asiatic provinces were represented in the first chamber by one deputy for every 162,148 male inhabitants (and Tripoli in Barbary was represented by one deputy for every 505,000 male inhabitants), while the European provinces as a whole were represented by one deputy for every 82,882 male inhabitants.[37]

The electoral process envisioned in the constitution was implemented only in the Ottoman capital. The authorities divided the city into twenty election districts, and entrusted resident ulema and district headmen with the nomination of candidates for an electoral college composed of two electors from each district. Taxpaying males aged twenty-five or older were eligible to vote. The forty elected members of the electoral college then held a secret ballot to elect deputies to the parliament. Participation was extremely low and, with the exception of the educated elite, most people were indifferent.

Elections in the provinces were held under a set of temporary regulations issued before the promulgation of the constitution and to a certain extent in conflict with its provisions.[38] The elected members of the existing local councils wrote a set number of names of Muslim and non-Muslim residents eligible to become deputies on ballots. Then regional election committees, over which governors presided, counted these ballots and forwarded lists of those who had won the most votes to the State Council in Istanbul for approval. Since the governors held sway over the local councils, they managed to manipulate the elections throughout the empire. As a result, the Chamber of Deputies contained numerous former officials and tax collectors favored by various governors. Although the Chamber was to have 130 deputies, only 119 were elected for the first session and 113 for the second. Of these, 71 deputies (64 in the second session) were Muslim, 44 (43) were Christian, and 4 (6) were Jewish. A Muslim deputy represented 133,367 (147,953) male inhabitants, a Christian represented 107,557 (110,058), and a Jew 18,750 (12,500).[39] Thus, Christians were slightly overrepresented. As for the Jews, a truly proportional system would have meant almost no representation at all.

[37] Robert Devereux, *The First Ottoman Constitutional Period: A Study of the Midhat Constitution and Parliament* (Baltimore: Johns Hopkins Press, 1963), pp. 138–41.

[38] *Düstûr*, II/1 (Istanbul, 1329 [1911]), pp. 14–15.

[39] Devereux, *The First Ottoman Constitutional Period*, p. 144.

FIGURE 10. Ottoman deputies 1877 (province/electoral district). a. Speaker of the Chamber of Deputies Ahmed Vefik Efendi (later pasha, senator, and grand vizier); appointed on February 5, 1877. b. Hacı Mehmed Mesʿud Efendi (Diyar-ı Bekir/Diyar-ı Bekir). c. Sayyid Aḥmad al-Barzanjī (the Hejaz/Medina). d. Georgios Athinadoros (Edirne/Tekfurdağı). e. Ahmed Muhtar (Erzurum/ Erzurum). f. Petraki Petrovitch (Bosnia/Sarajevo). Wikipedia.org/wiki/ image:Ahmed_Vefik; *Resimli Kitab*, 1/4 (December 1908), pp. 317, 320, 324–25, 332.

The first Ottoman parliament convened on March 19, 1877 on the brink of war. It survived less than a year, holding only two sessions: one from March 19 to June 28, 1877, and the other from December 13, 1877 to February 14, 1878. The sultan was quick to exercise the prerogatives granted him by the new constitution in order to dismiss Midhat Pasha and banish him from the empire soon after the failure of the Istanbul Conference. On February 13, 1878, once again relying on his constitutional rights, the sultan "temporarily prorogued" the parliament.[40] From this point on, the

[40] Hakkı Tarık Us, *Meclis-i Mebʾusan, 1293–1877*, 2 (Istanbul: Vakit Kütüphanesi, 1954), p. 407.

constitution remained confined to the pages of the official yearbooks, where it was published year after year, while the temporary prorogation of parliament lasted more than three decades. The first constitutional era (1876–78) can hardly be considered constitutional in the strict sense of the word. The sultan remained to a certain extent above the constitution, while the Ottoman parliament acquired real legislative powers only after 1909. Still, it served as an important precedent for the Second Constitutional Period (1908–18) and marks the starting point for the Turkish Republic's elongated journey toward democracy.

The Russo-Ottoman war of 1877–78 was a disaster for the Ottomans. Despite a heroic defensive battle at Plevne (Pleven) and sporadic successes on the Eastern front, their resistance was feeble. The Russians, free of the fear of British naval intervention, enjoyed their finest hour vis-à-vis the Ottomans, forcing them to sign one of the most severe peace treaties in history. The San Stefano Treaty of March 3, 1878 marked the high point of Russian expansion at the expense of the Ottoman Empire. Not only did the treaty award Russia certain territorial gains, it granted independence and additional territory to the ostensibly Ottoman states of Montenegro, Rumania, and Serbia. Moreover, the treaty stipulated the establishment of an autonomous Bulgarian principality on land stretching from the Danube to the Aegean. Finally, it committed the Ottoman government to the implementation of reforms in Bosnia and Herzegovina which it had rejected at the Istanbul Conference. Luckily for the Ottomans, the other Great Powers, and especially Great Britain and Austria-Hungary, were not prepared to accept this extensive revision of the status quo by fait accompli. Russian territorial gains at the expense of the Ottomans were one thing; the wholesale transformation of the Balkans into a Slavic federation under Russian hegemony was another matter altogether.

The Berlin Congress of June–July 1878 was one of the last great conferences convened to settle a major international problem in the era before the First World War. The attempt to resolve the Eastern Question once and for all was an ambitious one, from which the Ottomans emerged very much the losers. From Iran to Montenegro, states gained territory at Ottoman expense. During the lead-up to the Congress, Great Britain secured Cyprus from the Ottoman Empire in return for a promise to defend the Asiatic provinces of the empire against any future Russian attack. Russia acquired parts of Bessarabia (ceded to Moldavia in 1856) and the provinces of Kars, Ardahan, and Batum. Austria-Hungary won the right to occupy Bosnia-Herzegovina and establish military control over Yenipazar (Novibazar), which divides Montenegro from Serbia; Montenegro, Serbia, and Rumania gained formal independence from the Ottoman Empire as well as territory hitherto under direct Ottoman control. The terms were sweetened somewhat by the shrinking of the Bulgarian principality envisioned in the San Stefano

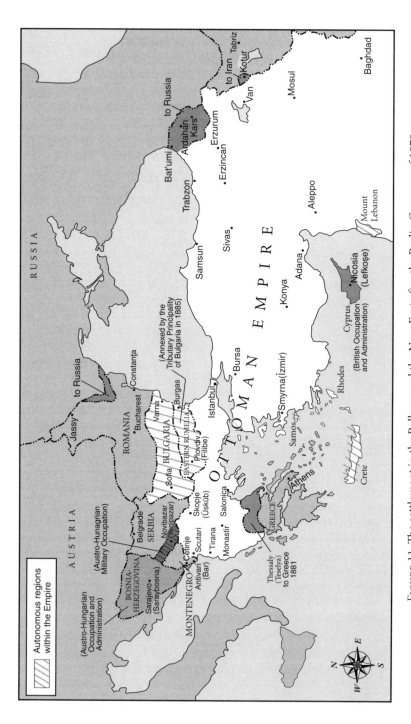

FIGURE 11. The settlement in the Balkans and the Near East after the Berlin Congress of 1878.

Treaty; the southern parts of Bulgaria were returned to the empire and became the autonomous province of Eastern Rumelia. The conference also agreed to restore Macedonia to the empire on condition that pro-Christian reforms would be implemented. In the Six Provinces of Eastern Anatolia, the empire was to enact reforms favoring the Armenians and take the measures necessary to protect them from Kurdish and Circassian encroachments.

Thus, although originally convoked to settle the Eastern Question by avoiding the mistakes of the past—that is, the creation of autonomous regions and demands for reforms favorable to certain ethnic or religious groups— the Berlin Congress ended up repeating them. Reformed Macedonia, in particular, was destined to saddle European diplomacy with a most burdensome problem in the decades to come, as it turned into a battleground for armed groups whose excesses were designed to provoke Ottoman retaliation, leading in turn to foreign intervention. Subsequent events in Macedonia played a significant role in the background to the Young Turk Revolution, the Balkan Wars, and the First World War.

THE HAMIDIAN REGIME

Following the effective dissolution of the parliamentary order, the sultan began to fashion new methods of administration that resulted in the longest-lasting regime in late Ottoman history. One of his confidants wrote a series of articles in which he described the new regime as one that granted freedoms within the strict boundaries of the law.[41] Ironically, the sultan, like his predecessors, the Tanzimat statesmen, believed in the idea of a Rechtsstaat, but he interpreted it quite differently.[42] In his view, the strict application of law could also provide the foundations for autocracy,[43] which should not be confused with the Islamic concept of despotism (*Istibdād/ İstibdad*) or with modern dictatorships.[44] Superimposing the Islamic principle of justice on this notion of a legal autocracy, he created an authoritarian regime that he believed to be the antithesis of absolutism.[45]

A key change brought about by the new sultan was the reduction of the Sublime Porte, which had grown over the preceding four decades into a powerful and independent branch of government, to its former role as a subservient administrative arm of the state. The bureaucrats of the Sublime Porte made their last bid for power in 1895 when, at the height of a crisis

[41] "Hürriyet-i Kanuniye," *Tercüman-ı Hakikat*, July 4, 1878.

[42] [Sidney] Whitman, "Abdul Hamid an Autocrat not a Despot," *New York Herald* (Paris), August 17, 1896.

[43] "Ahmed Midhat's Letter," *New York Herald* (Paris), September 4, 1896.

[44] "İstibdad," *Tercüman-ı Hakikat*, July 3, 1878.

[45] BOA-YEE, 5/1699/83/2; and "İstibdad," *Tercüman-ı Hakikat*, July 3, 1878.

FIGURE 12. Sultan Abdülhamid II in the early days of his reign. George Grantham
Bain Collection, Prints and Photographs Division, Library of Congress.
en.wikipedia.org/wiki/Image:Abdulhamid21890.jpg.

provoked by Armenian political demonstrations and subsequent armed clashes
in the capital, Mehmed Kâmil Pasha asked the sultan to restore responsible
governing practices. He was promptly dismissed, thereby dashing any remaining hopes for a return to the golden age of Sublime Porte paramountcy.[46]

[46] [Mehmed Kâmil], *Hâtırat-ı Sadr-ı Esbak Kâmil Paşa* (Istanbul: Matbaa-i Ebüzziya, 1329
[1911]), pp. 190–96.

Often derided as a simple reactionary, Abdülhamid II in fact envisioned efficient administration of the empire by a modern bureaucracy headed by a cadre of technocrats. Accordingly, bureaucratic reform picked up perceptible speed during his reign. At the sultan's behest, a host of new bureaucratic schools were established, including the Royal Academy of Administration, which became a college. These schools turned out bureaucrats and technocrats of different sorts, ranging from provincial governors to customs officials and veterinaries. In 1880, also at the sultan's urging, the statistical bureaus of the empire began to furnish information on a daily basis;[47] in 1897, Ottoman statisticians produced the first socioeconomic census of the realm.[48] Furthermore, in support of the vision of an efficient bureaucracy in control of the periphery,[49] Abdülhamid II linked the provinces to the center by means of a new invention, the telegraph.

The Hamidian regime reinstated an old Ottoman emphasis on personal loyalty. Whereas officialdom in the Tanzimat era had been bound by loyalty to the state, the bureaucrats of the Hamidian epoch owed their allegiance to their sovereign. The sultan viewed loyalty as an indispensable qualification for employment in the civil service. Abdülhamid II met with important appointees to emphasize that they owed their appointments to him and were responsible to him alone.[50] He granted extra ranks, decorations, and sometimes extravagant personal gifts, such as mansions, to high-ranking bureaucrats who proved exceptionally faithful[51]—often provoking storms of protest within officialdom and the military.[52] The lower rungs of the bureaucracy, however, obeyed a strict hierarchy little different from that found in parallel European institutions.

Abdülhamid II's regime also exploited the power of a modern press to cement loyalty to the state and stifle dissent. The mechanism of censorship developed during this period was one of the strictest in modern times. Ottoman censorship was more capricious[53] than the repressive machinery assembled by Prince Metternich and placed under the oversight of Count Sedlnitzky between 1815 and 1848. Its apparatus was likewise considerably more arbitrary than the Russian *Tsenzurnyi Ustav* of 1828,[54] and its severity

---

[47] *Düstûr*, I/4 (Istanbul: Matbaa-i Âmire, 1295 [1880]), pp. 670–72.

[48] *Devlet-i Aliyye-i Osmaniye'nin Bin Üç Yüz On Üç Senesine Mahsus İstatistik-i Umumîsidir*, IUL, Turkish Mss., no. 9184.6.

[49] BOA-Divân-ı Hümayûn: Muharrerat-ı Umumîye, 83/no. 7 [November 1, 1893].

[50] Tahsin Paşa, *Abdülhamit Yıldız Hatıraları* (Istanbul: Muallim Ahmet Halit Kitaphanesi, 1931), p. 6.

[51] See, for example, BOA-YP, 13 R 1314/no. 6320.

[52] BOA-YEE, 31/111-26/111/86, and BOA-Y.Mtv. 22 Ca 1314/no. 3885.

[53] Comte Am. de Persignac, "Les gaîetes de la censure en Turquie," *La Revue*, 67/2 (1907), pp. 384–94, 521–37.

[54] Mikh[ail] Lemke, *Ocherki po istorii Russkoi tsenzury i zhurnalistiki XIX stolietiia* (St. Petersburg: Knigoizdatel'stvo M.V. Pirozhkova, 1904), p. 186.

surpassed even the particularly harsh wave of Russian repression that followed 1848. When exercised over a community of authors and journalists already adept at self-censorship, the Hamidian censorship produced a press entirely committed to the service of the regime. Journalists stuck to nonpolitical issues unless instructed to criticize foreign governments.

The creation of an all-encompassing personality cult around the Caliph-Sultan coincided with a broader trend that peaked during the Hamidian regime: the re-invention of tradition. It was almost inevitable that an age of transformative reform, wholesale abandonment of old practices, and centralization of a once-loose confederation, should spark a hurried, sometimes artificial process of forming new traditions to replace those lost. The sources of inspiration were varied: often Europe provided the model, but usually old traditions were restyled to render them suitable for use by the renovated state.

Many of the "new" traditions were invented long before Abdülhamid II's ascension, but he reshaped them, broadened their use, and invested them with an imperial significance reminiscent of contemporary European courts. The imperial coat-of-arms, much refined and elaborated since the primitive designs in use under Mahmud II, began to appear on objects ranging from leather book binders and school maps to the backs of postcards and household silver decorations. Imperial yearbooks, which first appeared as slender handbooks in 1846, became copious volumes and a crucial medium through which new traditions were disseminated. Imperial orders, bestowed upon officials for outstanding service to the state, were created in 1832, and expanded in 1852 and 1861 with the introduction of the *Mecidî* and *Osmanî* orders. Under Abdülhamid II, a glittering array of special titles, medals, and decorations emerged (to be freely bestowed upon "vile men and scoundrels of the rabble," as one contemporary bureaucrat notes),[55] including the new *Şefkat* (Compassion) order for women. Celebration of the anniversary of a living sultan's ascension to the throne was also common practice in Ottoman history, but the twenty-fifth anniversary of Abdülhamid II's rule in 1901 was marked in a way unmistakably reminiscent of the golden jubilee of Queen Victoria in 1887—down to the erection of clock towers in the main squares of a host of provincial towns.[56]

Under the sultan's aegis, Ottoman tradition underwent a concerted process of re-invention. Some ancient rituals, such as visits to the holy relics, became pompous ceremonies. Even Friday prayers "acquired additional ceremonial trappings inspired by European examples."[57] The sultan's duties

[55] İnal, *Osmanlı Devrinde Son Sadrıazamlar*, 9, p. 1291.

[56] François Georgeon, *Abdülhamid II: Le sultan calife, 1876–1909* (Paris: Librairie Arthème Fayard, 2003), pp. 349ff.

[57] Selim Deringil, *The Well-Protected Domains: Ideology and the Legitimation of Power in the Ottoman Empire, 1876–1909* (London: I.B. Tauris, 1998), p. 22.

FIGURE 13. The first page of the journal *Terakki* (Progress) dated March 20, 1901, featuring the Ottoman coat of arms and a quatrain praising the sultan on the occasion of the Feast of Sacrifice.

as Caliph were also stressed. Though the title Caliph had been used previously by many sultans, Abdülhamid II created new traditions around it, like his request that officials refer to him foremost as "The Shelter of the Caliphate (*Hilâfetpenâh*)." As part of an attempt to re-mythologize the establishment of the state, tombs of comrades of Ertuğrul Bey (the father of Osman I, founding father of the Ottoman dynasty) were uncovered, named, and lavishly renovated.[58] The 600th anniversary of the foundation of the state was celebrated with enormous pomp and ceremony, and a new tradition inaugurated, which even the sultan's political rivals, the Young Turks, could not help but observe in exile.[59] In classrooms throughout the empire, new maps featuring the empire in its entirety broke an age-old Ottoman tradition of showing each continent separately and inspired youngsters to imagine an enormous transcontinental community.[60]

A candid assessment of the regime of Abdülhamid II would not conclude that it constituted a simple reversion to the patrimonial, pre-Tanzimat style of government. To be sure, the sultan wielded paramount authority; he often made arbitrary decisions; he emphasized personal loyalty to the sovereign; and he reduced the Sublime Porte to subservience. But at the same time he clearly sought to be more than the uppermost link in an inefficient chain of patronage. His self-image, which we need not confuse with reality in order to accept its significance, was that of enlightened reformer; articles written at the sultan's behest for publication in European journals emphasized Ottoman progress under the far-sighted leadership of Abdülhamid II, an Ottoman Peter the Great, who was taking the Tanzimat reforms to new horizons.[61] But beyond the propaganda, the regime's patrimonial façade was to a certain extent misleading. While the sultan himself would issue innumerable imperial decrees on issues ranging from decisions of life and death to the utterly trivial—he was, in other words, above the law—the actions of all other bureaucrats, including those of the grand vizier, were legally constrained. The sultan's ultimate source of authority was the "imperial will," but his civil servants were bound by the law.

Abdülhamid II was no simple-minded reactionary blindly presiding over the slow demise of a stagnant empire. He was a shrewd tactician. He lacked the imagination and courage needed for a wholesale transformation of his

[58] Ibid., p. 32.

[59] "İstiklâl-i Osmanî," *Türk*, no. 12 (January 20, 1904), p. 1; no. 66 (February 2, 1905), pp. 1–2; and no. 116 (February 1, 1906), p. 1.

[60] Benjamin J. Fortna, *Imperial Classroom: Islam, the State, and Education in the Late Ottoman Empire* (Oxford: Oxford University Press, 2002), p. 186.

[61] See, for example, Ibrahim Hakki, "Is Turkey Progressing?" *The Imperial and Asiatic Quarterly Review and Oriental and Colonial Record* 3/2 (April 1892), pp. 271–2.

anachronistic multinational state in the age of nationalism—not unlike his companions in this predicament, the Austrians and Russians. Instead he pursued an administrative solution to his problems at home, while maximizing the Ottoman Empire's weak potential abroad by staving off external threats to the empire through diplomacy. Indeed, it is often forgotten that Abdülhamid II's ambitious agenda of bureaucratic modernization at home ultimately depended on his ability to parry the external threats to the empire. With the military odds stacked heavily against the Ottoman state, and its enemies multiplying, shrewd diplomacy remained the only way to buy time.

Ottoman Foreign Policy under Abdülhamid II

Following the Congress of Berlin, Abdülhamid II pursued a pragmatic policy of noncommitment. Since the empire was militarily weak and domestically vulnerable, Ottoman leverage over the other Great Powers lay in exploiting their common fear of a disruption of the balance of power in Europe as a result of any one power gaining control or influence over the Ottoman territories. Accordingly, the sultan sought to stave off threats toward Ottoman territorial integrity and pressures for administrative reforms in favor of particular ethno-religious groups by playing off one Great Power against the other—without, however, committing the empire to an alliance with any one power or alignment of powers. To be sure, ideological considerations played a certain role as well. The sultan's opinion that the Western powers, with the exception of the United States and Brazil, formed a Union of Crusaders united against the Caliphate and bent on wresting its territory away from the believers (and even conniving to lure Shī'ite Iran into participation in this heinous scheme) was not wholly founded on realpolitik, but neither was it completely divorced from reality.[62] Ideology served to further the sultan's foreign policy goals, not the other way around. Above all, an acute consciousness of external constraints and internal limits guided Abdülhamid II's actions in the foreign arena.

After the Russo-Ottoman War of 1877–78, tension spread to new regions and posed greater difficulties than ever before. These were territories that included significant numbers of Muslims whom the Ottoman government could not simply abandon to their fate. Unlike his predecessors, Abdülhamid II had little inclination to implement reforms that might undermine the empire. In order to counter European pressure, the new sultan adopted a

---

[62] BOA-YEE, 8/2625/77/3.

two-pronged policy of Pan-Islamism. The first prong entailed knitting together the Muslim elements of the empire into a cohesive new core of identity. Due to the loss of territory heavily populated by Christians and the influx of Muslim refugees, the Muslim proportion of the Ottoman population had grown to 73.3 percent, according to the general censuses of 1881/2–1893.[63] By such gestures as the employment of numerous Arabs and Albanians in his service, the conferral of privileges and decorations on Albanian, Arab, and Kurdish chieftains, and the placement of Arab provinces at the top of the list in official yearbooks, Abdülhamid II attempted to forge a polyethnic brotherhood of Muslims. The second prong of his Pan-Islamist strategy was the use of Pan-Islamic propaganda as a wild card directed against colonial powers who ruled over substantial Muslim populations.

Ironically, the most avid takers of Abdülhamid II's Pan-Islamic rhetoric abroad were not Muslims but Europeans. Pundits like Valentine Chirol and Gabriel Charmes strove to convince their readers of the grave dangers posed by Pan-Islamism. Such assessments often fell on attentive ears, especially after the much-publicized Dinshawāy incident of June 1906—in which a clash with Egyptian peasants led to the death of one British officer and the wounding of another while they were out pigeon-hunting. Kaiser Wilhelm II's support for the sultan as spiritual leader of Sunnī Islam disquieted policy makers in Great Britain, France, and Russia. Abdülhamid II at one point even offered his services to the Americans as a mediator with the Philippine Muslims.[64] Underpinning all this posturing was the sultan's assumption that by securing the world's recognition of his status as spiritual leader of all Sunnī Muslims, he would gain bargaining power denied to him by military weakness. The sultan, whose adroit manipulation of European fears of an imagined Pan-Islamic threat attested to a shrewd tactical mind, was otherwise powerless to deflect Great Power pressure.

Aware of the limitations of his position, Abdülhamid II carefully evaded direct confrontations with the Great Powers and studiously avoided taking risks for regions only nominally under Ottoman control. The establishment of a de facto French protectorate in Tunisia in 1881, the British occupation of Egypt in 1882, and the Bulgarian annexation of Eastern Rumelia in 1885— all these drew no more than formal protests from the Ottoman government. And when, in 1897, the Ottomans defeated the Greeks in a war sparked by a rebellion on Crete, the Ottoman administration yielded swiftly to a Great Power scheme that enhanced the autonomy of the island's Christians.

[63] Kemal H. Karpat, *Ottoman Population, 1830–1914: Demographic and Social Characteristics* (Madison: University of Wisconsin Press, 1986), pp. 148–50.

[64] Chargé d'affaires Spencer Eddy to the Secretary of State, John Milton Hay, Therapia, September 27, 1902 (Private and confidential telegram); Dispatches from U.S. Ministers to Turkey (1818–1906), 72 (July 1–December 29, 1902).

But the ability of Abdülhamid II to pursue his delicate balancing act was severely constrained by an indirect outcome of the Russo-Ottoman War of 1877–78: the end of active British support for the Ottoman Empire. The strategic commitment of Britain to Ottoman defense, like all its continental obligations, was inherently in tension with two strong currents in British tradition: an isolationist mentality that abhorred commitment unless British security was directly threatened, and a moralizing tendency that condemned policies of support for regimes considered less than liberal. The war and the events surrounding it inaugurated a new ascendancy of the moral component in British policy toward the Ottoman Empire, fueled especially by vocal criticism of Ottoman policy emanating from the liberal wing of British public opinion. The practical implications for Ottoman foreign policy were a diminished assurance of British intervention in time of crisis and heavier external pressure for reform. The liberal critique of the empire intensified during the Armenian crises of 1895 and 1896, in which Armenian revolutionaries stepped up acts of violence and sabotage in the hope of provoking European intervention. The heavy-handed suppression of these activities by the Ottoman authorities, and ensuing attacks by mobs on Armenian civilians, played a role in the subsequent formulation of contingency plans for the partition of the Ottoman Empire by the Marquis of Salisbury, who bluntly remarked that the British "sympathies with Turkey have completely changed and she would never again make great sacrifices for a government which she so thoroughly distrusts."[65]

The liberal assault on the British-Ottoman relationship coincided, unhappily for the Ottomans, with a reassessment of British defense policy which diminished the importance of Ottoman territorial integrity for the defense of the British Empire. The opening of the Suez Canal in 1869 and the British occupation of Egypt in 1882 were milestones on the road to an inevitable reevaluation of policy, culminating in Salisbury's landmark decision of 1896 to base the defense of British interests in the Near East on Egypt rather than on efforts to preserve the status quo at the Straits.[66] Thus, the internal turmoil of 1895–97, which so negatively affected British public opinion toward the Ottomans, also marked a broader turning point in Ottoman-British relations, as a result of the drastic reduction of the importance of the Ottoman Empire in the eyes of British policy makers.

The opening of the Suez Canal also greatly enhanced the strategic importance of the Red Sea Coast, which became the object of Great Power rivalry. The British occupation of Egypt meant de facto British domination

---

[65] A report regarding the Marquis of Salisbury's response to Graf Deym, dated January 23, 1897, Royal Archives, (M) H 39.

[66] M[atthew] S[mith] Anderson, *The Eastern Question, 1774–1923: A Study in International Relations* (London: Macmillan, 1966), p. 261.

over the Sudan, which was recognized in the Anglo-Egyptian Condominium of 1899. The Italians mounted a bolder and more direct challenge to Ottoman control of Eritrea, landing troops at Massawa in 1885. Despite raucous Ottoman protests, they expanded the area under their occupation and, following the Treaty of Wichale of 1889 between the Ethiopian Emperor Menelik II and the Italian government, proclaimed Eritrea an Italian colony in 1890. Great Power control of the African Red Sea coast posed a strategic threat to the Ottomans, rendering virtually impossible the defense of the coastlines of ʿAsīr, Yemen, and even the Ḥijāz.

The loss of a dependable British option led to a natural Ottoman gravitation toward Germany and even Russia. As the events of 1877–78 had shown, Britain could no longer be depended on to save the Ottomans from Russia; nor was the British navy of much use against increasingly land-based threats to the heart of the empire.[67] The Ottoman refusal during the Penjdeh crisis of 1885 to allow the British fleet to pass through the Straits in the event of an Anglo-Russian war strained relations and heightened suspicions on both sides still further. At the same time, Bismarck's disdain for the Ottomans—memorably captured in his assessment that their empire was not worth "the sound bones of a single Pomeranian Grenadier"—no longer fit in with Germany's *Drang nach Osten*. Whereas Bismarck had ignored the pleas of Ottoman diplomats at the Berlin Congress and saw utility mainly in promising their territory to rival European powers, Wilhelm II thought that German economic and political penetration of the Caliph's empire—with his cooperation—would prove to be an invaluable asset in Germany's quest for global power. Despite striving for friendly relations with Germany, Abdülhamid II did not wish to limit his options by establishing a formal alliance with Germany and Austria-Hungary. Moreover, a necessary condition for such an alliance, from the Ottoman perspective, remained unfulfilled: the combined military strength of Germany and Austria-Hungary in Europe had to be sufficient to deter Russia from attacking the Ottomans in Asia.[68] In any case, Russia had achieved as great a territorial expansion as was tolerable to the other European powers. As a result, the Russian option remained open alongside the German one. It is in this light that we must understand such developments as the granting of the Baghdad Railway concession to the Société Impériale Ottomane du Chemin de Fer de Baghdad (established by a convention between the Ottoman government and the Deutsche Bank in 1903), the Black Sea Agreement of 1900 (which promised Russia exclusivity with regard to railway concessions on the Ottoman side of the Russo-Ottoman border), and more generally, Ottoman

[67] F[eroz] A[bdullah] K[han] Yasamee, *Ottoman Diplomacy: Abdülhamid II and the Great Powers, 1878–1888* (Istanbul: Isis Press, 1996), p. 256.
[68] Ibid.

flirtation with the *Dreikaiserbund*. But noncommitment from a position of military weakness required constant appeasement of all the powers and proved unsustainable in the long run. When the Penjdeh crisis and the Mediterranean Agreement of 1887 thrust the Ottoman Straits to the top of the international agenda, a non-negotiable Ottoman interest was affected. Faced with the prospect of a hostile takeover of the Straits in the event of an Anglo-Russian war, the sultan felt compelled to abandon passive noncommitment, based as it was on the impossibility of securing the defense of the empire through an alliance with a single European power, and had to shift to a more assertive policy of armed neutrality. Inter alia, this entailed substantial outlays on fortifying the Straits and supplying a large army to defend the empire against a Russian invasion.[69]

The Japanese victory over Russia in 1905 significantly reduced the primary land-based threat to the Ottoman heartland. At the same time, Britain—the traditional guarantor of Ottoman security—now emerged as the principal threat to Ottoman territorial integrity. This was particularly true in the Near East, where Ottoman and British interests clashed most consistently, and where Ottoman territory was most vulnerable to the exercise of hostile sea power. To defuse this threat, Abdülhamid II authorized major concessions to the British in negotiations over a line of demarcation between Ottoman Yemen and the British protectorate in Aden.[70] The resulting Anglo-Ottoman agreement of 1905 was a substantial achievement that did much to relieve tensions between the two powers (and to ease the Ottoman policy of armed neutrality). But soon another dispute flared up over the Egyptian-Ottoman border in Sinai (the Ṭābā crisis of 1906), demonstrating that British and Ottoman interests in the Near East had become fundamentally incompatible. Leaks of British plans to force the Straits in the event of war with the Ottoman Empire[71] further underscored the new danger from Great Britain, hitherto associated mostly with benevolent aid in time of need. With its impotent navy, which had proven its worthlessness against the Greeks in 1897, the Ottoman Empire simply could not defend a coast that stretched from the Dardanelles in the north to al-Ḥudaydah in the south against the Royal Navy. Accordingly, Ottoman defense planners focused on the protection of the Dardanelles, which would deny Britain an easy victory, and compel it to contemplate the dispatch of a large expeditionary force to the Levant.

Another major foreign policy headache Ottoman statesmen acquired in the 1880s was the emergence of an autonomous Bulgarian entity in Rumelia. Serbia, Montenegro, and Greece posed no serious military threat to the

---

[69] Ibid., p. 257.
[70] BOA-DUİT, 69, 3–45.
[71] PRO/CAB. 38/11 (1906)/no. 27 (secret).

empire, even in combination. But the establishment, in 1878, of an autonomous Bulgarian principality that was Ottoman in name only, and its unification with Eastern Rumelia in 1885, altered these calculations in an alarming way. As Abdülhamid II foresaw in 1886,[72] an effective army deployed in the Bulgarian principality would threaten both Istanbul and Salonica, and be in a position to score a swift victory before Ottoman mobilization was complete and troops from the Anatolian and Arab provinces could be transferred westward. His prophecy was to be fulfilled in 1912–13. In the meantime Bulgarian meddling in Macedonia was a constant irritant. To reduce the menace, the sultan exerted considerable effort to forge an alliance with Greece, Serbia, and possibly Rumania to encircle Bulgaria and contain it. Concurrently, the Ottoman administration turned a blind eye to Greek band activity in Macedonia so long as it targeted the Macedonian Slavs. At the time of the Young Turk Revolution, Abdülhamid II was vigorously pursuing such a Balkan alliance,[73] but lost power before he could achieve it. With the exception of one stillborn attempt to achieve a Serbo-Ottoman alliance in 1908, his successors abandoned these efforts, with disastrous consequences.

Although Abdülhamid II consistently avoided a major conflict with the Great Powers over regions only nominally under Ottoman control—such as Tunisia, Egypt, and Eastern Rumelia—there was one notable exception to this policy of accommodation: the Arabian Peninsula. The sultan fiercely defended Ottoman rights in the birthplace of Islam with the limited means offered him by diplomacy without the backing of force. When, for instance, Germany attempted to establish a base in the Red Sea archipelago of Farasan in 1900 (ostensibly to supply her China-bound ships with coal), the Ottomans did not hesitate to bring the crisis with this friendly government to the brink of serious conflict. Only when Germany accepted the condition that it must unequivocally recognize Ottoman sovereignty did the Ottomans move to defuse the crisis by offering a rental contract for a coal depot on the islands.[74] The sultan responded with equal resolve to a British challenge to Ottoman sovereignty over Kuwait in the fall of 1901. In an attempt to nudge the Ottomans out of their precarious position of influence, British officials attempted to prevent an Ottoman frigate from anchoring in the harbor of Kuwait, and then recommended to the Kuwaiti sheikh that he replace the Ottoman banner with a black and white striped flag. The sultan did not

[72] BOA-YEE, I/156-32/156/3.

[73] See Galip Kemali Söylemezoğlu, *Hariciye Hizmetinde Otuz Sene, 1892–1922*, 1 (Istanbul: Şaka Matbaası, 1950), pp. 131–2. See also Geshof to Kniaz Ferdinand, Tsarigrad, December 19, 1906 [January 1, 1907]; and a report prepared in Belgrade and submitted to the Prince on October 2[15] 1906, TsDA, fond. 3, op. 863, a.e. 863, ff. 71–4 and 20–21, respectively.

[74] BOA-HR.SYS 98/3 (1900-1901).

back down on either issue, continuing to protest until the British provided assurances of respect for Ottoman suzerainty.[75]

Abdülhamid II's dexterous acrobatics in the field of foreign policy helped the empire adjust to major changes in the balance of power and stave off a large-scale conflict that might have gravely damaged its territorial integrity or even triggered its collapse. Given the impossibility of obtaining a significant European ally, this was a major achievement.

THE ECONOMY

Two-thirds of the lifespan of the Hamidian regime coincided with the Great Economic Depression of 1873–96, the greatest long-term price deflation in modern history. Despite rendering Ottoman manufacturing more competitive, this deflation caused a host of political and cultural problems in addition to widespread economic instability and serious damage to Ottoman external trade and foreign investment. Notwithstanding the turbulence of the times and the persistence of serious structural deficiencies, the Ottoman economic system under Abdülhamid II shed its peculiar dualism and became a modern economy.

In spite of the sultan's determined efforts to downsize the bureaucracy and balance the budget, the Ottoman debt ballooned after the Russo-Turkish War of 1877–78, precipitating a grave financial crisis. In 1879, the government formed a special administration to manage the payment of interest and amortization on a loan of Lt 8.72 million borrowed from Galata bankers. This authority collected certain taxes and monopoly revenues to pay off the debt. In 1881, the sultan decreed a restructuring of the Ottoman debt. Consequently, the debt was reduced from Lt 239.5 million to Lt 125.3 million, and yearly interest and amortization payments dropped from Lt 13.2 million to Lt 7.6 million. A new Public Debt Administration, formed in 1881 in fulfillment of one of the stipulations of the Berlin Congress, was to administer all Ottoman debt, including the payment of war indemnities to Russia. Its management consisted of a representative of the Galata bankers as well as delegates from the Netherlands and all the Great Powers but Russia. The Administration assumed collection duties for various Ottoman revenues, such as those accruing from the salt monopoly, the fisheries, and the tobacco tithe, and used them to pay off 5 percent of the Ottoman debt each year (consisting of 1 percent principal and 4 percent interest). Between 1881–82 and 1911–12, the income of this body rose from Lt 2.54 million to Lt 8.16 million, and its share in the total revenues of the state from

---

[75] *Kuveyt Meselesi* (Istanbul: Matbaa-i Âmire, 1334 [1917]), pp. 5ff.

17 percent to 27 percent.[76] Negative public reaction to the Public Debt Administration played a significant role in the emergence of Turkism and, later, of Turkish nationalism.

An additional major problem, which was not new, was the perennial trade deficit. The emergence of the United States as a major exporter of agricultural products and raw materials to Europe, and the consequent decline in the prices of goods that constituted a major portion of Ottoman exports, was one exacerbating factor. Another was the fact that the prices of Ottoman imports, primarily industrial goods and military hardware, did not decline to the same extent. However, the state managed to prevent trade imbalances from getting out of hand. As a result, the overall foreign trade deficit remained steady over this period (1.161 million gurushes in 1878–79, as compared with 1.299 million gurushes in 1908–9). Several factors account for this success. First, the state managed to maintain the parity of the Ottoman lira with major foreign currencies. Second, the period saw a considerable increase in European demand for Ottoman raw materials. The export of chromate, for instance, rose from 3.5 tons in 1885 to 17.7 tons in 1909; that of boracites, from 4.0 tons to 15.3 tons during the same period.[77] Third, the regime continued to employ an array of protectionist policies adopted during the last decade of the Tanzimat. These were designed to shield the empire from global competition, boost Ottoman industrial and agricultural production, and increase exports within the constraints imposed by the capitulations.

To promote agriculture, the state founded agricultural schools, established model farms, and provided tax relief to farmers who grew produce desired in foreign markets.[78] In 1888, the government established the Agricultural Bank (Ziraat Bankası), with a nominal capital of Lt 10 million, by consolidating all existing state-backed funds for public improvement.[79] The bank served two major purposes. First, it provided mainly agricultural credits; the value of total loans issued by the bank increased from Lt 162,832 in 1889 to Lt 1,097,469 in 1907. In this capacity, the bank served as the principal financier of agricultural reform.[80] Second, the Agricultural Bank became the state's embryonic, unofficial national bank in competition with the foreign-owned Ottoman Bank. By the end of the Hamidian period, the Agricultural Bank had provided 602 million gurushes in credit on the basis

[76] Vedat Eldem, *Osmanlı İmparatorluğunun İktisadi Şartları Hakkında Bir Tetkik* (Istanbul: Türkiye İş Bankası Kültür Yayınları, 1970), pp. 259–65.

[77] Ibid., pp. 182–3.

[78] Donald Quataert, "Dilemma of Development: The Agricultural Bank and Agricultural Reform in Ottoman Turkey, 1888–1908," *IJMES* 6/2 (April 1975), p. 211.

[79] *Ceride-i Mahakim*, no. 750 [November 1, 1890], pp. 8245–9, and no. 751 [November 8, 1890], pp. 8257–61.

[80] Quataert, "Dilemma of Development," pp. 219ff.

of a mere 48 million gurushes in deposits, as compared to 1,587 million gurushes in credit on the basis of 1,772 million in deposits provided by the Ottoman Bank.[81] The manufacturing sector also benefited from Hamidian economic policy. Despite the allocation of substantial portions of the gross national income to military expenditure[82] and interest payments on debt, the state managed to launch major infrastructural investments, such as the Baghdad and Ḥijāz railroads, a large irrigation project in the Konya Valley, and telegraph lines connecting the Ottoman provinces with the center. The development of a more advanced railroad network, in particular, facilitated the efficient delivery of goods to domestic markets or ports of export. Partly as a result, production levels of silk, carpets, tiles, glass, and other goods increased. Heavier industrial production, such as that of gas, minerals, and cigarettes, also rose. Nevertheless, these increases did not amount to a major boom in the development of Ottoman industry. Between 1881 and 1908, only forty-seven new joint-stock industrial companies were founded, with a total capital of Lt 11.9 million (almost a quarter of which belonged to the Société de la Régie coïnteressée des Tabacs de l'Empire ottomane—the monopoly that exploited the Ottoman tobacco industry through its position as sole subcontractor for the Public Debt Administration).[83]

Abdülhamid II's government made a second attempt to introduce banknotes to the empire. The decision to print money, taken prior to Abdülhamid II's accession to the throne, was implemented between 1876 and 1878, and helped finance the Russo-Ottoman War. The banknotes were intended for circulation throughout the empire, with the exception of the Ḥijāz, Yemen, and Tripoli of Barbary.[84] But once again, a rash of counterfeits, combined with popular mistrust of the innovation, especially in the provinces, caused rapid depreciation of the value of the notes on the market, leading to their withdrawal from circulation in March 1879. To compensate for the loss, the government raised certain taxes on consumption.[85] In 1881, the empire announced a switch from bimetalism to a loose gold standard (a full switch took place in April 1916), under which silver coins continued to circulate at a rate set by the state but linked to a gold reserve.[86] This move, which predated similar decisions by Russia (1893), Japan (1897), and the United States (1900), illustrates the intent to integrate the Ottoman Empire into the global economy. The scarcity of gold limited its

[81] Eldem, *Osmanlı İmparatorluğunun İktisadi Şartları Hakkında Bir Tetkik*, p. 234.

[82] [Mehmed] Rıza, *Hülâsa-i Hâtırat* (Istanbul: s.n., 1325 [1909]), appendices.

[83] Eldem, *Osmanlı İmparatorluğunun İktisadi Şartları Hakkında Bir Tetkik*, p. 122.

[84] Süleyman Sûdî, *Usûl-i Meskûkât-ı Osmaniye ve Ecnebiye* (Istanbul: A. Asadoryan, 1311 [1893]), p. 228.

[85] Ibid., pp. 128–32.

[86] Ibid., pp. 243–4.

use to the execution of foreign trade transactions, while silver remained the primary medium of domestic exchange.

INTELLECTUAL AND CULTURAL DEVELOPMENTS

Among the many ironies of the Hamidian regime, one of the most striking is certainly the triumph of materialist ideas under the most pious sultan of late Ottoman history. For while Abdülhamid II was laboring to fashion Islamist modernity in opposition to the West, a large number of Ottoman intellectuals were increasingly being drawn to the European doctrine of scientific materialism. The penetration of German *Vulgärmaterialismus*—a peculiar mixture of materialism, scientism, and Social Darwinism—had already begun during the Tanzimat, and gained considerable traction in the 1870s and 1880s. Its proponents propagated these imported ideas through popular scientific journals that, being apolitical, were spared by the censor. Ludwig Büchner, whose *Kraft und Stoff* was regarded as a sacred text by many Ottoman intellectuals, became the idol of a generation of Ottoman recipients of Western-style education. Littréian Positivism seemed more influential only because of its prominence among the leaders of the Committee of Union and Progress, who had at one point made *ordre et progrès* their motto. Likewise Spinoza, once the target of criticism by traditional Ottoman scholars bent on exposing the evils of materialism,[87] became an object of lavish praise by the 1880s as "one of the foremost philosophers to adorn the history of philosophy."[88] A bibliography of all Turkish books and translations published in Istanbul between 1876 and 1890 lists only 200 of roughly 4,000 titles as dealing with religious topics. By contrast, it features approximately 500 works on science, the majority of which promoted materialism in a more or less explicit fashion. Much of the remainder of the list is made up of legal and literary works.[89] The importance of the acceptance of a hybrid doctrine based on eighteenth-century French materialism and nineteenth-century German *Vulgärmaterialismus* by a large segment of the Ottoman intelligentsia should not be underestimated. This was one instance where ideas mattered a great deal: for the winds of materialism continued to blow long after the Young Turk Revolution and into Republican times, exerting a profound influence on the Weltanschauung of the founders of the Republic and on the ideology they fashioned to build modern Turkey.

Many members of the new intellectual elite expected the Darwinian triumph of science over religion in their time. One Ottoman statesman

---

[87] *Spinoza Mektebine Reddiye*, TPL, H. 372.

[88] Hüseyin Avni, "Spinoza—Hayat ve Mesleği," *Güneş* 1/5 [1883], pp. 255ff.

[89] Server R. İskit, *Türkiyede Neşriyat Hareketleri Tarihine Bir Bakış* (Istanbul: Maarif Vekâleti, 1939), p. 102.

expressed these sentiments in a giddy poem entitled "The Nineteenth Century," which he wrote in elation after the Paris Fair of 1878:

The light of comprehension has touched the summit of perfection;
Many impossibilities have become possibilities.

Elementary substances have become complex, complexity has become elementary;
Many unknowns have become familiar through experience.

The truth has become figurative, that which was once figurative has become true;
The foundations of old knowledge have collapsed.

Now the sciences are astronomy, geology, physics, and chemistry,
Not misconceptions of the mind, conjectures, and analogies.

. . . .

Wise men have probed the depths of the earth,
Treasures of buried strata furnish the proofs of creation.

. . . .

Neither the belief in metamorphosis nor the fire of the Magians has survived,
The Holy Trinity is not the *Qibla* of fulfillment for the intelligent.

. . . .

Atlas does not hold up the earth, nor is Aphrodite divine,
Plato's wisdom cannot explain the principles of evolution.

. . . .

'Amr is no slave of Zayd, nor is Zayd 'Amr's master,
Law depends upon the principle of equality.

. . . .

Alas! The West has become the locus of rising knowledge,
Neither the fame of Anatolia and Arabia nor the glory of Cairo and Herat remains.

This is the time for progress; the world is the world of sciences;
Is it possible to uphold society with ignorance?[90]

As the materialist movement gained traction within the Ottoman elite, it evolved into a peculiar form of scientism that rejected religion and

[90] Sâdullah Paşa, "Ondokuzuncu Asır," in Mehmed Kaplan (ed.), *Şiir Tahlilleri: Âkif Paşadan Yahya Kemal'e Kadar* (Istanbul: Anıl Yayınevi, 1958), pp. 59–60.

attributed European progress to the alleged adoption of materialist doctrine in Europe. The rejection of religion was perhaps more tempting for
the non-Muslims of the empire, who embraced European ideas before their
Muslim counterparts. While the adherents of materialism in the capital
were mostly Muslim, in the Arab provinces they were most often Christians. It was from among the latter that a challenge to the ulema on the
subject of Darwinism first emerged.[91] But the initial assaults on religion
were cautious. During the Tanzimat era, the scientistic critique of religion
was typically presented by drawing seemingly innocuous comparisons between modern science and traditional methods for the pursuit of knowledge, for example, by contrasting the usefulness of geology and history as
tools for understanding the human past.[92] Such articles delivered, between
the lines, the same subversive message that was conveyed openly in Sir
Charles Lyell's *Elements of Geology* and *The Geological Evidences of the An-
tiquity of Man*. Beginning in the 1870s, a popular scientistic press emerged,
which imitated European journals like *Science pour tous* and *Die Natur*,
thus helping to spread the gospel among ever wider audiences. Not every
disciple of scientism was as radical as Beşir Fu'ad who, as an experiment,
cut his veins in a bathtub, continuing taking notes on his condition until
losing consciousness—all to prove that human life was ephemeral and
material;[93] or Dr. Şerafeddin Mağmumî, who proposed to destroy every
work of traditional Ottoman poetry ever written on the grounds that these
works were not scientific.[94] Nevertheless, a generation of secular materialists
emerged in the capital of the Caliphate and, as self-assured bearers of the new
truth, made an impact on Ottoman intellectual life quite disproportionate
to their numbers.

Despite the pronounced Islamist flavor of the sultan's rhetoric, Islamist
intellectuals suffered immensely under his reign. The sultan, who feared the
potent capacity of the ulema to legitimize criticism of his regime, banished a
large number of them. At the same time, the censor curtailed any serious religious debate. The Islamist opposition worked with the Young Turks abroad,[95]
while the Salafi movement flourished in Syria.[96] It was only after the Young

---

[91] See, for instance, Dr. Shiblī Shumayyil's *al-Ḥaqīqah wa-hiya risālah tataḍamman rudūdan li-ithbāt madhhab Darwin fī'l-nushū' wa'l-irtiqā'* (Cairo: al-Muqtaṭaf, 1885); and *Rudūd al-'ulamā' 'alā madhhab Darwin fī'l-irtiqā'* (Beirut: Maṭba'at al-Mursalīn al-Yasū'īyīn, 1886).

[92] Münif, "Mukaddime-i İlm-i Jeoloji," *Mecmua-i Fünûn* 1/2 (July–August 1862), p. 65.

[93] M. Orhan Okay, *Beşir Fuad: İlk Türk Pozitivist ve Natüralisti* (Istanbul: Hareket Yayınları, 1969), p. 93.

[94] Şerafeddin Mağmumî, *Başlangıç* (Istanbul: İstepan Matbaası, 1307 [1888–1890]), pp. 22–3.

[95] M. Şükrü Hanioğlu, *The Young Turks in Opposition* (New York: Oxford University Press, 1995), pp. 49ff.

[96] David Dean Commins, *Islamic Reform: Politics and Social Change in Late Ottoman Syria* (New York: Oxford University Press, 1990), pp. 49ff.

Turk Revolution of 1908 that Islamist intellectual activity began to thrive in the capital and the imperial heartland.

One of the intellectual realms from which the dualism of the Tanzimat all but disappeared was literature. Ottoman literary figures under Abdülhamid II engaged wholeheartedly in debates that mirrored those taking place in Europe. European literary forms, such as the sonnet, became standard, while classical forms were all but forgotten. Naturalist, Parnassian, Realist, and Symbolist influences abounded. The New Literature (*Edebiyat-ı Cedîde*) movement, started in 1891 by the proponents of *l'art pour l'art*, and succeeded by the Impending Dawn (*Fecr-i Âtî*) current, dominated the scene during this period. By 1900, major Ottoman literary figures were presenting images of a new modernist vision informed by French literature. Works such as Tevfik Fikret's poem "Sis" (Fog, 1902) expressed the moral decay of late Ottoman Istanbul, where "a stubborn smoke has shrouded its horizons."[97] The Ottoman novel developed rapidly during the 1890s. One particularly appealing example was Halid Ziya (Uşaklıgil)'s "*Aşk-ı Memnu*'" (Forbidden Love, 1900), a psychological study of adultery in a Bosporus mansion. It constituted an allegory on the decline of the empire and a model in theme and structure for much Turkish literature of the twentieth century.

Attitudes toward European manners and mores, summed up in the phrase Alla Franca, continued to evolve under Abdülhamid II. This sovereign's own attitude was ambivalent. While the "pious sultan" protested vigorously against the notion that he was an ardent admirer and blind emulator of "Frankish civilization,"[98] his lifestyle betrayed the internalization of many Alla Franca values. His secret passion for European classical music and theater, for example, brought many stars to perform privately at his palace. These included such famous opera singers as the Belgian soprano Blanche Arral and legendary actresses like French tragedienne Sarah Bernhardt. Following the Young Turk Revolution, fiercely nationalistic anti-Western sentiments replaced the Hamidian regime's official Islamic abhorrence of Western mores. Accordingly, the derisive attitudes toward the adoption of Western fashions and habits common in the late nineteenth century gave way to more severe ones, as Alla Franca came under attack as a moral pestilence to be exterminated.[99] By then, however, the habits it denoted had already become firmly ensconced among educated people and members of the upper and middle classes of the empire.

---

[97] Tevfik Fikret, *Rubab-ı Şikeste* (Istanbul: Tanin Matbaası, 1327 [1911]), p. 295.

[98] Ahmed Salâhi, *Osmanlı ve Avrupa Politikası ve Abdulhamid-i Sanî'nin Siyaseti*, IUL, Turkish Mss., D. 2/9521 (1303 [1885]), p. 4.

[99] See, for example, M.S., *Alafranga Bir Hanım: Ahlâk-ı Nisvâniyeyi Musavvir Romandır* (Istanbul: Artin Asadoryan, 1329 [1911]), passim.

The Emergence of Nationalism among Muslims

Turkism (to be discussed in the next section) was not the only proto-nationalist movement to flourish during the Hamidian era. It was merely one of the last in a series of similar movements to emerge among Muslim Ottoman groups, such as the Albanians, the Arabs, and the Kurds. Even small Muslim communities, like the Circassians, exhibited a rise in nationalist sentiment. The level of national consciousness varied considerably within each of these movements. The nationalisms of the Albanians and Arabs were the most developed. Both the Albanian *Rilindja* (Rebirth) and the Arab *Nahḍah* (Renaissance) movements focused on re-awakening the dormant "nation" with the aid of a new approach to history and literature centered on the recovery of a glorious past. The key role played by non-Muslim Arabs and Albanians in this effort contributed to the emergence of national identities apparently free of religious affiliation. The proto-nationalisms of the Kurds and Circassians, by contrast, were less developed and depended heavily on the Islamic heritage.

Abdülhamid II's efforts to redefine Ottomanism and give it a Muslim coloring, as well as his domestic use of Pan-Islamic ideology, were directed mainly at curbing nascent proto-nationalist activities among Muslim Ottomans. In a multinational empire, crumbling most dangerously on its Christian periphery, Islam potentially represented a last line of defense against the corrosive effects of nationalism. The state could theoretically survive the loss of parts of some provinces to Christian nationalist movements, but if the Muslims of the empire—who by 1900 accounted for three-quarters of the total population—were to split along ethnic lines, the Ottoman polity was doomed.

The sultan's Islamist policies certainly won over the hearts and minds of a large segment of the elite in various Muslim Ottoman communities which feared the likely alternatives to Ottoman rule: colonial administration by one of the Great Powers or minority status in small nation-states backed by these powers and dominated by Christian populations formerly under Ottoman rule (such as the Greeks, the Serbians, or the Armenians). But other members of these same elites, often disenfranchised or harboring long-standing grievances against the Ottoman administration, could envision more positive scenarios. Some thought of autonomous regions which would remain loosely attached to the empire; others were bolder still, dreaming of independent nation-states under their own control. From their ranks came the leaders of proto-nationalist activity in this period.

By the end of the Hamidian era, these movements—like the nascent Turkism that fed the ideological base of the major opposition organization, the CUP—had succeeded in converting ideological coherence into political strength, dominating intellectual debate within their respective communities both in the press and on the street. One theoretical advantage they had over the sultan was that as nationalist movements, they could envision a community that included non-Muslim compatriots excluded by Abdülhamid II's Islamic Ottomanism. The redefining of the political community along linguistic or ethnic lines proved very important for the subsequent popularization of proto-nationalist ideas in the Arab communities of the empire, and especially among the Albanians. The center suffered from a further disadvantage in competition with these groups: its failure to create a *Homo Ottomanicus* in the wake of the Tanzimat, coupled with its pressure for ever more centralization, fostered grave tensions with the non-Turkish periphery, tensions which proto-nationalist intellectuals were only too ready to exploit. Although the extent to which these movements penetrated the masses was apparently limited, they were regarded within the various Muslim communities as serious alternatives in the event of an Ottoman collapse or a drastic deterioration in imperial policy toward them.

It was certainly no coincidence that the treaty of San Stefano and the Berlin Congress of 1878 marked the starting point of Albanian proto-nationalism. The casual award of what Albanians considered their territory to Balkan nation-states demonstrated to Muslim Albanians that Ottoman rule was slipping away, perhaps irretrievably, lending support to the nationalist thesis that the Albanians had to take their destiny into their own hands. This reasoning lay behind the formation of the Prizren League, which ruled Albania between 1878 and 1881. The scale of Armenian revolts in the last decade of the nineteenth century had a similar impact among the Anatolian Kurds, although their movement toward nationalism was more hesitant and gradual than that of their Albanian counterparts. Kurdish expatriates in Cairo launched the bilingual journal *Kurdistan* in 1898. Hedging their bets, they invoked the notion of a nation with a glorious past that transcended the Ottoman experience in time and space, while simultaneously defining the Kurds as "one of the most distinguished peoples composing the eternal Ottoman state," and describing them as a bulwark against Russian and Iranian encroachments.[100] Syrian intellectuals expressed a similar ambivalence. On the one hand, they highlighted Arab superiority over the Turks in administration and culture (repeating the familiar cliché that the Turks had lacked "language, poetry, science, and tradition" until they acquired them by force from the Arabs[101]). On the other, they often expressed their preference for continued Ottoman rule because, as one

---

[100] See "Kürdistan ve Kürdler," *Kürdistan*, no. 25 [24], [September 1, 1900], pp. 3–4; and [Mikdad Midhat Bedirhan], "Şevketlû, Utûfetlû Sultan Abdülhamid-i Sânî Hazretleri'ne Arz-ı Hâl-i Ubeydânemdir," *Kürdistan*, no. 4 [June 2, 1898], p. 1.

[101] "Mawḍūʿ taʿammul ilā ikhwāninā al-Sūriyyīn," *Turkiyyā al-fatāt*, no. 3 (January 10, 1896), p. [1].

writer put it, "Arabs would not be secure in their welfare and future if Istanbul" were not in the hands of the Turks.[102] Circassian intellectuals, too, insisted on their duty to defend the integrity of the empire, despite Ottoman mistreatment, while vowing to persevere in their struggle for cultural autonomy.[103]

As these examples illustrate, by and large proto-nationalist movements under the Hamidian regime exercised a great deal of caution. This prudence was one of several factors inhibiting their development into fully fledged nationalist movements. There were individual exceptions to this rule, such as Najīb ʿAzūrī, who passionately advocated an independent Arab nation free of the Ottoman yoke in his book *Le réveil de la nation arabe dans l'Asie turque* (1905), and in his journal *L'Indépendance arabe* (1907–1908); another was Fan Stylian Noli, who called for an independent Albanian nation first in Egypt and then in the pulpit of the Albanian Orthodox Church in Boston. But such extremists—both, significantly, Christian—expressed radical views shared only by a handful of followers. More mainstream proto-nationalist organizations, like the Albanian *Bashkimi* (Union) Society, the *Comité Turco-Syrien*, the Kurdish *Azm-i Kavî* (Strong Will) Society, and the *Cemiyet-i İttihad-ı Çerâkise* (the Committee for Circassian Union), remained within the scope of Ottomanism, although they stretched the boundaries of this concept considerably. Yet over time, such groups laid the groundwork for the emergence of full nationalist movements during the Second Constitutional Period, as the twin threats of centralization by a Turkist-dominated state and conquest by foreign powers exposed the incoherence of the halfway position as untenable. Under such conditions, proto-nationalist groups that already enjoyed a degree of representation and publicity rapidly evolved into national separatist movements, turning the post-1908 period into a stark struggle between competing nationalisms.

OPPOSITION AND THE YOUNG TURK REVOLUTION

The various strands of opposition to the regime of Abdülhamid II are commonly, and wrongly, lumped together under the rubric of the Young Turks. In reality, opponents of the sultan were a motley array of ulema, bureaucrats, and nationalists who shared a common enemy, but not a common agenda. For example, there was resentment against the regime among members of the educated class who viewed the preference given to loyalty over merit as unfair. In this sense, a very large segment of the educated elite, even

[102] Khālīl Ghānim, "al-qānūn al-asāsī," *Kashf al-Niqāb*, no. 8 (January 10, 1895), pp. [1–2].
[103] "Kelimeteyn," *İttihad Gazetesi*, no. 1 [October 15, 1899], pp. 2–4.

low-ranking bureaucrats serving in the first chamberlain's office, espoused what may loosely be termed "Young Turk" ideology.[104] However, not everyone who aspired to replace the sultan's "neo-patriarchy" with one based on merit was a political conspirator.

Although a significant number of individuals shared the general worldview of the Young Turks, the movement itself was more sharply defined. The politically active dissidents were members of secret committees, based in Europe and British-ruled Egypt, and dedicated to the overthrow of Abdülhamid II. Their modus operandi until shortly before the revolution consisted largely of the publication of journals and their clandestine dissemination throughout the empire. The major Young Turk organization was the Union of Ottomans, founded by a group of medical students at the Royal Medical Academy in 1889. Ahmed Rıza, a staunch positivist who intermittently led the Young Turk movement from 1895 to the revolution, gave the organization its more familiar name, the Ottoman Committee of Union and Progress. This committee functioned as an umbrella organization under which various groups collaborated loosely in opposing Abdülhamid II. One major faction, led by Ahmed Rıza, advocated nonrevolutionary change; another supported revolutionary action to topple the Hamidian regime; a cluster of medical doctors, scientist disciples of German *Vulgärmaterialismus*, wanted to create a utopian society governed by the dictates of materialism; a number of ulema, who controlled the Egyptian branch of the Young Turk organization, challenged the sultan's regime on religious grounds; while a group of former statesmen with pro-British inclinations dreamed of restoring the dominance of the Sublime Porte in Ottoman politics. Leadership of the umbrella organization changed hands several times between 1895 and 1902.

Until 1902, non-Turkish Muslims played significant roles in the umbrella organization. Ironically, none of the original founders of the committee was of Turkish origin. However, all of the founders represented Muslim groups threatened by Christian communities who enjoyed European backing: Albanians, Circassians, and Kurds. It was, therefore, not surprising that the committee adopted a Muslim variant of Ottomanism quite similar to the ideology promoted by Abdülhamid II. The contest for leadership of the movement, and the debate over the strategy to be pursued against the sultan, reached a peak at the Congress of Ottoman Liberals in 1902. Convened with the purpose of uniting all opponents of the sultan, including the Armenian committees, the Congress ended in schism, as an argument over

---

[104] This did not escape the sultan's notice. In 1901, he issued an imperial decree which noted that "the Young Turks act as if they were members of a distinct social class." The designation "Young Turk," wrote the sultan, ought to be replaced with "conspirators" or "agitators." BOA-BEO/ Mahremâne Müsveddat, no. 129 [July 8, 1901]; and Münir Bey to Müfid Bey, July 17, 1901/no. 30, Archives of the Turkish Embassy in Paris, D. 244.

Figure 14. The Congress of Ottoman Liberals in Paris (February 1902).
Osmanlı, no. 104 (April 16, 1902), p. 1.

the merits of soliciting European intervention exploded in discord. As a result, two major factions emerged along the fault line of the debate: the non-
Turkish organizations joined the former statesmen in support of external
intervention, while Ahmed Rıza took charge of the group championing
independent action from within.

Members of the first group worked toward staging a coup with British
assistance. They failed ignominiously. In 1905, Sabahaddin Bey, a nephew
of the sultan, reconstituted this faction as the League of Private Initiative
and Decentralization. Inspired by Edmond Demolins's ideas on private
initiative and decentralization, and by the *Science sociale* movement, the
League was largely ineffective. Sabahaddin Bey and his followers looked
down on their Turkist rivals because they lacked a serious sociological
theory, likening them to an "extinct animal species, eternal losers in the
perpetual theater of the struggle for life."[105] In fact, Sabahaddin Bey's rivals
had a firmer grasp of the realities of power; above all, they understood that
no revolutionary movement could succeed without the support of army
officers—many of whom had developed Turkist, anti-imperialist inclinations and viewed decentralization as a proxy for partition. Sabahaddin
Bey's promotion of administrative decentralization as a scientific remedy
for Ottoman illnesses thus attracted only a handful of dissidents among the
Young Turks. But various other Ottoman political movements interested in
regional autonomy accepted an expansive interpretation of the concept and
supported him against the increasingly Turkist Committee of Union and
Progress. Not surprisingly, the League's most important collaborators were

[105] M[ehmed] Sabri, "Anadolu Kıyamları," *Terakki*, no. 11 [July 1907], p. 3.

Armenian revolutionary organizations. The League did provide crucial assistance to local revolts in Anatolia in 1906 and 1907. But beyond that its influence was negligible.

The Turkist faction of the Young Turk movement, renamed the Ottoman Committee of Progress and Union (the title used by the committee from late 1905 until the summer of 1908, hereafter CPU), underwent substantial reorganization after the split. It emerged as an activist committee with a highly developed network of branches along the periphery of the empire. Its major activity was the dissemination of propaganda. Turkism was promoted not only by the CPU (and by a more radical intellectual faction of the Young Turks, which published the journal *Türk*[106]), but also by many unaffiliated intellectuals throughout the empire. In 1904, a Young Turk intellectual of Tatar descent, Yusuf Akçura, asserted that there were three ideological paths open to the Ottoman administration: Pan-Ottomanism, Pan-Islamism, and Pan-Turkism. The best alternative, he thought, was "to pursue a Turkish nationalism based on race."[107] Although no such thesis could yet be openly advocated in official circles, cultural Turkism flourished among intellectuals during this period.[108]

A significant stepping stone on the path to revolution was the merger in 1907 between the CPU and a secret association of Ottoman officers and bureaucrats, established in Salonica in 1906 under the name of the Ottoman Freedom Society. The merger enabled the CPU to expand its membership base immensely within the army and to turn its focus to Macedonia, then undergoing civil war and in danger of European-sponsored partition. The new focus compelled the CPU to tone down the Turkist element in its propaganda and switch to Ottomanism, a platform better suited to staging a rebellion in the ethnic mélange of Macedonia. The plan called for the conversion of Ottoman military units into sizeable armed bands, similar to the nationalist guerrilla groups fighting each other in Macedonia at the time (including Macedo-Slav, Bulgarian, Greek, Serbian, Kutzo-Vlach, and Albanian groups), and led by officers loyal to the CPU. These bands, in conjunction with a CPU gendarme force of self-sacrificing volunteers, were to assassinate high-ranking Ottoman officials, seize control of key points in major Macedonian towns, and demand the reinstatement of the constitution. Although success hinged on an alliance with the Albanians—who now formed a majority among the Muslims of European Turkey, and without whom victory was inconceivable—the CPU counted on at least tacit support from the non-Muslim bands of Macedonia, in order to portray the revolt as

[106] M. Şükrü Hanioğlu, *Preparation for a Revolution: The Young Turks, 1902–1908* (New York: Oxford University Press, 2001), pp. 62–73.

[107] Yusuf Akçura, *Üç Tarz-ı Siyaset* (Cairo: Matbaa-i İctihad, 1907), pp. 4, 12.

[108] David Kushner, *The Rise of Turkish Nationalism, 1876–1908* (London: Frank Cass, 1977), pp. 20ff.

FIGURE 15. The Young Turk Revolution in Monastir, July 23, 1908. *Manastır'da İlân-ı Hürriyet, 1908–1909: The Proclamation of Freedom in Manastir* (Istanbul: Yapı ve Kredi Yayınları, 1997), picture no. 12.

an all-Ottoman revolution and thereby forestall the threat of European intervention.

As should be evident by now, the so-called Young Turk Revolution was not, as the name suggests, a large-scale popular uprising of young Turks throughout the empire; nor was it a liberal reform movement, as was assumed by many at the time. Rather, it was a well-planned military insurrection, conceived and executed in Macedonia by a conspiratorial organization whose leadership harbored a quintessentially conservative aim: to seize control of the empire and save it from collapse.[109] Two pieces of news precipitated the CPU's decision to act in July 1908. First, rumors reached the CPU leadership of a new Anglo-Russian initiative for ambitious, large-scale

[109] For more on the CPU and the background to the revolution, see my *Preparation for a Revolution*, passim.

reform in Macedonia, threatening to deprive the Ottoman Empire of its tenuous foothold in Europe. Second, intelligence of a preemptive strike planned by the sultan's security apparatus to crush the committee and nip the rebellion in the bud was received at CPU headquarters. Starting on July 3, 1908, the so-called National Battalions, which were Ottoman military units that defected under the command of CPU members, took to the mountains. Several of the local Macedonian bands joined the rebels, as did many Ottoman military units, including the crucial reserve divisions sent by the sultan from Anatolia to crush them. On the political front, the CPU, in conjunction with several Albanian committees, managed to stage a gathering of Albanians and portray it as a mass "Ottoman" demonstration demanding the reinstatement of the constitution. Other demonstrations followed throughout European Turkey, and all major military divisions in the area declared their sympathy with the rebels.

By mid-July, the movement had gained such strength that the CPU leaders were convinced they could lead the Second and Third Ottoman Armies in a march on the capital—just as the Rumelian notables had done exactly one hundred years earlier, ousting sultan Mustafa IV and imposing the Deed of Agreement on Mahmud II. The desperate sultan attempted to thwart the revolution by creating a state of war with Bulgaria, ostensibly an Ottoman principality. But on the Bulgarian prince's refusal to collude with this scheme, the sultan finally yielded.[110] On July 23/24, 1908, he issued an imperial decree for the convening of a new chamber of deputies. Incredibly, the revolution was so localized at the outset that news of it did not reach the public in Istanbul, the Asiatic provinces, or Tripoli of Barbary until after the reinstatement of the constitution. It was only at this point that people began to pour out into the streets of towns all over the empire and that the rebellion in Macedonia began to take on the form of a Pan-Ottoman popular revolution. Ordinary citizens in various parts of the empire seized the opportunity to rid themselves of all vestiges of imperial authority, such as irksome officials and burdensome taxes. But they soon confronted the restored power of the state under a reclusive band of "revolutionaries" whose immediate preoccupation was the restoration of law and, more especially, order.[111]

[110] See Hanioğlu, *Preparation for a Revolution*, pp. 275–7.

[111] CUP communiqués issued during July 1908 give some indication of official unease concerning the revolution's radical connotations. Labeling their action an "implementation" (*icra'at*), a "period of implementation and activity" (*devre-i icra'at ve fa'aliyet*), or a "movement for radical transformation" (*harekât-ı inkılâbiye*), they deliberately refrained from using the word for revolution, *ihtilâl*. See an undated CPU communiqué of this period, Private Papers of Dr. Bahaeddin Şakir. After the fact, publications by leading CUP members employed the term "*inkılâb*," meaning radical transformation. See, for instance, Ahmed Niyazi, *Hâtırat-ı Niyazi yahud Tarihçe-i İnkılâb-ı Kebîr-i Osmanîden Bir Sahife* (Istanbul: Sabah Matbaası, 1324 [1908]); and Ahmed Refik, *İnkılâb-ı Azîm* (Istanbul: Asır Matbaası, 1324 [1908]).

From Revolution to Imperial Collapse:
The Longest Decade of the Late
Ottoman Empire

THE YOUNG TURK Revolution overthrew the Hamidian regime under the banner of "Liberty, Equality, Fraternity, and Justice." In its place, the revolutionaries promised a constitutional monarchy founded on the rule of law. They envisioned a parliamentary democracy headed by a responsible government and administered by a meritocratic bureaucracy. They expected political parties to replace age-old institutions, such as notable houses and religious orders, as the principal medium of political participation. They stood for a new fraternal Ottoman identity, united against European intervention in the affairs of the empire. They spoke of a free press, and of virtually unlimited individual liberties. Very little of this came to pass.

It was not that the revolution manqué produced no change—it set in motion radical transformations in many fields—but rather that the changes it brought about, like those of most revolutions, differed markedly from the expectations of its true believers. The 1908 Revolution was unprecedented in three respects. For one, its heroes were conservatives, who viewed their essential task as conservation and survival. Somewhat hastily labeled "liberals" by sanguine Europeans, the CUP leaders viewed themselves primarily as saviors of the empire. Second, its aim was accordingly not destruction but restoration. Unlike the French revolutionaries of 1789, the CUP leaders did not destroy an ancien régime in order to build a new one in its stead; unlike the Iranian revolutionaries of 1905–1906, they did not replace an absolutist monarch with a novel constitutional regime; nor could they even take credit for inaugurating a brand new consultative body, such as the Russian Gosudarstvennaia Duma that emerged from the 1905 Revolution. Formally, the conservative leaders of the CUP brought about a *restoration* of the constitutional sultanate established in 1876 and subsequently

FIGURE 16. Elections of 1908. Crowds carrying ballot boxes to counting centers.
Resimli Kitab 1/4 (December 1908), p. 384.

suspended in practice. Third, the Young Turk Revolution resulted in the gradual emergence of a radically new type of regime that was to become frighteningly familiar in the twentieth century: one-party rule. The CUP retained the sultan, but reduced his stature. It reintroduced the parliament, but kept it under tight control. In the palace, in the bureaucracy, and within the military, it was the Committee that, working from behind the scenes through the existing institutions of government, came to pull the levers of imperial power.

To fulfill the revolutionary pledge to "restore" parliamentary rule, the CUP instructed the transitional government to schedule the elections promised by the sultan in his capitulatory decree. These elections, held in November–December 1908, were remarkably fair; indeed, they may be considered the first and last true elections of this period. In principle, all tax-paying males over the age of twenty-five were eligible to vote. A minimum age of thirty and knowledge of the Turkish language were required of deputies. Every 500 voters in a given district elected a representative to an electoral college, selecting him from a list of candidates drawn up by municipal administrators. Each 50,000 electors selected one of their own to be sent to the Chamber of Deputies.[1] The number of deputies in the chamber fluctuated according to changes in the size of the population; the parliament

[1] *Düstûr*, II/1 (Istanbul, 1329 [1911]), pp. 18ff.

FIGURE 17. Ottoman deputies 1908 (province/electoral district). a. Deputy Speaker
of the Chamber of Deputies, Mehmed Talât Bey (later pasha, grand vizier)
(Edirne/Edirne). b. Nesim Mazliyah (Aydın/İzmir). c. Sulaymān al-Bustānī (later
senator) (Beirut/Beirut). d. Esʿad Pasha Toptani (Scutari in Albania/Durazzo). e.
Muḥammad Makḥafi (Yemen/Ṣanʿāʾ). f. Grigor Zōhrab (Istanbul). *Resimli Kitab*
2/1 (July 23, 1909), pp. 984, 986–7, 992, 1002, 1007.

of 1908 had 275 deputies, that of 1912, 278, and the one following the 1914
elections, only 255.

The major bone of contention between the CUP and the various ethno-
national communities was the method of representation. Many nationalist
organizations, with the Greeks in the forefront, vigorously protested the
system of universal representation, maintaining that it would work to the
disadvantage of minorities and give Muslims, and especially Turks, disproportionate representation. They demanded quotas for ethno-religious
groups,[2] and even threatened to boycott the elections. In the event, deputies
of Turkish origin obtained half of the seats in the parliament, while other
Ottoman communities received fair proportional representation despite
the absence of quotas.

[2] "Rumların Programı," *Sabah*, September 2, 1908.

Election day itself was celebrated in a carnival atmosphere; huge crowds escorted ballot boxes to the counting centers bearing flags and placards. The CUP's immense popularity in the wake of the revolution, and its untouchable position as a *comité de salut public*, virtually guaranteed a landslide victory. Still, the free nature of the elections introduced into the chamber many independent-minded deputies, who later formed the core of the opposition to the CUP. This was a lesson the CUP never forgot.

Whatever liberal affinities the CUP leaders harbored prior to and immediately following the revolution quickly gave way to authoritarian tendencies. Ensuring the survival of the empire in the face of internal and external predators, they felt, necessitated and therefore justified strong measures, including the restriction of fundamental liberties. In any case, it was perhaps inevitable that a conspiratorial committee that had carried out a revolution through the exercise of raw power should seek to dominate the post-revolutionary political playing field, as Jamāl ʿAbd al-Nāṣir's Free Officers showed almost half a century later in Egypt. If the anarchic aftermath of the revolution was one development that diminished the CUP's appetite for liberalism, concern over the outcome of the elections was another.

Although the CUP enjoyed a majority in the first Chamber of Deputies and successfully kept the government on a short leash, its hold on power was far from absolute. As the novelty of the revolution began to wear off, opposition emerged. There were liberals who complained of the CUP's heavy-handed rule; bureaucrats, led by Mehmed Kâmil Pasha, who still dreamed of restoring the supremacy of the Sublime Porte; nationalist and proto-nationalist societies that took issue with the CUP's narrow definition of Ottomanism; local groups frustrated at the increasing centralization of power and the revocation of privileges granted under the old regime; Islamists critical of the secular attributes of the new regime; and socialists who took issue with its socioeconomic policies. From very early on, the CUP faced repeated demands by political opponents that it relinquish its elusive and untouchable status at the pinnacle of power. The insistence of the Central Committee on wielding power from the shadows provoked outcries both from opportunist opponents and from genuine proponents of liberalism. Specific complaints centered on the claims of the Committee to special status as savior of the fatherland and the numerous prerogatives it exercised, ranging from the right to send telegrams free of charge to its habit of bypassing official channels to offer guidance to central and local governments.

The emergence of opposition confronted the CUP with a dilemma, for they could not squash it without betraying the ideals of the revolution. But to accept opposition as a fact of life threatened to undermine their hold on power. As a solution to this conundrum, the CUP, soon after the revolution, attempted to absorb or co-opt rival organizations. Some, like Sabahaddin Bey's League of Private Initiative and Decentralization, were falsely declared to have voluntarily merged with the CUP;[3] professional associations, like the merchants' unions, were subsumed under the CUP organizational framework;[4] CUP sections were created to cater to key interest groups like women[5] or the ulema;[6] and various nationalist organizations were targeted for co-option.[7]

But such measures could not completely stifle dissent. Many organizations, especially those representing various nationalist groups, refused to play along with the CUP. They sought to maintain their independence and contested CUP hegemony. Faced with the impossibility of eliminating opposition through persuasion, the CUP leaders resigned themselves—much like the sultan, whose efforts to dissolve the CUP and all political organizations in the aftermath of the revolution met with rejection[8]—to the existence of independent organizations, including rival political parties. New parties began to emerge soon after the revolution, covering the entire range of the political spectrum. Among these were the religious-conservative Mohammedan Union Party, the center-left Democratic Party, the Liberal Party, and the Moderate Freedom-Lovers' Party. However, none of these parties was strong enough to mount an independent challenge to the CUP, and they accordingly tended to coalesce in heterogeneous opposition blocs. The inescapable fact of one-party rule within an ostensibly multiparty system produced tensions that tore apart the fragile fabric of parliamentary democracy. Relations between the CUP and the opposition began to follow a pattern of oppression and conspiracy. In fact, during the entire Second Constitutional Period, not once was power transferred peaceably. And for much of it, power was not really transferred at all.

In April 1909, an improbable combination of old regime supporters, Islamists, liberals, and non-Turkish nationalists, exploiting tensions in the armed forces provoked by CUP-led purges of the sultan's army, came together in support of a military uprising in the capital. The CUP reacted swiftly and decisively, organizing an "Action Army" composed of military units and volunteers to march on the capital from Macedonia and restore order.

The challenges mounted against the CUP between the Revolution and April 1909 prompted its leaders to crack down on political opposition as such. Prevailing upon a reluctant parliament, they pushed through a series of controversial measures designed to curtail fundamental liberties that posed

---

[3] "Osmanlı İttihad ve Terakki Cemiyeti Merkezi'nden," *Sabah*, August 23, 1908.

[4] "İttihad ve Terakki Cemiyeti'nin İtimadnâmesi," *Sabah*, September 4, 1908.

[5] Emine Semiye, "İsmet Hakkı Hanımefendi'yle Bir Hasbihâl," *İkdam*, August 29, 1908.

[6] *Takvim-i Vekayi'*, no. 3571 (June 10, 1335 [1919]), p. 133.

[7] [Ahmed Cemal], *Cemal Paşa Hâtıratı, 1913–1922* (Istanbul: Ahmed İhsan ve Şürekâsı, 1339 [1922]), pp. 246–7.

[8] Grand vizier's office to the inspector general in Salonica, [July 24, 1908]/no. 1012, BOA-BEO/Şifre Telgrafnâme, 981-61/15.

FIGURE 18. The Action Army in Istanbul, April 24, 1909. *Resimli Kitab* 2/9 (June 1909), p. 939.

a threat to CUP domination. To restore order and put a stop to political demonstrations, they imposed martial law, a tool used with increasing regularity in later years. To halt labor disobedience, they drafted the heavy-handed Law of Strikes, which banned strikes in all public services and dissolved the labor unions in this sector.[9] To stifle dissent, they issued the Press Law, which restricted freedom of the press.

But opposition continued. In November 1911, elements as diverse as ulema and non-Muslim liberals came together to form a new umbrella party, the Liberal Entente. Its formation was a watershed. Not only did the party pose the first serious democratic challenge to CUP rule; from this point on politics became a bipolar struggle, as even parties and nationalist clubs that did not join the Liberal Entente backed it as the major political vehicle for opposition to the CUP. Within twenty days of its formation, to everyone's amazement, the Liberal Entente won a significant victory in a by-election held in the capital. Many provincial representatives elected on the CUP ticket saw which way the wind was blowing and submitted their resignations to the Committee. To stem the tide, the CUP engineered snap general elections, held between February and April 1912. Determined to avoid a repetition of the experience of 1908–1912, it adopted new

[9] The ban on strikes began with a temporary law on September 8, 1908 and, after minor adaptations, became regular law on August 9, 1909. See *Düstûr*, II/1, pp. 88–90; and 433–6.

measures to control these elections (nicknamed, for this reason, "The Elections with the Stick"). These included direct intervention in the campaign process, arrest of political opponents, banning of opposition meetings, shutdown of opposition newspapers, use of government resources to support CUP candidates, and finally, corruption of the ballot-counting process. CUP intervention was almost certainly responsible for the crushing defeat of the opposition, which managed to retain a mere six seats in the 278-seat Chamber of Deputies.

Frustrated yet again by CUP control of the democratic process, the dissidents, supported by a clandestine organization of army officers opposed to the CUP, resorted once more to force. In an echo of 1908, they capitalized on a nationalist uprising in Albania to induce various Albanian commanders in the Ottoman military to mutiny in July 1912. This provoked a major cabinet crisis, in the course of which first the recalcitrant minister of war and then the entire CUP-backed government resigned only one day after receiving their inaugural vote of confidence. The opposition then formed a new government under the leadership of the decorated war hero Gazi Ahmed Muhtar Pasha, and proceeded to dissolve the Chamber of Deputies, thereby nullifying the election's results.

In effect, the putsch of July 1912 marked the end of the Ottoman parliamentary experiment. Significantly, the CUP was not the organization responsible for its termination. The Chamber of Deputies would not meet again until after the elections of 1914, but by then the CUP had established a virtual one-party regime. Thereafter, as the dominant political organization shifted power from the legislative to the executive, the parliament lost much of its potency and met with decreasing frequency. This process was exacerbated following the Ottoman entry into the Great War. During the decade-long Second Constitutional Period, the chamber was in session for only four-and-a-half years, with several interruptions. Between December 1908 and July 1912, it held 473 sittings, whereas from May 1914 to December 1918, it held only 253 sittings.[10]

Shorn of its most efficacious political weapon (an obedient legislature) and faced with opposition from within its main power base (the army), the CUP had no choice but to capitulate in 1912. The force of the opposition revealed the fragility of CUP control, both civilian and military, four years after the revolution. For a brief period, from August 1912 to January 1913, the CUP, defeated and humiliated, rejoined the ranks of the opposition. The government of Gazi Ahmed Muhtar Pasha, and its successor under Mehmed Kâmil Pasha, worked hard to crush the Committee. But the panic and state of emergency surrounding the Balkan crisis of late 1912 provided an

---

[10] Tarık Zafer Tunaya, *Türkiye'de Siyasal Partiler, 3: İttihat ve Terakki, Bir Çağın, Bir Kuşağın, Bir Partinin Tarihi* (Istanbul: Hürriyet Vakfı Yayınları, 1989), p. 170.

opportunity for the CUP to launch a comeback. As the crisis reached a fever pitch, the Committee organized mass rallies in support of war and launched a massive propaganda campaign designed to underscore the government's lack of determination in the face of the threat. Although it failed to realize its main ambition and topple the government, its vocal campaign contributed to the outbreak of the disastrous Balkan Wars, in the course of which enemy forces penetrated far enough to threaten Istanbul.

It was the threat of imminent defeat in war that provided the occasion for the recovery of power by the CUP. On January 23, 1913, a CUP strike force raided the grand vizier's office, forced him to resign, and compelled the sultan to rubber-stamp the appointment of a new cabinet. The opposition struck back six months later, on July 11, 1913, when a group of hired assassins murdered the Grand Vizier Mahmud Şevket Pasha. This action, however, proved insufficient to dislodge the CUP, which launched a harsh campaign of repression in the course of which a large number of dissidents, ranging from ulema to socialists, were rounded up and sent into exile. A thorough purge of the armed forces followed, justified by the poor performance of the CUP's opponents in the First Balkan War. The CUP generals Enver and Cemal Pashas became minister of war and minister of the navy, respectively, symbolizing the final assertion of Committee control over the military. One-party rule was solidified and CUP control remained effectively unchallenged until the empire surrendered.

Political Life under the CUP

The Committee chose to rule initially from behind the scenes. The conspiratorial mind-set of the CUP leaders, their conservative predilections and reluctance to confront tradition, the protection afforded by the continuity of time-honored institutions, and a disinclination to expose their young, unknown, and inexperienced cadre to the risks of public scrutiny—all these considerations may have played a role in their decision to stay in the shadows. Whatever the reasoning behind it, the decision not to publicize the names of the central committee members shrouded the CUP in mystery, laying the foundations for an institutional cult that would replace the personality cult that had surrounded Sultan Abdülhamid II. The Committee regarded itself—and wanted to be seen by others—as the sacred agent of imperial redemption and the guarantor of the empire's future security. The veil was lifted somewhat during the first open congress of the CUP in 1909, but the aura of secrecy remained till the end of the empire. In any event, the decision meant that the very fact of CUP power—its physical hold on the reins of government—was hidden from the public view at the outset. At first the Committee did not visibly take over the traditional institutions

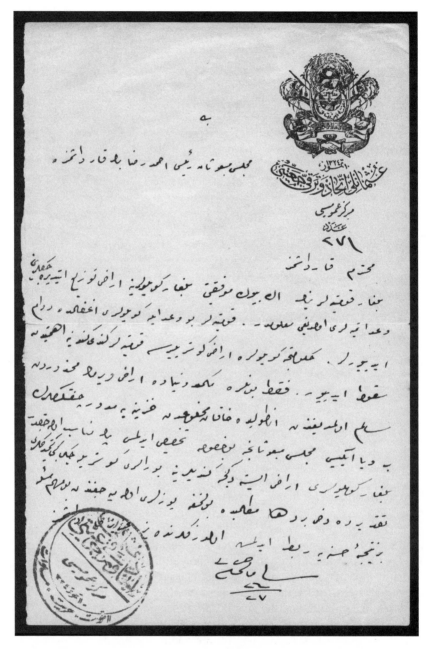

FIGURE 19. A CUP central committee note dated June 8/9, 1909 and sent to the Speaker of the Ottoman Chamber of Deputies, Ahmed Rıza. The author's private collection.

of power—the court and the Porte. But it did control their actions. Thus, if a governor seemed unreliable, the CUP would order the grand vizier to fire him. If a military unit was suspected of disloyalty, the Committee had the minister of war carry out a purge. The capricious edicts of the sultan were thus replaced by equally whimsical decrees issued by the anonymous members of the Central Committee. In addition, starting with the appointment of Talât Bey (Pasha) as minister of the interior and of Mehmed Cavid Bey as minister of finance in 1909, the CUP gradually began to exercise direct control over important offices, a process which ended in its total domination of the bureaucracy in 1913.

Despite the secrecy, some details about key individuals within the CUP leadership have come to be known. The crucial reshaping of the CUP on the road to revolution was carried out by Dr. Bahaeddin Şakir, a representative of the activist faction, in 1905–1906. The shift to an activist platform marginalized the hitherto predominant intellectuals within the Committee. Dr. Bahaeddin Şakir, frequently described as the Stalin of the CUP, and Dr. Nâzım, another of the architects of the reshaping, became the *éminences grises* of the organization. Although they distanced themselves from intellectual debate, they represented the Turkist ideological strand within the Committee. The hand of the men of action was strengthened by the merger with the Ottoman Freedom Society in 1907, following which Talât Bey, organizer of dissident activity in Salonica, rose to prominence. The revolution itself naturally strengthened the position of military men within the Committee. Two officers in particular, Enver and Cemal Beys (later Pashas), stood out and became the military leaders of the CUP. Though scholarship has spoken of a triumvirate of Enver, Cemal, and Talât Beys (Pashas), the situation in reality was more complex. First, Dr. Bahaeddin Şakir and Dr. Nâzım continued to be very influential in decision-making in the early years following the revolution. Second, as the CUP came to control more areas of government and society, new leaders appeared. The need to deal with such fields of specialized policy making as economics and social mobilization pushed to the fore men like Mehmed Cavid Bey, a financial expert, and Kara Kemal Bey, an organizer of societies, guilds, and cooperatives. Finally, the renewed need for an ideological framework for action brought Ziya Gökalp to the fore. A self-taught sociologist and devout follower of Durkheim, he was awarded a seat on the Central Committee in 1912. There were few men of charisma among the senior leadership. The military hero Enver Bey was an exception, but he gained disproportionate power as an individual only during the Great War. As a rule, decisions were taken collectively and there was no deviation from the discipline required for the projection of the institutional cult. The shared interest in thwarting the rise of any one individual to a position of prominence ensured that this did not change.

The very nature of the Committee of Union and Progress as an organization remained rather murky in the aftermath of the revolution. On the one hand, it grew into something approaching a mass party. At the same time, it retained its conspiratorial qualities and avoided the full institutionalization of one-party rule. The CUP never formally abolished or outlawed rival parties or nonparty organizations in the empire. Ostensibly, all Ottoman political organizations were equal before the law throughout the Second Constitutional Period. To maintain the pretence of a free, multiparty system, the CUP in 1909 resorted to a fictitious distinction between the "committee" (*cemiyet*) and the parliamentary group supporting it, which was the "party" (*fırka*). There was little substance to this distinction, as the committee nominated all deputies and senators in its parliamentary faction. In 1913, the CUP expanded its definition of "the party" to include the committee itself as well as the organization's press organs.[11] But by then, its control of the political system was assured.

Incredibly, the seat of the central committee of the CUP remained in Salonica until 1912, and the annual congresses were also held there. This fact helps to explain the tenuousness of the CUP's position in the early post-revolutionary years and emphasizes the extent to which the organization was a Macedonian phenomenon. After the revolution, as the CUP transformed itself from a highly compartmentalized and conspiratorial organization into something approaching a mass party, the composition of its membership changed and its center of gravity shifted eastward. As the doors of access to the lower levels of the organization were thrown open to mass membership, notables and merchants flocked to join the proliferating local branches of the CUP across the empire. Overwhelmed by a flood of applications for membership, the CUP center tended to approve petitions for the establishment of local branches on the basis of superficial information concerning their members.[12] By late 1909, the number of CUP branches across the empire had multiplied from 83 on the eve of the revolution (several of them minor cells) to 360, while membership had grown roughly from 2,250 to 850,000.[13] Although the CUP had clearly become a mass organization, the extent of central control over this unwieldy structure was debatable. In any case, the provincial appendages of the CUP were largely cut off from the process of policy formulation at the center. They were also

---

[11] *Osmanlı İttihad ve Terakki Cemiyeti Program ve Nizamnâmesidir: 1329 Senesi Umumî Kongresi'nde Tanzim ve Kabul Olunmuşdur* (Istanbul: Matbaa-i Hayriye ve Şürekâsı, 1329 [1913]), p. 14.

[12] "Osmanlı İnkılâb-ı Kebîri Nasıl Oldu?" *Musavver Salnâme-i Servet-i Fünûn*, 1 [1910], pp. 102–3.

[13] "Osmanlı İttihad ve Terakki Cemiyeti," *Haftalık Şûra-yı Ümmet*, no. 203 [January 23, 1909].

institutionally detached from its implementation, which was still in the hands of the traditional bureaucracy.

Although the CUP grew and became increasingly institutionalized, it never became a true mass party within which power could be rendered legitimate and participatory in the Bolshevik or Nazi sense. On the surface, this was due to the lack of charismatic leadership; the CUP never produced a Lenin or a Hitler. But just as significantly, this failure may be traced to the same combination of ideological deficiencies and structural barriers that had thwarted earlier attempts of predecessors to establish a sound political basis for a modern Ottoman state. The main task that the CUP leaders took upon themselves was the preservation of the multinational empire. There were two problems with this objective. For one, it was essentially a conservative platform that held little potential for galvanizing the masses into undertaking a vast effort of destruction and reconstruction. Second, the status quo held little appeal for large segments of the population. There was a fundamental incompatibility between the aims of the Turkist core of the CUP and those of the non-Turkish populations of the empire. Indeed, the main threat to the survival of the empire came from separatism on the periphery. To win over the separatists, the CUP adopted a prudent policy of inclusiveness. But the inclusion of diverse population groups with little in common within the ranks of a single party inevitably led to ideological incoherence. There was no class or ethnic basis for membership. There was only a vague and varying interpretation of Ottomanism. Not surprisingly, the political platforms of the various branches contradicted each other and that of the central committee, which controlled them only weakly. In this sense—as well as in the conservative agenda buried under the revolutionary rhetoric—the CUP resembled the *Partido Revolucionario Institucional*, which dominated Mexican politics for much of the twentieth century. Ultimately, the CUP's power depended on its control over the army and on the perception that it was the only force capable of defending the empire. Under the near constant threat of war from abroad and rebellion at home, this was a strong case.

The tugging and pulling between political parties masked a more fundamental set of changes in the traditional balance of forces brought about by the CUP within the Ottoman political system. These affected the court, the Porte, the legislature, and the military. Abdülhamid II, who had barely escaped deposition by belatedly making himself the father of the constitutional regime, prudently assumed a low profile immediately after the revolution. But this did not mean that he accepted its results. On the contrary, he resented his diminished stature in the new regime and his role as a legitimizing figurehead charged with rubber-stamping Central Committee decisions. A showdown was therefore inevitable, and it was not long in coming. In early August 1908, the sultan provoked an open confrontation with the Committee by claiming the constitutional authority to nominate the ministers of the navy and of war, in addition to the grand vizier and Şeyhülislâm. The CUP, overruling him, forced the cabinet to resign. To make sure the message was understood, the Central Committee dispatched a delegation with detailed policy instructions to the new government,[14] and provided the minister of war with a list of key military appointments he was to make.[15] But the obstructionism of the sultan convinced the CUP leaders that Abdülhamid II had to go. The "counter-revolution" of 1909 provided them with an ideal pretext to depose Abdülhamid II, which they did on April 27, 1909. The final reduction of the court to insignificance was completed with the accession of Abdülhamid II's weak successor, Mehmed V (Reşad, r. 1909–18), who displayed little inclination to intervene in affairs of state. Although the CUP leaders initially sought to limit the power of the sultan through constitutional amendments in 1909, they came to realize that a subservient sultan, empowered to act on their behalf, could be of great use in maintaining the façade of a constitutional monarchy. Further amendments, proposed in 1912 and approved in 1914, restored several of the sultan's more convenient executive powers, such as the authority to prorogue a recalcitrant chamber of deputies. Mehmed V's successor, Mehmed VI (Vahideddin, r. 1918–22), exploited the humiliation of the Mudros armistice in 1918 to try to reinstate the power of the court, but to no avail. The institution of the sultanate, for centuries at the heart of Ottoman might and identity, was effectively dead.

Similarly, the Sublime Porte, already cut down to size by Abdülhamid II, lost all hope of restoring the bureaucracy's former stature in the aftermath of the revolution. At first, the CUP manipulated the traditional rivalry between the court and the Porte by taking away powers from the former, in accordance with its overall strategy of weakening the sultan, and giving them to the latter. But these were minor concessions, such as the restoration of official control over provincial governors, whom Abdülhamid II had required to report directly to the palace.[16] The key to the weakening of the bureaucracy lay in the new restraining effects of representational politics. First, the CUP balanced its wariness of a robust legislature with a willingness to use it, within limits, to control the bureaucracy. Second, the very conditions brought about by the restoration of a Chamber of Deputies, turned the bureaucracy's dreams of a return to unfettered rule into fantasy as Russia was discovering at about the same time. As bureaucrats soon found out, simply ignoring the deputies was not an option. When Mehmed Kâmil Pasha (who had led the last effort of officialdom to restore responsible

---

[14] See the undated, twenty-article instructions given to Rahmi Bey, who led the CUP delegation, Private Papers of Dr. Bahaeddin Şakir.

[15] BOA-A.AMD.MV 90/1 [August 9, 1908].

[16] BOA/BEO, file 265634 [May 6, 1909].

government in 1895)[17] attempted to place the Sublime Porte above the parliament and the CUP, he received the first vote of no confidence in Ottoman history, on February 13, 1909. A third factor that weakened the bureaucracy was its increasing subservience to the CUP. Although actual membership of the CUP—unlike membership of the Communist Party of the Soviet Union—never became a condition for service, loyalty to the Committee was now a key criterion for advancement. And while the CUP did not carry out any significant purge of officialdom during the Second Constitutional Period, it did finally assert its direct control in 1913, when leading Committee members took over virtually all important posts in the bureaucracy.

Likewise, the parliament, the prime institutional product of the constitution, soon withered away. Although it was the harbinger of constitutional revolution, the CUP, once in power, developed a distaste for strong legislatures. As adherents of Gustave Le Bon's *Psychologie des foules*, CUP leaders looked down on the motley crowd that filled the chamber of deputies.[18] More important, they came to share Abdülhamid II's concern over the ability of a strong parliament to undermine the regime and aggravate ethno-religious conflict. Yet the CUP could not afford to betray their revolution by abolishing the parliament; nor were they prepared to sacrifice the parliament's legitimizing benefits, as the supposed voice of the people, by openly confronting it. Instead, the CUP managed to bypass the legislature by means of the cabinet. Enver Pasha is once said to have remarked: "If there is no law, make one."[19] The cabinet began to issue so-called temporary laws confirmed by imperial decrees at times when the parliament was not in session. Over time, temporary laws overtook legislation in the parliament as the principal lawmaking mechanism of the state. Many important decisions were confirmed as temporary laws, without any discussion in the Chamber. Examples include the grant of autonomous fiefdoms to local Arabian leaders,[20] passage of the controversial Family Law of 1917 (discussed in the next section), and above all the farcical dismissal of parliament on the very day that the fateful German-Ottoman alliance was signed, August 2, 1914. As these examples demonstrate, the CUP was not prepared to tolerate any

---

[17] [Mehmed Kâmil], *Hâtırat-ı Sadr-ı Esbak Kâmil Paşa* (Istanbul: Matbaa-i Ebüzziya, 1329 [1911]), pp. 190–96.

[18] Enver Bey (Pasha) to a German woman with whom he frequently corresponded, ʿAyn al-Manṣūr, September 2, 1912, Ernst Jäckh Papers, Yale University, MSS 466, Box 1, Folder 40.

[19] Tunaya, *İttihat ve Terakki*, p. 386.

[20] See the temporary law of January 22, 1912, which ratified the Daʿʿān contract granted to Imām Yaḥyā on October 20, 1911. BOA-DVN 37/1. See also the temporary law of September 10, 1914, which ratified the contract granted to ʿAbd al-ʿAzīz ibn Saʿūd on May 28, 1914. BOA-DH.SYS 25/103.

consequential role for the legislature in a debate on policy, let alone in its formulation.

But if the CUP outmaneuvered its new competitors and reduced the old nineteenth-century contenders for state power to subservience, it also restored to prominence a power broker not heard of in Ottoman politics for more than eighty years: the army. The role played by the armed forces in Ottoman politics, often in alliance with the ulema, had traditionally been a decisive one. It was to become so once again. Indeed, the very success of the CUP, first in mounting a revolutionary challenge to the ancien régime, and then in the struggle to remain in power, rested on its ability to penetrate the armed forces and stage the return of the military to politics for the first time since the destruction of the Janissaries in 1826. The CUP was a militarized political organization even before the revolution. The overwhelming majority of its members prior to July 1908 were army officers. When the sultan gave in to the CUP's ultimatum in July 1908, he surrendered not to a group of starry-eyed idealists in exile, but to the effective commanders of a substantial portion of the Ottoman officer corps. Militarization of the organization, in both structure and spirit, continued after the CUP seized power. Shortly after the revolution, the CUP converted the units of self-sacrificing volunteers into a paramilitary force that coexisted uneasily with the military and the constitutional regime. It also established a network of military clubs, through which thousands of new officers swelled the ranks of the organization's membership.

To the CUP, the army was above all an indispensable tool against domestic and foreign opponents. The opposition's attempts to sunder the strong ideological ties that bound the military to the CUP ultimately failed. Despite legislative measures sponsored by the opposition which prohibited the involvement of military personnel in politics, the CUP managed to maintain its dual political-military character up until the collapse of the empire. But the CUP leadership regarded the military as far more than just an instrument of power. For them, it embodied the institutional core of Baron Colmar von der Goltz's idea of "A Nation in Arms." The Committee assigned to the military a significant role in shaping a new, militarized Ottoman society.[21] This was made explicit very early on. As one of the Committee leaders put it in 1908: "The two powers, the CUP and the Ottoman Armed Forces, which have been formed by the great majority of the Ottoman nation, can annihilate the supporters of tyranny at any time."[22] The outbreak

---

[21] See Ali Fu'ad, "Ordu ve Millet," *Asker* 1/1 [September 3, 1908], p. 16, and Ahmed Refik, "Von der Goltz: Hayat ve Âsârı," *Servet-i Fünûn* [July 15, 1909], pp. 138-9.

[22] "Osmanlı İttihad ve Terakki Cemiyeti ve Osmanlı Ordusu," *Şûra-yı Ümmet*, October 18, 1908.

of the Great War provided the CUP with an opportunity to realize its vision of a nation in arms. One example of this policy was the mobilization of youth within a paramilitary framework;[23] another was the establishment of a paramilitary Special Organization composed of CUP leaders and self-sacrificing volunteers directly attached to the Ministry of War.

Having displaced the traditional loci of power within the Ottoman political system, the CUP employed new legitimizing devices to buttress its rule. The military ethic was the first. The second was the concept of "the people." The claim to rule on behalf of the people was no innovation, although the term employed, *hakimiyet-i milliye* (national sovereignty), was a new one coined by the CUP. But the Committee proved more skillful at giving substance to this fiction than the old regime had ever been, especially through the adroit manipulation of an elected legislative body. The need to bolster authoritarian rule with the appearance of popular sovereignty was the single most important factor behind the CUP's persistence down the constitutional path, even though the parliament caused the CUP nearly as much grief as it had caused Abdülhamid II. The following anecdote is telling. When Lieutenant-Colonel Enver Bey stormed the Sublime Porte at the head of CUP volunteers in the coup d'état of 1913, he forced the grand vizier to draft a letter of resignation at gunpoint. The grand vizier accordingly wrote that he had been compelled to resign "at the demand of the armed forces." But Enver Bey insisted that he amend the letter to read: "at the demand of *the people* and the armed forces [emphasis added]."[24] Elitism in the political thought of the CUP thus coexisted with an acute awareness of the symbolic power of the notion of the people.

The third device that the CUP leaders used in consolidating power was the press. Here again, they were not creating something unknown under the old regime. But as members of a conspiratorial organization in exile, dependent on the clandestine dissemination of smuggled journals and propaganda pamphlets to communicate their political message, the CUP leaders were especially aware of the capacity of the press to form public opinion, and exceedingly skilled at its manipulation. Upon coming to power, they launched a host of official and semi-official organs, and a series of other publications, to help them broadcast their message, monopolize public space, and consolidate their hold on power. Following the precedent set by Abdülhamid II, they also maintained a strict regime of censorship, beginning in 1913. The combination of a skillful propaganda machine, a loyal press, and effective restrictions on freedom of speech ensured that CUP

---

[23] Zafer Toprak, "İttihat ve Terakki'nin Para-Militer Gençlik Örgütleri," *Boğaziçi Üniversitesi Beşeri Bilimler Dergisi* 7 (1979), pp. 93–113.

[24] BOA-A.AMD 1345/41 (1331.S.14) [January, 23, 1913].

Figure 20. Demonstrations before the Sublime Porte immediately after the CUP raid on January 23, 1913. *Resimli Kitab* 8/46 (December 1912–January 1913), p. 719.

policy gained a favorable reception among considerable parts of the literate population, while the opposition, which initially posed a fierce challenge to the CUP-sponsored press, was effectively silenced, particularly after 1913.

The post-revolutionary era also witnessed important changes in the way the central government interacted with the empire's various religious and ethnic communities. The relative freedom of the first few years after 1908 did not resolve existing tensions; on the contrary, it aggravated them. CUP policies only made things worse. The cancellation of all privileges of non-Turkish Muslim groups, the launching of an aggressive centralization campaign, and the demand that all citizens place their Ottoman identity above any other—all these were bound to provoke a strong reaction. As the CUP itself became increasingly penetrated by Turkist ideas, the difference between "Ottoman" and "Turkish" became increasingly blurred. And as the dominant culture emerged from the convenient ambiguity of Ottomanism, non-Turks began to feel less and less comfortable. Attitudes in the periphery hardened, and the appeal of the alternatives offered by various Christian and Muslim ethno-nationalist organizations grew accordingly. Greek, Bulgarian, and Armenian nationalisms were already strong at the time of the revolution. Under the CUP, Albanian and Arab nationalisms became significant movements, while Kurdish and Circassian proto-nationalist sentiments gained momentum. Between a center predisposed to view all demands for the recognition of difference as evidence of separatism, and a periphery decreasingly inclined to compromise, all-out war was inevitable. A strongly Turkist version of Ottomanism faced off against increasingly intransigent nationalisms that at best sought to reduce Ottoman identity to an unimportant, secondary symbol. To be sure, this was primarily a struggle among overrepresented intelligentsias; it did not yet infect the more established classes within many of the non-Turkish communities. Even those who had opposed the Hamidian régime—like the Armenian Amira class of rich artisans and bankers—continued to reject the nationalist calls for independence outside the Ottoman framework up until 1915. Nevertheless, the consequences are evident in the political map of the post-Ottoman Balkans and Near East.

The Foreign Policy of the CUP

The CUP leaders inherited Abdülhamid II's expensive policy of armed neutrality. They moved swiftly to replace it with an alliance with a major European power. Such a pact would not only better secure the territorial integrity of the empire; it would also make possible the diversion of scarce resources into economic development. As early as August 18, 1908, the CUP made its first overtures to the German and British monarchs.[25] The very initiation of such contacts with the Germans, loathed for their support of the Hamidian regime, and with the British, abhorred as a major imperialist supporter of Ottoman separatists, showed how swiftly pragmatic considerations of power trumped the ideological proclivities of these revolutionaries. But the CUP underestimated the weakness of its hand. Neither Britain nor Germany saw the value of extending guarantees to an economically unstable, militarily weak empire riven by Christian separatist forces. Moreover, the Ottoman offer of support for Germany in a future European war, in exchange for a guarantee of territorial integrity,[26] could scarcely be reconciled with the long-standing ambitions of the two key German allies, Italy and Austria-Hungary, to annex Ottoman territories in the Balkans and North Africa. As for Great Britain, its strategic decision to base the defense of the Near East on Egypt made the Ottoman Empire a nuisance at best. At the same time, the British aim of preserving and, if possible, expanding its foothold on the Arabian Peninsula did not sit well with recognition of Ottoman territorial inviolability. The inevitable rejection, particularly by the British Foreign Secretary, Sir Edward Grey, surprised and

[25] See Ahmed Rıza's letters to Edward VII and Wilhelm II in PRO/FO. 371/545, file 28993 and Abschrift zu A. 13323, Nachlaß Fürsten von Bülow, Bundesrachiv (Berlin), nr. 82.

[26] Lancken to Bülow, Paris, August 18, 1908 (A.13323), ibid.

humiliated the proud leaders of the CUP, who had imagined themselves rulers of the "Japan of the Near East."[27]

The attempts to reach out to these European powers did not mean that Ottoman anti-imperialism, one of the key ideological tenets of the revolution, was dead. Indeed, following the revolution, ideology joined fresh perceptions of the national interest to reinforce the CUP's resolve to resist the accelerating fragmentation of the empire. In particular, the CUP consistently opposed European settlements based on carving out autonomous regions from the narrowing fringes of the empire. When the Bulgarian Principality declared its independence and Austria-Hungary announced the annexation of Bosnia and Herzegovina only seventy-four days after the revolution, frustration in the ranks of the CUP knew no bounds. However, the anti-imperialist outlook of the CUP was swiftly tempered by recognition of the constraints imposed on the conduct of Ottoman policy by the reality of European supremacy. Like Abdülhamid II, the CUP leaders typically stood up to foreign pressure until further resistance became futile; they then strove to reach the best possible accommodation.

Yet at the outset, the CUP had exhibited a predilection for fighting against insuperable odds rather than accepting a European diktat that left a region only nominally under Ottoman sovereignty. Such was the case in Tripoli. In 1911, the Ottoman government turned a deaf ear to Italian offers of minor privileges in Tripoli of Barbary in return for recognition of the Italian administration.[28] As a consequence, between September 1911 and October 1912, the Ottomans fought a forlorn war against the Italians in Tripoli and Cyrenaica.

Tripoli of Barbary and Cyrenaica, which formed the Ottoman Province of Tripoli, were among the most underdeveloped regions of the empire. But as the last African territories still ruled from Istanbul, they possessed a sentimental value that far outweighed their strategic significance. Italy's long-standing designs on Tripoli stemmed from two motives: the wish to compete in Africa with France, which had established a protectorate over Tunis in 1881, and the need to compensate for the ignominious defeat at the hands of Menilek II of Ethiopia in 1896. Over the course of almost two decades, the Italians managed to persuade one after another of the Great Powers of Europe to acquiesce in this disturbance of the balance of power. Once they had obtained agreement from all their Great Power partners by 1909, the issue was reduced to one of timing. The CUP's acerbic anti-imperialist rhetoric and resolute defensive measures—for example, a ban on land purchases by

---

[27] Grey to Lowther, November 13, 1908 (private), PRO/F.O. 800/79.

[28] Mahmud Muhtar, *Maziye Bir Nazar: Berlin Muʿahedesi'nden Harb-i Umumî'ye Kadar Avrupa ve Türkiye Münâsebâtı* (Istanbul: Matbaa-i Ahmed İhsan ve Şürekâsı, 1341 [1925]), pp. 118ff.

FIGURE 21. The Banco di Roma branch in Tripoli of Barbary (ca. 1909). *Resimli Kitap* 7/42 (July 1912), p. 433.

Banco di Roma in the province of Tripoli—provided ample excuses for the Italian government. On September 28, 1911, it issued a twenty-four-hour ultimatum to the Ottoman government. Announcing imminent invasion of the province and demanding Ottoman nonintervention, the ultimatum was clearly meant to be rejected.[29] The surprisingly conciliatory response from the Ottomans, which provided assurances for Italian "economic expansion of interests in Tripoli and Cyrenaica," was to no avail, as the decision to invade had already been made.[30]

The defense of distant Tripoli proved no easy matter for the Ottomans, whose performance was closely monitored by the restless new powers of the Balkans. Their principal problem was one of supply and reinforcement. North Africa could be reached by sea across the Mediterranean or by land via Syria and Egypt; the superior Italian navy blocked the first route, while the British in Egypt impeded the second. Incredibly, the small local garrison and an Ottoman-trained militia led by Ottoman officers smuggled into the region (including the military hero of the 1908 Revolution, Enver Bey) managed to put up an effective resistance, compelling the Italians to confine their operations to the coastal strip under naval cover. To break the military

[29] "Ultimatum from Italy to Turkey Regarding Tripoli," *American Journal of International Law* 6/1 (January 1912), pp. 11–12.

[30] "The Turkish Reply to Italian Ultimatum Regarding Tripoli," ibid., pp. 12–14.

stalemate, the Italians opted to expand the war and put military pressure on Ottoman possessions elsewhere, occupying Rhodes and other islands of the Dodecanese, bombarding Ottoman towns on the Mediterranean and Red Sea coasts (such as Beirut and al-Qunfudha), and increasing military aid to Muḥammad ʿAlī al-Idrīsī, a local challenger to Ottoman authority who had established a small Ṣūfī state in parts of the subprovince of ʿAsīr. But the Ottomans held firm, yielding little ground in the Ottoman-Italian talks at Ouchy in Switzerland in August and September 1912.

The sudden emergence of a new threat in the Balkans dramatically altered Ottoman calculations. The danger of a two-front war compelled Ottoman negotiators to liquidate the lesser conflict and come to terms with the Italians. A final agreement was concluded on October 18, the very day major hostilities began in the Balkans. The settlement squeezed out of the Italians allowed the Ottoman side to save face and maintain the pretense of continued sovereignty. The Ottoman sultan appointed a viceroy and a qāḍī to enforce the sharīʿa and announced the grant of extensive autonomy to Tripoli of Barbary and Cyrenaica.[31] But in reality, Tripoli became an Italian colony. The last of the Ottoman lands in Africa was lost.

The Italo-Ottoman war exposed the difficulty of defending the empire's long coastlines. That even a second-tier European power could occupy Ottoman islands, bombard coastal towns, and dispatch troops all around the Mediterranean and Red Sea at will pointed to a mortal weakness. One possible remedy was to build a modern navy; but to construct a fleet almost from scratch was a time-consuming and vastly expensive undertaking. Thus, Ottoman ruling circles concluded once again that it was absolutely vital to secure the protection of a Great Power, preferably one with a strong navy. The lessons learned in North Africa were reinforced by the course of events in the Balkans.

A Balkan alliance against the Ottoman Empire was one of the least expected developments of the early twentieth century. The mutual hostility of Serbs, Bulgarians, and Greeks and the irreconcilability of their aspirations in Ottoman Macedonia made a tripartite alliance all but inconceivable. Abdülhamid II had attempted to form a Balkan League with Greece, Serbia, and Rumania to check the rise of Bulgaria, which, thanks to extensive military reform, was on the road to becoming a major regional power. Serbian leaders, sensing the turning of the tide, frustrated Abdülhamid II's early plans and formed an alliance with Bulgaria in 1904. The CUP leaders continued the sultan's efforts when, in 1908, they attempted to exploit the crisis over the annexation of Bosnia-Herzegovina to entice Serbia back into an alliance with Montenegro and the Ottoman Empire against Bulgaria and Austria-Hungary, but without success.

---

[31] See *Düstûr*, II/4 (Istanbul: Matbaa-i Âmire, 1331 [1913]), pp. 690–91.

Meanwhile, Russia's growing involvement in the Balkans, stoked by rising fear of Germany, almost produced a broad Balkan alliance with Ottoman participation. But Balkan hostility toward the Ottoman Empire was such that this was not possible. Moreover, with the Ottomans embroiled in a hopeless attempt to ward off the Italians in North Africa, the Balkan states sensed weakness and decided to make the most of it. The negotiations sponsored by the Russians produced the worst possible result from the Ottoman perspective: a Serbo-Bulgarian accord, reached in March–April 1912. Then, in May 1912, Greece and Bulgaria, the two archrivals in the struggle for Macedonia, concluded an alliance, and the circle of hostility was complete. Subsequent Serbo-Montenegrin, Greco-Montenegrin, and Bulgarian-Montenegrin understandings rounded off the preparations for an assault on the remaining European domains of the Ottoman Empire with a view to their final partition.[32]

It was clear from the start that this alliance of rivals would not last. Accordingly, pressure mounted for an immediate opening of hostilities. Seizing on the pretext of the Ottoman failure to comply with the 23rd article of the Berlin Congress of 1878, which called for Macedonian reform, the Balkan allies rushed toward war. The Ottoman government, caught unprepared and fearful of another military disaster, adopted a conciliatory attitude and promised reforms. But this merely worsened its position at home—where it was already under pressure from the CUP in opposition—and did nothing to propitiate its Balkan predators. Great Power warnings against modifications to the status quo failed to prevent the allies from launching hostilities. Montenegro took the lead on October 8, followed by the three larger Balkan states on October 18, 1912.

In the ensuing war, the Balkan allies inflicted the most humiliating defeats on the Ottoman armies. Within weeks, all of European Turkey was lost, with the exception of three besieged fortress cities, Scutari in Albania, Janina, and Edirne; and the victorious Bulgarians were on the march against the final Ottoman defense line at Çatalca, a mere thirty-seven miles from Istanbul. Ottoman appeals for Great Power intervention proved unavailing. From the European perspective, the situation had the dangerous potential for a Russo-Austrian conflagration, which could easily set the entire continent ablaze. The Great Powers, accordingly, focused on forcing a cease-fire and convening a conference to discuss the future of the Balkans.

The armistice of December 3 paved the way for two parallel conferences in London. At the first, Ottoman and Balkan delegates met to discuss the future of European Turkey and the Northern Aegean islands. At the second,

---

[32] E[rnst] Christian Helmreich, *The Diplomacy of the Balkan Wars, 1912–1913* (Cambridge, MA: Harvard University Press, 1938), pp. 87–9.

Figure 22. Partition of the European provinces of the empire after the Balkan Wars of 1912–13.

the ambassadors of the Great Powers debated a general settlement in the Balkans. The first set of negotiations broke down on January 6, 1913. The second resulted in a note to the Ottoman government, warning it to sign a peace treaty or face the consequences alone. All the while, Edirne, a city that had served as the capital of the empire before the conquest of Constantinople, remained under siege. The CUP took advantage of the situation to carry out its coup and return to power under the banner "Free Edirne!" In February, hostilities resumed but Ottoman efforts to relieve the siege of Edirne failed, and the city fell on March 26, 1913. Defeated on the battlefield, the CUP-led government had no choice but to sue for peace. The Treaty of London of May 30, 1913 heralded the end of the Ottoman presence in Europe. It also signaled the beginning of a major conflict between the Balkan allies over the division of the spoils.

The Bulgarian surprise attack on its erstwhile allies on June 29/30 backfired, as Greece, Rumania, and Serbia declared war on Bulgaria and scored decisive victories in the battles that ensued. It also provided the Ottomans with the opportunity to recover some of their losses. Defying the warnings of the Great Powers, the Ottoman army marched on Edirne, recapturing the city on July 22. The Ottoman government signed peace treaties with Bulgaria, Greece, and Serbia in September 1913, November 1913, and March 1914, respectively. No peace treaty was concluded with Montenegro.

Many historians consider the Balkan Wars an essential link in the causal chain leading to the Great War. They were certainly a major disaster for the Ottomans. A defeat of this magnitude at the hands of former subjects was a very difficult pill to swallow. Reducing an empire of three continents to an Asiatic state, it shattered Ottoman pride and self-confidence. In addition to the humiliation, the Ottoman government had to deal with an immense financial drain resulting from the losses of territory and materiel, and the difficulty of resettling hundreds of thousands of refugees pouring in from the lost regions. The renunciation of territories with large non-Turkish populations, and the ensuing atrocities against Muslims in those lands, dealt the Ottomanist ideal a shattering blow, giving the upper hand to the Turkists in the internal debate over the basis of loyalty in the empire. Inevitably, the loss of the European lands prompted an innovative view of the geographical character of the empire among the Ottoman ruling elite. For centuries, the empire had rested on two central pillars, Rumelia and Anatolia, between which nested the imperial capital. Suddenly, the Arab periphery became the only significant extension of the empire outside its new Anatolian heartland. Some influential thinkers went so far as to propose the removal of the capital from Istanbul to a major town in central Anatolia or northern Syria.[33]

---

[33] Tunaya, *İttihat ve Terakki*, pp. 480–83.

FIGURE 23. Muslim refugees from the Balkans in the capital (December 1912). *Resimli Kitab* 8/46 (December 1912–January 1913), p. 764.

Ottoman statesmen learned three principal lessons from the Balkan Wars. First, the wars underscored the fact that without a Great Power protector, the empire's days were numbered. The Ottoman-German alliance of the following year must be seen in this context. Second, the wars proved the futility of written assurances from the Great Powers as a group. Events made a mockery of the prewar European diplomatic note stating that the Great Powers would not tolerate any change in the status quo in the event of war.[34] Only a formal alliance based on mutual interest would do. Third, the wars demonstrated to the Ottomans that they had to do everything in their power to eliminate major sources of confrontation with the Great Powers of Europe, and come to terms with their foremost domestic rivals on the periphery, if they were to avoid further war and foreign intervention.

In 1911,[35] and again in 1913,[36] the Ottomans knocked on the door of the British Foreign Office, only to be rebuffed time and again by Sir Edward Grey.

[34] Poincaré à MM. les Ministres de France à Sofia, Belgrade, Athènes, Cettigné, October 7, 1912, *Documents diplomatiques: Les affaires balkaniques, 1912–1914*, 1 (Paris: Imprimerie nationale, 1922), p. 99.

[35] Joseph Heller, *British Policy towards the Ottoman Empire, 1908–1914* (London: Frank Cass, 1983), p. 80.

[36] PRO/F.O. 371/1263, file 48554 (October 31, 1911).

Thereafter, up until the outbreak of the Great War, they approached all possible powers begging for an alliance. Austria-Hungary rejected Ottoman appeals in February 1914; Russia in May 1914; and France in July 1914. The crisis brought on by the Sarajevo incident gave impetus to Ottoman efforts to secure an alliance that would both protect Ottoman territorial integrity and enable the empire to recover a portion of the territories recently lost to Greece and Bulgaria. The universal expectation of a short war combined with the perception of Ottoman military weakness to preclude a positive response in London, Paris, or St. Petersburg. Although the Germans maintained a military mission in Istanbul, they, too, proved lukewarm regarding the prospect of an alliance with the Ottoman Empire. Having refused similar Ottoman démarches in late 1912 and early 1913, Germany began to reassess its traditional response to Ottoman overtures only after the onset of the crisis of July 1914.[37] In the end, the kaiser, under pressure from his Austrian allies, prevailed on the German government to accept the Ottoman offer. After negotiations hastened by the approaching war, the Ottoman government finally concluded a treaty with Germany on August 2, 1914. The German-Ottoman alliance, which is often erroneously portrayed as the result of German pressure on the Ottoman Empire, must be regarded in this larger context. Ottoman entreaties, not German designs, formed the essential background to the German-Ottoman partnership in the Great War.

The second major diplomatic initiative undertaken by the Ottomans in the aftermath of the Tripolitan and Balkan debacles was a proactive attempt to reduce tensions in trouble spots that might prompt fresh rounds of armed conflict. One such area was eastern Anatolia. In February 1914, after protracted diplomatic negotiations, and under intense Russian pressure, the Ottoman government accepted a settlement providing for a pro-Armenian reform program, to be implemented by two European inspector-generals (Dutch East Indies administrator Louis Constant Westenenk and Norwegian officer Nicolas Hoff) in the six Eastern provinces.[38] Another area in which the CUP sought to preempt conflict was Arabia. The Anglo-Turkish conventions of 1913 and 1914 formalized the division of the Arabian Peninsula between the British and the Ottomans.[39] In return for Ottoman recognition of agreements signed between the British and local tribal leaders, whereby British protectorates were created de jure in southern and eastern Arabia,

[37] Mustafa Aksakal, "Defending the Nation: The German-Ottoman Alliance of 1914 and the Ottoman Decision for War," Unpublished Ph.D. dissertation, Princeton University (2003), pp. 63ff.

[38] *Die Große Politik der europäischen Kabinette*, 38: *Neue Gefahrenzonen im Orient, 1913–1914* (Berlin: Deutsche Veragsgesellschaft für Politik und Geschichte, 1926), pp. 1–189; and BOA-DH. KMS 2/2-5 [April 28, 1914].

[39] BOA-Muahedenâme, 242/11; 242/14; 376/2; and 369/2.

Chapter Six

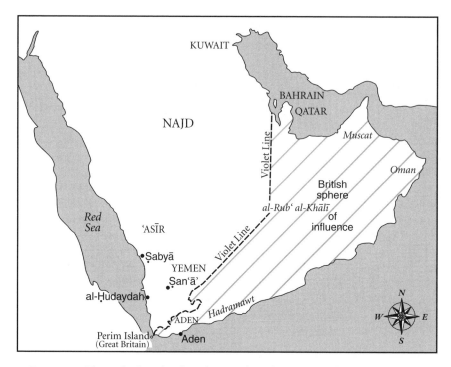

FIGURE 24. The violet line dividing the British and Ottoman spheres of influence
according to the 1914 Anglo-Ottoman Convention.

the British recognized Najd, a vast area under the rule of ʿAbd al-ʿAzīz ibn
Saʿūd, as Ottoman territory. The violet line separating the Ottoman and
British spheres of influence represented a settlement beneficial to both parties. The British obtained international legitimacy for their holdings in the
Peninsula, something they had sought for decades, while the Ottoman government forced a strong and rebellious leader to accept Ottoman sovereignty. The demarcation of a border in Arabia was part of a larger Ottoman-British effort to liquidate all outstanding disputes between the two
governments, including rights of navigation on the Tigris and the Euphrates,
and Ottoman customs duties.[40]

Caught between the Ottomans and the British, local rulers in Arabia
were forced to come to terms with one or other dominant power. ʿAbd
al-ʿAzīz ibn Saʿūd, for example, was left high and dry by the British accommodation with the Ottomans, and signed a contract with the Ottoman
government in May 1914 making him the hereditary governor of Najd.[41]
Imām Yaḥyā had already benefited from a similar arrangement, offered by

[40] BOA-A.AMD. MV 103/53.
[41] BOA-DH.SYS 25/103.

the Ottoman administration in 1911, which made him autonomous ruler of the mountainous, Zaydī-populated parts of the province of Yemen.[42] Muḥammad ibn ʿAlī al-Idrīsī of ʿAsīr, who received aid from the Italians, rejected a similar Ottoman offer;[43] but, surrounded as he was by the then pro-Ottoman Sharif Ḥusayn ibn ʿAlī in the Ḥijāz on the one hand, and by Imām Yaḥyā in the highlands of Yemen on the other, he did not pose a serious threat to Ottoman sovereignty.

THE OTTOMAN EMPIRE IN THE GREAT WAR

By June 1914, when the sultan ratified the Anglo-Turkish convention,[44] it seemed that the Ottoman Empire had at last secured a breathing space—with no major domestic or international conflict on the horizon—in which to heal the wounds of the Tripolitan and Balkan wars, reorganize the military, and prepare for another round against the Balkan powers who had seized so much of the empire's territory. It was not to be.

The outbreak of war in Europe in August 1914 did not automatically entail Ottoman participation, for the carefully worded treaty with Germany did not make Ottoman entry into the war a definite obligation. Accordingly, on August 3, the Ottoman government merely declared armed neutrality and initiated a full military mobilization. The Ottomans aimed to mobilize within the thirty-nine days scheduled for the execution of the first phase of the Schlieffen plan against France, so that the Ottoman army would be ready to lend a helping hand to the Germans when they turned eastward against Russia. But as soon as the Germans ran into difficulties on the Western front, they began to apply heavy pressure on the Ottomans to enter the war, open up new fronts against Russia and Great Britain, and declare a global *jihād* against the Allies. The Ottomans, however, were disinclined to move until the mobilization process was complete, German success in the West was certain, and an overland route of communication with the Central Powers (through Rumania and Bulgaria) was open.

Ottoman neutrality became more precarious with time, particularly after the cabinet authorized the passage of two German men-of-war, the Panzerkreuzer *Goeben* and the Kleiner Kreuzer *Breslau*, into Ottoman territorial waters on August 5. The cruisers, originally requested by Enver Pasha, Ottoman minister of war and leader of the pro-German faction within the CUP, had been pursued by the entire British Mediterranean fleet to the mouth of the Dardanelles. But now the Ottomans threatened either to take

[42] BOA-A.DVN.NMH 371/1.

[43] BOA-MV 174/no. 928 [1913]; BOA-BEO/ file 309254 [December 15, 1913]; 333431 [December 23, 1916].

[44] BOA-Muahede ve Mukavelenâme, 369/2 (1914).

over the ships by force or to leave them to British mercy. The Germans, caught between Scylla and Charybdis, chose the lesser evil. To preserve the two cruisers, they granted the Ottoman government six valuable concessions, including incorporation of the ships into the Ottoman navy, support for the abrogation of the capitulations, a commitment not to conclude peace until all Ottoman territory that might be occupied in the current war had been liberated, and the guarantee of any territorial gains achieved by the Ottomans in the course of the war.[45] On August 10, the two cruisers entered the Sea of Marmara. The next day, their fictitious purchase by the Ottoman government was announced. The German crews, donning fezzes and flying Ottoman colors, surrendered the newly named Yavuz Sultan Selim and Midilli to nominal Ottoman control. The Entente Powers opted to accept this bold fait accompli rather than declare war.

The *Goeben* and *Breslau* episode brought the Ottoman Empire tangible political benefits, and added to its obsolete navy two powerful men-of-war (worth 50 million German Marks, an amount twice the entire annual budget of the Ottoman Ministry of the Navy). But it also lost the empire any semblance of freedom of action. The acquisition of the cruisers considerably strengthened the German military mission in the capital and the hand of the pro-German faction within the government and CUP. The two men-of-war were the very vessels that spearheaded the surprise attack on Russia carried out by the German Admiral Wilhelm Souchon on October 29, 1914 despite the opposition of several key figures in the CUP. There was no turning back.

The expectations of the Ottoman leaders from the war were fourfold. First, they hoped to secure a more advantageous treaty of alliance from Germany, one that would provide them with protection against both European and Balkan powers. The renewable, five-year German-Ottoman defensive alliance of January 11, 1915 addressed this need, providing for German protection against an attack by Russia, France, or Great Britain, as well as "a coalition composed of at least two Balkan states."[46] At the time, this seemed like a major diplomatic success for the Ottomans, though of course the eventual defeat of Germany was to expose it as a major strategic blunder.

The second expectation from the war was that full Ottoman control would be reestablished over the various autonomous regions of the empire. The Ottoman abolition of the self-governing status of Mount Lebanon in July 1915 provided a hint as to what lay in store for many such regions in the event of victory. The Ottoman Foreign Ministry conducted extensive

---

[45] Aksakal, "Defending the Nation," pp. 117–18.

[46] *Recueil des traités, conventions, protocoles, arrangements et déclarations signés entre l'Empire ottoman et les Puissances étrangères, 1903–1922*, 1 (*1903–1916*), ed. Sinan Kuneralp (Istanbul: The Isis Press, 2000), p. 314.

preparatory work on the history and legal circumstances of autonomous regions such as Kuwait, Qatar, Najd, Bahrein, and even Hadramawt and Oman, in anticipation of the extension of Ottoman central control over these areas. The disappearance of the British from the Arabian Peninsula, it was assumed, would make possible the fulfillment of the age-old Ottoman aspiration for full sovereignty while at the same time satisfying German strategic interests. The reestablishment of central control over Egypt and the Sudan was deemed unrealistic (the ambassadors who were commissioned to prepare a memorandum on this subject commented that Egypt and the Sudan could legally be restored to the empire, but that in the light of "almost one century of autonomous rule," it would be preferable to maintain their current status);[47] but their attachment to the empire might be strengthened. Algeria and Tunis could also be drawn closer to the center. As for the Bosporus and Dardanelles, either they would return to full Ottoman control, or the status quo that had existed between 1856 and 1871—providing for the neutralization of the Black Sea—would be restored.[48] Of course, none of this came to pass.

The third set of Ottoman expectations in 1914 related to the opportunity for territorial gains in the war. If Greece entered the war on the Allied side, the Ottomans hoped that the northern Aegean islands occupied during the First Balkan War could be recovered for the empire. They had similar designs on Cyprus, which had been administered by the British since 1878. The Italian entry into the war in 1915 raised additional hopes for the restoration of Tripoly of Barbary, Cyrenaica, and the Dodecanese, which had been either acquired or occupied by Italy in 1912. On the eastern front, the Ottomans sought the restoration of three Anatolian provinces lost to Russia in 1878, as well as expansion into the Caucasus. Tellingly, one of the Ottoman conditions for allowing the German cruisers into the Dardanelles was that "Germany must secure a small border change in Eastern Anatolia that would allow for direct contact with the Muslims of Russia."[49] It seems plausible that the CUP leaders were thinking in terms of laying the groundwork for a "Great Turanian Empire" linking the Caucasus to Central Asia by means of direct Ottoman control or a chain of dependent states (like the Northern Caucasus Republic, declared upon the Ottoman conquest of Derbent in October 1918).[50]

[47] Rauf Ahmed and Ragıb Raif, *Mısır Meselesi* (Istanbul: Matbaa-i Âmire, 1334 [1918]), pp. 177–9.

[48] Rauf Ahmed and Ragıb Raif, *Boğazlar Meselesi* (Istanbul: Matbaa-i Osmaniye, 1334 [1918]), pp. 42–4.

[49] Aksakal, "Defending the Nation," p. 118.

[50] Nâsır Yüceer, *Birinci Dünya Savaşı'nda Osmanlı Ordusu'nun Azerbaycan ve Dağıstan Harekâtı: Azerbaycan ve Dağıstan'ın Bağımsızlığını Kazanması, 1918* (Ankara: Genelkurmay ATASE Yayınları, 1996), pp. 127–8 and 147.

The final hope harbored by the Ottoman leadership at the outset of the war was that it would provide the opportunity to break the humiliating shackles of the foreign capitulations once and for all. They assumed that the removal of economic and legal constraints would free the empire to establish state monopolies on materials such as petroleum and sugar and fix customs tariffs at will, thereby marshalling the resources required to launch an ambitious program of economic development that would foster the growth of an Ottoman industrial sector capable of holding its own against European competition.[51] Of all their hopes and expectations, this was the only one that was to be fulfilled to any appreciable degree, although economic ruin and imperial collapse removed many of the potential benefits associated with the end of the capitulations.

In the war that ensued, Ottoman military performance wholly surpassed the expectations of European experts. Ottoman armies fought effectively on multiple fronts—in the Caucasus, Mesopotamia, and Palestine—in addition to fending off a major onslaught on their capital through the Dardanelles. At the request of the German High Command, the Ottoman IVth Army also launched two somewhat quixotic offensives against the Suez Canal in 1915 and 1916; both ended in utter failure.[52] Minor operations were carried out in ʿAsīr, the Yemen, Tripoli of Barbary and Cyrenaica, and Iran. The Ottomans also provided valuable help to the war effort in the European theater, with Ottoman units serving on fronts in Galicia, Rumania, and Macedonia. By contrast, the Ottoman declaration of jihād on November 14, 1914 did not result in any significant rebellions by the millions of Muslim subjects under Allied rule. Although the steady attrition of British power seemed the most crucial contribution of the Ottoman war effort at the time, its most radical impact on world history was in Russia. The unexpected Ottoman victory at the Dardanelles paved the way for the success of the Bolshevik Revolution and the subsequent collapse of the Eastern Front in 1917, as Russia bled to death for lack of the material support that its allies could have supplied through the Straits and the Black Sea. Over the course of the war, Great Britain deployed 2,550,000 troops on the Ottoman fronts, constituting 32 percent of the total number of British troops in the field; at one point, the British had 880,300 men fighting the Ottomans, or 24 percent of the British armed forces. The Russians initially mobilized 160,000 troops on the Caucasian front. By September 1916, they had 702,000 troops facing the Ottomans in Anatolia and Iran, out of a total force of 3.7 million. Additionally, 50,000 French troops fought the Ottomans, mainly at the Dardanelles. The Italians dispatched an expeditionary force of 70,000 soldiers

---

[51] Mehmed Nâbi and Rumbeyoğlu Fahreddin, *Gümrük Resmi'nin Yüzde On Beşe İblâğı, Ecnebî Postaları ve Kapitülâsyon* (Istanbul: Matbaa-i Âmire, 1334 [1917]), p. 6.

[52] [Friedrich] Kreß von Kressenstein, *Mit den Türken zum Suezkanal* (Berlin: Otto Schlegel, 1938), pp. 85ff.

to quell a rebellion of the local militia in Tripoli and Cyrenaica aided by the Ottoman government. Total Allied casualties on the Ottoman fronts amounted to a massive 650,000.[53] In short, the Ottoman war effort imposed on the Allied powers a substantial diversion of troops that could otherwise have been used on the major European fronts.

The cost of this achievement was nonetheless immense. Ottoman losses on all fronts wreaked havoc throughout the empire. During the Great War, the empire put 2,608,000 men in uniform.[54] Approximately 15 percent of the entire population, or almost one out of two adult males outside the civil service, was called to arms. By 1918, Ottoman casualties had reached the appalling figure of 725,000 (325,000 dead and 400,000 wounded). In addition, the Allies (mainly Great Britain and Russia) took 202,000 Ottoman prisoners of war on various fronts. More than a million deserters, constituting almost half of the total number of draftees, wreaked social havoc throughout the empire, especially in rural areas. On the day the Mudros armistice was signed, out of 2,608,000 men put into uniform, only 323,000 were still at their posts.[55] Of those who remained, a majority were noncombatants or fresh recruits not ready for combat. As early as 1916, draft regulations were stretched to the extent that the age of soldiers in the infantry regiments varied between sixteen and fifty. By 1918, almost all Ottoman divisions existed on paper only.[56]

The war was also devastating from an economic perspective. The government spent an estimated total of Lt 389.5 million (equivalent to 9.09 billion gold French francs)[57] on expenses related to the war effort—or an average of Lt 97 million (2.3 billion gold French francs) per year. Given that the Ottoman budget for the fiscal year 1914 was Lt 34 million (or 1.5 billion gold French francs), out of which 44 percent went to the Public Debt Administration,[58] the total additional burden of expenditure imposed by the war amounted to ten times the net annual budget after debt repayments.

---

[53] M[aurice] Larcher, *La guerre turque dans la guerre mondiale* (Paris: E. Chiron, 1926), pp. 617–34.

[54] This figure does not include 32,000 commissioned officers of different ranks, the Shammar Bedouin of Ḥāʾil, the Zaydī militia in the Yemeni Highlands and ʿAsīr, the Kurdish tribal regiments, the irregular units set up by the Special Organization, 1,400 German naval personnel, 7,500 German soldiers including those in the Deutsche Asien-Korps and in the Sonderkommando detachment, and 650 German officers, medical personnel, and officials of the Military Mission.

[55] Cemalettin Taşkıran, *Ana Ben Ölmedim: Birinci Dünya Savaşı'nda Türk Esirleri* (Istanbul: Türkiye İş Bankası Kültür Yayınları, 2001), pp. 47–8.

[56] [Otto] Liman von Sanders, *Fünf Jahre Türkei* (Berlin: August Scherl, 1920), pp. 155–6.

[57] By comparison, Great Britain spent 235.7 billion gold French francs, Germany 243.1 billion, Belgium 5.9 billion, Bulgaria 3.6 billion, and Serbia 3.2 billion. See Larcher, *La guerre turque*, p. 636.

[58] *Düstûr*, II/6 (Istanbul: Matbaa-i Âmire, 1334 [1916]), p. 1081.

To this extraordinary level of expenditure, once must add catastrophic losses in revenues. The strain of wartime finances was clearly staggering.

The Russian collapse on the eastern Anatolian front in the upheaval brought about by the Bolshevik Revolution prolonged Ottoman hopes of ultimate victory. But the ambitious Ottoman thrust into the Caucasus in the summer and fall of 1918, following the formal withdrawal of Russia from the war under the terms of the Brest-Litovsk Treaty of March 1918, proved unsustainable. As the Anatolian heartland came under threat from British advances in the Near East, as the German offensives in Western Europe failed, and as a major Allied attack resulted in the collapse of the entire Bulgarian front, it became clear that the empire could no longer depend on its Great Power ally. The combined impact of these developments resulted in the Ottoman capitulation to the Allies at Mudros on October 30, 1918. The surrender of the Ottoman government and the subsequent flight of the leading members of the CUP meant the end of the Second Constitutional Period and, more broadly, the Ottoman period as a whole.

One of the most tragic events of the war was the deportation of much of the Armenian population of Anatolia. Faced with the prospect of total collapse on the Ottoman eastern front early in the war the government apparently decided to deport all Armenians of the Armenian Apostolic Church living in and around the Ottoman-Russian war zone, on the grounds that the Armenian revolutionary committees were rebelling against the Ottoman Empire and providing crucial assistance to the advancing Russian armies.[59] However, the finer details of this decision were abandoned in practice with the result that almost all Armenian populations affiliated with the Apostolic Church were deported, with the exception of those residing in Istanbul, İzmir, certain smaller cities such as Kütahya, and some Arab provinces. In addition, the government deported scores of leading members of the Armenian elite of the capital and other major cities, including numerous intellectuals and professionals, on the grounds that they were clandestinely serving the rebellious Armenian committees.[60] Many prominent politicians, including various Armenian members of the Ottoman Chamber of Deputies, later shared the same fate. The deportation of the Armenians (mainly to Dayr al-Zawr in Syria) was carried out with large-scale violence and under conditions of extreme weather and hunger, leading to massive loss of life. It effectively ended Armenian existence in much of Anatolia.

---

[59] See the temporary law "Vakt-i Seferde İcraat-ı Hükûmete Karşı Gelenler İçün Cihet-i Askeriyece İttihaz Olunacak Tedâbir Hakkında Kanun-i Muvakkat," *Takvim-i Vekayi'*, May 19, 1331 [June 1, 1915]. Deportations in fact began before this temporary law was issued.

[60] Minister of the Interior Talât Bey's coded telegram dated April 11, 1331 [April 24, 1915], BOA-DH.EUM, 52/96–98.

INTELLECTUAL LIFE UNDER THE CUP

The post-revolutionary period witnessed the most far-ranging intellectual debate in late Ottoman history. During the early days of relative freedom under the CUP, pundits of all ideological hues—ranging from Islamic modernism to socialism—vied for attention in the public sphere. Intellectual life in the Ottoman capital, which under the old regime had lost its preeminence to Cairo and Beirut, once again flourished after the revolution. Other cities, such as Salonica, Damascus, and Baghdad, also witnessed a revitalization of intellectual life.

Nationalist literary movements dominated Turkish, Albanian, Arab, Armenian, and Greek intellectual circles. One such group, the Young Pens (Genc Kalemler), advocated literature that reflected social realities, focused on national problems, and employed simple language; this became the most popular approach to literature during this period. Similar approaches predominated in the nationalist literary journals of other Ottoman communities, such as the Armenian journals *Mehean* and *Nawasard* (Istanbul), the Albanian journal *Koha* (Korçë), the clandestinely circulated Arab journal *Lisān al-ʿArab/al-Muntadā al-ʿArabī* (Istanbul), and the literary sections of the Kurdish journals *Rōj-i Kurd* and *Hetav-i Kurd* (Istanbul).

Publications devoted to the concerns of women also proliferated throughout the empire during this period. During the Tanzimat, women's publications, such as the supplement to the journal *Terakki*, launched in 1869, centered on the narrow concerns of the Westernized elite. During the Hamidian era, the palace-sponsored *Hanımlara Mahsus Gazete* (Ladies' Gazette), in accordance with the innovative emphases of Ottomanism, promoted a new idealized image of a Muslim mother and wife, who shopped at Muslim stores and raised obedient, pious children. The new post-revolutionary women's press, by contrast, gave vent to more liberal voices, and discussed a much broader range of issues, including sensitive ones like feminism, universal suffrage, and gender discrimination.[61]

Women's organizations multiplied as well. Principal among them was the Society for the Defense of Women's Rights. In 1913, its leader, Belkıs Şevket, a staunch defender of gender equality in all aspects of life, flew aboard a chartered military plane on behalf of Ottoman and Muslim women to demonstrate to her female compatriots that they need not be excluded from any human activity. Belkıs Şevket struck a defiant pose, insisting that "Oriental women will not accept a position that falls behind that of their Western sisters."[62] Although participation in women's movements was significantly

---

[61] Serpil Çakır, *Osmanlı Kadın Hareketi* (Istanbul: Metis Yayınları, 1994), pp. 120ff.

[62] Belkıs Şevket, "Tayarân Ederken," *Nevsâl-ı Millî: 1330*, ed. T. Z. (Istanbul: Artin Asadoryan, 1330 [1914]), pp. 438–40.

FIGURE 25. Belkıs Şevket, a leading Ottoman feminist, aboard an Ottoman Bleriot XI/B with Captain Fethi Bey, before embarking on the first flight of a Muslim and Ottoman female (December 1, 1913). *Nevsâl-i Millî*, ed. T. Z. (Istanbul: Artin Asadoryan, 1330 [1914]), p. 450.

greater than in previous periods, it was still strictly an elite activity. As such, it cannot be compared to the scale of suffragette activity in the Western world. Though gender-based, the movement supported the larger Otto-manist cause, inviting women of different ethnic backgrounds and religious affiliations to participate; at the same time, it also benefited nationalist or-ganizations, which came to dominate national women's clubs and organiza-tions under the CUP.

Socialism never achieved the status of a mainstream movement in the Ottoman Empire. The socialist movement, popular among the Christian population of the empire, relied mainly on the support of a handful of intellectuals of Armenian, Bulgarian, Macedonian, or Serbian background. The Ottoman Socialist Party, established in 1910 to create a mainstream movement with the participation of Muslims, fell far short of making any impact on politics. Unique at the time in its attempt to reconcile Islam with socialism, the Ottoman Socialist Party did, however, set a precedent for modern Islamic socialist movements.[63]

The one ideological component of socialist dogma that did make its way into mainstream Ottoman thought was materialism. The Ottoman materialist movement, which had begun under the Tanzimat and gained momentum during the Hamidian regime, came into its own under the CUP. Full translations of Büchner's *Kraft und Stoff* now appeared[64] as well as many works on Darwinism.[65] The first major Ottoman philosophical journal, *Felsefe Mecmuası*, promoted German *Vulgärmaterialismus* with a strong bias toward Ernst Haeckel's Monism. Various journals linked materialism to Westernization (*Garbcılık*), portraying it as the driving force behind the material progress of the West. The most prominent of these, *İctihad*, also waged a war of ideas against Islam and ridiculed many Muslim practices.[66] Indeed, Sharif Ḥusayn of Mecca listed the attacks on Islam published in the pages of *İctihad* among the factors that prompted his revolt against the Ottomans in 1916.[67] More important, the Westernization agenda vigorously advocated by this journal provided a blueprint for the radical reforms later implemented by Mustafa Kemal (Atatürk), the first president of the Turkish Republic.[68] Following the Balkan Wars, a major schism took place within the Ottoman Westernization movement. One faction combined support for cultural Westernization with vigorous opposition to Western imperialism,[69] while another advocated wholesale acceptance of Western civilization, "with its roses and its thorns."[70]

---

[63] Mete Tunçay, *Türkiye'de Sol Akımlar, 1908–1925*, 1 (Istanbul: BDS Yayınları, 1991), p. 33.

[64] Louis [Ludwig] Büchner, *Madde ve Kuvvet*, 1–3, tr. Baha Tevfik and Ahmed Nebil (Istanbul: Teceddüd-i İlmî ve Felsefî Kütübhanesi, [1911]).

[65] Subhi Edhem, *Darwinizm* (Monastir: Beyn'el-milel Ticaret Matbaası, 1327 [1911]).

[66] Abdullah Cevdet, "Softalığa Dair," *İctihad*, no. 60 [April 17 1913], p. 1304.

[67] Sulaymān Musā, *al-Ḥusayn ibn ʿAlī waʾl-thawra al-ʿArabīya al-kubrā* (Amman: Lajnat Tārīkh al-Urdunn, 1992), p. 134.

[68] [Kılıçzâde Hakkı], "Pek Uyanık Bir Uyku," *İctihad*, no. 55 [March 6, 1913], pp. 1226–8; no. 57 [March 20, 1913], pp. 1261–4.

[69] Celâl Nuri, "Şime-i Husumet," *İctihad*, no. 88 [January 22, 1914], pp. 1949–51.

[70] Abdullah Cevdet, "Şime-i Muhabbet," *İctihad*, no. 89 [January 29, 1914], pp. 1979–84.

Islamist movements, which had suffered persecution at the hands of Abdülhamid II, enjoyed a period of relative growth and tranquility under the CUP. The most important of these was the one inspired by Muḥammad ʿAbduh's ideas on the reconciliation of Islam with science and modernity. Supporters of ʿAbduh strongly defended constitutionalism, but criticized Turkism on the grounds that "Islam does not allow nationalism."[71] They denounced the Westernizers (*Garbcılar*) for seeking to dupe Muslims into accepting a "new religion."[72] The ulema as a whole strove (without much success) to reclaim their former position in political and intellectual life. Initially, the religious establishment maintained cordial relations with the CUP, which for its part set up an ulema party branch to keep the mainstream religious figures under its control. But the relationship deteriorated over time, especially after the attempted counterrevolution of 1909, which the CUP abused to consolidate its hold on power and marginalize the ulema. As a substitute for public religion sanctioned by the ulema, the CUP pushed for the transformation of religion into a private affair; in 1909, for example, the government banned the hearing of private law cases by shariʿa courts in instances where a prior judgment from a civil court existed.[73] In 1917, it issued the "Temporary Family Law," a cautious but significant step toward the adoption of a civil law code. The statute granted a limited right of divorce to Muslim women by means of a liberal interpretation of Ḥanbalī law; and it limited the practice of polygamy by allowing women to stipulate monogamy as a condition in their marriage contracts.[74] This legislation was the product of proposals put forth by a group of intellectuals, labeled the Turkist-Islamists, who published the journal *İslâm Mecmuası* (Islamic Review). These thinkers advocated the construction of a modern Islam that limited itself to matters of private faith and rituals. They believed it could be construed by entrusting the *ulu'l-amr* (those vested with authority) with extensive legislative authority, broadening the basis and applicability of *ʿurf* (custom), and liberally interpreting traditional Islamic sources.[75] In this manner, Islamic practices that could not be reconciled with modernity, such as polygamy, would be eliminated.[76] Especially during the Great War, such theses found an attentive ear in the corridors of power, as the CUP supported the use of a modernist Islam to rally religion to the national cause and project

---

[71] Ahmed Naʿim, *İslâmda Daʿva-yı Kavmiyyet* (Istanbul: Tevsiʿ-i Tıbaʿat Matbaası, 1332 [1914]), pp. 5ff.

[72] Ferid, "Tarih-i İstikbâl," *Sebilʾür-Reşad*, 11/283 [February 12, 1914], p. 358.

[73] *Düstûr*, II/1 (Istanbul: Matbaa-i Osmaniye, 1329 [1911]), pp. 192–4.

[74] *Düstûr*, II/9 (Istanbul: Evkaf Matbaası, 1928), pp. 762–81.

[75] Ziya Gökalp, "Dinin İctimaʿî Hidmetleri," *İslâm Mecmuası* 2/34 [August 26, 1915], pp. 741–3; no. 36 [September 23, 1915], pp. 772–6; no. 37 [October 7, 1915], pp. 791–6.

[76] See, for instance, Mansurizâde Saʿid, "İslâm Kadını: Taʿaddüd-i Zevcât İslâmiyetde Menʿ Olunabilir," *İslâm Mecmuası* 1/8 [1914], pp. 233–8.

a "Religion for a Turk."[77] However, the mainstream ulema, as well as the more radical Islamists, rejected such views as unwelcome innovations.[78]

Despite these tensions, the regime's legitimacy deficit repeatedly forced the CUP to seek compromises with the liberal wing of the ulema whenever it felt challenged by conservatives, and, more generally, to fall back on the traditional legitimizing power of Islam. One example is the Islamization of the Ottoman Constitution following the counterrevolution.[79] An amendment to article 10 added "sharī'a" to a clause that originally read: "Except for the reasons and under the conditions prescribed by the law [qānūn], no one shall be arrested or punished on any pretext whatsoever." A similar alteration in article 118 of the constitution made fiqh a major source for new legislation. Analogous political calculations led the State Council in 1909 to recommend a wholesale ban on the import of alcoholic beverages to the province of Yemen (so as to avoid a backlash from "the local population, which is inclined toward conspiracy," ran the proposal).[80] Ironically, the implementation of this recommendation prompted an unforeseen backlash from Yemen's non-Muslims, whose right to drink alcohol—recognized by the "reactionary" Abdülhamid II—was thus inadvertently annulled. In general, the CUP tended to appeal to Islam when it was convenient to do so, as when bureaucrats explained the shutdown of socialist organizations on the grounds that their regulations violated the sharī'a (in addition to "fundamental principles").[81]

The Turkism that had flourished among Ottoman expatriates in Cairo, the capital cities of Europe, and other parts of the empire during the later years of Abdülhamid II went from strength to strength after the revolution. Once in power, the CUP everywhere backed Turkist organizations, such as the Turkish Hearths; and leading CUP members wrote for Turkist organs, such as *Genc Kalemler* and *Türk Yurdu*, thereby broadening their appeal. The Turkist attitude to Islam and Islamic reform was radically new. Epitomized by Ziya Gökalp's motto, "to become Turkish, Muslim, and modern," Turkism advocated reconciliation with both Islam and secularism.[82]

---

[77] Ziya Gökalp, "Türk'e Göre: Din," *İslâm Mecmuası* 2/22 [March 10, 1915], p. 552.

[78] See, for example, İzmirli İsmail Hakkı, "Fıkh ü Fetâvâ: Örfün Nazar-ı Şer'deki Mevki'i," *Sebil'ür-Reşad* 12/293 [April 23, 1914], pp. 129–32; and Ahmed Na'im, "Müdafa'at-ı Diniye," *Sebil'ür-Reşad* 11[12]/ 298 [May 28, 1914], pp. 216–21 and 12/300 [June 11, 1914], pp. 248–50.

[79] *Mu'addel Kanun-i Esasî ve İntihab-ı Meb'usan Kanunu*, ed. Tevfik Tarık (Istanbul: İkbal Kütübhanesi, 1327 [1912], pp. 3–11.

[80] BOA-ŞD, 2267/12 (1905–1909).

[81] See the draft memorandum to be sent by the ministry of the interior to the acting governor of Istanbul, [January 29, 1913]/no. 624, BOA-DH.İD., 126/44.

[82] Ziya Gökalp, *Türkleşmek, İslâmlaşmak, Mu'asırlaşmak* (Istanbul: Yeni Matbaa, 1918), pp. 3ff.

But perhaps the most important effect of the surge in Turkist thought was the reconstruction of the official ideology of Ottomanism. Much as Abdül-hamid II's reinterpretation of Ottomanism had stressed the solidarity of the empire's Muslim subjects, the CUP's new Ottomanism now allocated a dominant role to its Turks. And just as Abdülhamid II's emphasis on Islam transcended the boundaries of the empire, so too did the new emphasis on the Turkish race. Thus Ottomanism, which originally envisioned an egalitarian supranational identity that would supersede other religious or ethnic affiliations and bind the empire together, ended up as the ideological foundation for a society dominated by Turks—not unlike Arkadii Prigozhin's vision of a *narod-patron*, in which a multinational Soviet community was in fact to be run by Russians. "Turks who had lived an unconscious life under the Ottoman flag" were called upon to acquire a "national awareness" and, as the dominant nation of the state, to reinvigorate the empire. At the same time, they were asked to extend a helping hand both to Turks living under foreign rule and to Muslims in other parts of the world.[83]

Some Turkists took these notions one step further, advocating a Pan-Turkist union of Turkic peoples, most of whom were held to be chafing under Russian domination. The ideal future homeland of all Turks, "Turan," was, however, for the most part a fantasy entertained by a handful of intellectuals. In a poem on this theme composed in 1911, Ziya Gökalp wrote: "Neither Turkey nor Turkistan is a fatherland for the Turks / The fatherland is an enormous and eternal country: Turan."[84] Only during the war did it become fashionable to discuss the union of all Turks as a practical possibility to be realized on the ruins of the Russian Empire.

The intellectual ferment of the period found new modes of expression. Political demonstrations, workers' strikes, and economic boycotts directed at Western powers dotted the political landscape of this era. Debates such as that on Westernization raged on into the early months of the First World War, when the government finally put an end to freedom of speech, suspending *İctihad* and other controversial journals. As the war progressed, the administration placed increasing restrictions on political activities of all kinds, limiting demonstrations, outlawing political organizations, and manipulating anti-Western sentiments for its own purposes.

The Economy

The militant prerevolutionary rhetoric of the Turkist faction of the CUP gave no indication what economic policy could be expected after the revolution.

[83] Köprülüzâde Mehmed Fu'ad, "Türklük, İslâmlık, Osmanlılık," *Türk Yurdu* 4 (1329 [1913]), p. 695.

[84] Tevfik Sedad [Ziya Gökalp], "Turan," *Genc Kalemler*, no. 6 [March 1911], p. 167.

Talk of declaring an economic boycott against the treacherous Armenians,[85] of shunning the Public Debt Administration as an *imperium in imperio*,[86] of resisting aggressive European capitalists and exploiters who "go wild when they see money"[87] died down quickly as revolutionary extremism gave way to more realistic attitudes following the assumption of power by the CUP. Although early CUP decisions revealed a certain tendency to support domestic production, such as viticulture on the Aegean coast, against foreign companies,[88] fears of an immediate shift to extreme étatism favoring Muslims and Turks proved unfounded. Instead, the CUP surprised everyone by adopting a liberal policy conceived by one of its leading members, Mehmed Cavid, a scholarly champion of liberalism.[89] Between 1908 and 1913, the number of Ottoman joint stock companies established with foreign capital (and usually in partnership with European or non-Muslim Ottoman entrepreneurs) actually increased.[90] Still, economic liberalism clearly contradicted the Weltanschauung of the CUP; as such, it represented merely a temporary compromise with reality.

The surge of anti-Western sentiments under the impact of the Balkan Wars helped the CUP leaders readjust their economic policy and shift to a new agenda more in line with their beliefs. The new policy, labeled "National Economics," was a blend of corporatism, protectionism, and strict state control over the economy. It had its intellectual roots in the thinking of Friedrich List and the German Historical School. The coming of war facilitated the adoption of such measures, and the 1916 General Congress of the CUP heralded the full adoption of this platform as official policy. It was significant that Mehmed Cavid, who abhorred the German Historical School, stayed on to preside over the implementation of these new policies as the CUP's minister of finance or in other key positions within the financial establishment. Clearly, the Turkist and étatist party line overrode individual intellectual preferences.

The Ottoman government unilaterally abrogated the capitulations on September 11, 1914,[91] much to the dismay of its German ally. This act,

---

[85] Uluğ, "Ermeniler," *Türk*, no. 110 (December 21, 1905), p. 2.

[86] Ali Muzaffer, "Düyûn-i Umumiye-i Osmaniye Varidat-ı Muhassasa İdaresi yahud Hükûmet İçinde Hükûmet," *Kanun-i Esasî*, no. 39 [May 30, 1899], pp. 4ff.

[87] "Dinleyiniz!" *Şûra-yı Ümmet*, no. 119 (July 30, 1907), p. 1.

[88] See the CUP İzmir branch's memorandum to the Central Committee, June 15, 1325 [June 28, 1909]/no. 379, and the CUP special commission's report dated July 3, 1325 [July 16, 1909], Private Papers of Ahmed Rıza.

[89] Mehmed Cavid, *İlm-i İktisad*, 1 (Istanbul: Matbaa-i Âmire, 1326 [1910]), p. 53.

[90] Zafer Toprak, *Türkiye'de "Milli İktisat," 1908–1918* (Ankara: Yurt Yayınları, 1982), p. 86.

[91] The imperial decree issued on September 8, 1914 was set to go into effect on October 1, 1914. *Düstûr*, II/6, p. 1273.

coupled with the virtually total economic isolation imposed by the war, produced a protectionist environment that favored domestic producers. The government further strengthened protectionism by increasing customs tariffs from 8 percent to 11 percent in October 1914,[92] and then raising them again to 30 percent in May 1915.[93] Despite these measures, however, conscription of almost half of the adult male population prompted a drastic decrease in domestic production in both the agricultural and nonagricultural sectors; because of the military monopoly over the use of the railways, the main means of transportation, only a small portion of production could be brought to major markets. At the same time, wartime conditions sharply limited the available export market. Moreover, severe shortages of everything imaginable emerged, leading to rampant black-marketeering and the formation of a new class of war profiteers. But these circumstances did permit the CUP to alter the balance of economic forces within the empire in favor of Muslims, and especially Turks. As the war wore on, the goal of creating of a national Muslim/Turkish bourgeoisie, at the expense of foreign capital, non-Muslims, and non-Turks, became official policy. The CUP helped Turkish entrepreneurs establish companies and banks with the word "national" in their titles. It supported the launching of a grander project to replace the Ottoman Bank with a national central bank. The new institution, named "Ottoman National Honor," was established in 1917,[94] but the collapse of the Ottoman war effort shattered hopes for its future. The CUP also created an array of other economic institutions in support of their policies, such as cooperatives for Muslim and Turkish manufacturers and societies of artisans. Such organizations supported the goal of "nationalizing the economy," while at the same time deepening organized political support for the CUP. The Temporary Law for the Encouragement of Industry, issued in 1913, sought to provide advantages to local entrepreneurs through the selective award of customs, tax, and land privileges, with the unstated aim of fostering the emergence of a Muslim bourgeoisie.[95] Until the full switch to "National Economics," the results of this legislation were meager; in 1915, Muslim entrepreneurs owned only 42 companies in the empire, as compared with 172 firms listed under non-Muslim ownership. In March 1915, the government amended the law to reinforce its unwritten agenda, restricting privileges to "Ottomans," which in practice meant Muslims, and to Ottoman joint stock companies.[96] As a consequence, by 1918 the picture had changed dramatically. A host of new

---

[92] Ibid., pp. 1276–77.

[93] *Düstûr*, II/7 (Istanbul: Matbaa-i Âmire, 1336 [1918]), p. 610.

[94] *Düstûr*, II/9 (Istanbul: Evkaf Matbaası, 1928), pp. 42–3; 184–5.

[95] *Düstûr*, II/6, pp. 108–14.

[96] *Düstûr*, II/7, pp. 535–6.

companies and factories established by Muslims gave them the upper hand in the economy, though the defeat nullified this development.[97]

It is not easy to put together an accurate economic picture of the CUP era because of the unstable conditions arising from successive wars. The upheaval caused by the First World War was particularly disruptive. For example, price indices of basic consumption in the wartime economy rose a record 1,953 percent.[98] To meet the extraordinary expenses of war, the government first obtained German credits and sold domestic bonds. But eventually, to resolve the shortage of cash, the government had no choice but to print money. In order to do so, it had to reintroduce banknotes for the third time in Ottoman history. From 1915 to the end of the war, the Ottoman Bank issued seven series of notes, amounting to Lt 161 million (more than three times the value of the metal currency circulating in the Ottoman economy), underwritten for the most part by German treasury bonds. In 1916, in an attempt to stabilize the Ottoman currency, the government issued the Temporary Law of Standardization of Metal Coins, which established a full gold standard and sought to put an end to the varying exchange rates of coins in the different regions of the empire.[99] To underscore the serious intent behind these reforms, the government made failure to accept paper notes a crime.[100] However, on the street nobody took them at face value or respected the stipulated 1:1 ratio against gold. As a result, two parallel money markets emerged. Resistance to giving change in coins for payments in notes compelled the government to authorize the practice of cutting Lt 1 and Lt 5 bills into two and using them as Lt 0.50 and Lt 2.5 notes, respectively.[101] Eventually, it was forced to issue banknotes worth as little as 5 gurushes. For still smaller amounts, the government allowed the use of revenue stamps.[102] In some towns, governors took matters into their own hands, issuing paper notes in small denominations.[103] The failure of the attempt to control the exchange rate between paper and metal is evidenced in the following statistic: in May 1917, a paper bill worth Lt 1 circulated at the rates of 0.35, 0.30, 0.25, 0.10, and 0.08 metal gurushes in Istanbul, Konya, Aleppo, Mosul, and Baghdad, respectively.[104] The farther one got from the capital, the less paper money was worth; by 1918, it was almost worthless in many areas. Despite the dire economic conditions, the

[97] Toprak, *Milli İktisat*, pp. 191ff.

[98] Ibid., p. 333.

[99] *Düstûr*, II/8 (Istanbul: Evkaf Matbaası, 1928), pp. 892–4.

[100] Ibid., p. 674.

[101] Ibid., p. 677.

[102] *Düstûr*, II/9, p. 183.

[103] Zafer Toprak, *Türkiye'de Ekonomi ve Toplum, 1908–1950: İttihat-Terakki ve Devletçilik* (Istanbul: Yurt Yayınları, 1995), p. 24.

[104] Ibid., p. 23.

sale of Ottoman treasury bonds, purchase of which was declared a patriotic duty, turned out to be a success, as the government sold Lt 18 million worth of bonds in the last year of the war.

THE COLLAPSE OF THE EMPIRE

Ottoman defeat entailed the final dissolution of the empire. But the process of dismemberment had begun several years before. On November 3, 1914, Great Britain recognized Kuwait as an independent state under British protection. Two days later, it officially annexed Cyprus. In December, it declared Egypt a protectorate. Although these acts signified no more than the formal termination of Ottoman suzerainties over territories that had long before slipped away from central control, they were a signal of more serious things to come. From 1914 onward, the Allies coordinated a series of plans for the partition of the Ottoman Empire, each of which was rapidly overtaken by wartime developments. The Constantinople agreements of 1915 between Great Britain, France, and Russia, which awarded the Ottoman Straits to Russia (on the condition that Istanbul remain a free port), became a dead letter following the Bolshevik Revolution. Other wartime sketches of the possible fault lines of partition were the Treaty of London (1915), the Sykes-Picot agreement (1916), and the Agreement of St. Jean de Maurienne (1917). Woodrow Wilson's famous Fourteen Points of 1918 set three principles of partition: sovereignty for the Turkish portion of the empire; security of life and an unmolested opportunity for autonomous development for the non-Turkish nationalities; and the permanent opening of the Dardanelles under international guarantees as a free passageway for the ships and commerce of all nations.[105] Such lofty principles appeared easily applicable on paper; in practice, however, their implementation was no simple matter. Anglo-French conflict over some of the grey areas in these various plans, compounded by the subsequent American disengagement from the area, constituted the primary external obstacles to the smooth partition of the empire. Among the other factors that complicated its division were British commitments to Arab leaders in the Ḥijāz, Najd, and ʿAsīr in 1915–16, separate reassurances given to Sharif Ḥusayn of Mecca in January 1918, promises made to seven other Arab leaders domiciled in Egypt in June 1918, the undertaking toward world Jewry embodied in the Balfour Declaration of 1917, and the territorial demands of Greeks, Armenians, and Kurds, not to mention fierce Turkish nationalist resistance.

---

[105] [Woodrow Wilson], *Woodrow Wilson: The Essential Political Writings*, ed. Ronald J. Pestritto (Lanham, MD: Lexington Books, 2005), pp. 259–64.

After the conclusion of the war, a new Near East arose from the ruins of the Ottoman Empire, shaped and dominated by British and French power, but seething with underlying tensions of local origin. Recognizing the irretrievable loss of empire brought about by defeat in the Great War, Turkey's pragmatic leaders renounced all formal rights of empire outside of Anatolia, including all claims to Egypt, the Sudan, Libya, and Cyprus. Syria, the hotbed of Arab nationalist intellectual activity during the last years of the empire, came under French mandate in July 1920. Contrary to nationalist aspirations, some districts hitherto ruled from Damascus, as well as the northern parts of the Ottoman province of Beirut, were annexed to Mount Lebanon to form "Grand Liban," also under French mandate, in 1920. In 1921, over Turkey's strong objections, the British fused the province of Mosul with two other former Ottoman provinces, Baghdad and Basra, to form the mandate, and then state, of Iraq.[106] The British also controlled both banks of the Jordan River, the Holy Land destined to pose one of the most acute partition challenges in former Ottoman lands. In 1922, the British divided the Palestine Mandate into two artificial entities: on the East Bank, they created the Kingdom of Transjordan, which became the enduring refuge of the Hashemite family, driven out of Arabia by their rivals, the Saudis; and on the West Bank, they continued to administer the reduced mandate of Palestine, bitterly contested between Jews and Arabs ever since.

In the Arabian Peninsula, Imām Yaḥyā, who during the conflict had remained loyal to the Ottoman Empire, secured for himself an independent state in Yemen following the war. Another pro-Ottoman semi-independent leader, Saʿūd ibn ʿAbd al-ʿAzīz, amīr of the House of Rashīd in Ḥāʾil, was assassinated in 1920, following which the Rashīdī dominion was overrun by the Saudi ruler ʿAbd al-ʿAzīz ibn Saʿūd. The latter then embarked on a bitter struggle for the domination of northern Arabia against his archrival, Sharif Ḥusayn; this ended in Saudi domination of the Ḥijāz by 1925, and the ouster of the Hashemite line from the Arabian Peninsula. The Idrīsī Ṣūfī state in ʿAsīr suffered a similar fate at Saudi hands in 1930. Other beneficiaries of British protection under the 1914 Anglo-Ottoman convention shed their remaining ties to the Ottoman state at various stages of the war.

In Anatolia, the Turkish nationalists led by Mustafa Kemal Pasha ferociously resisted partition of the Anatolian core of the empire. Their success in overturning the peace settlement breezily imposed by the Allies at the end of the Great War is an astonishing episode in world history, and one which has received far less attention than it deserves. The defiance of the Turkish nationalists signified the first major challenge to the new world order and served as a harbinger of things to come.

---

[106] Mosul was officially awarded to Iraq by the League of Nations in December 1925.

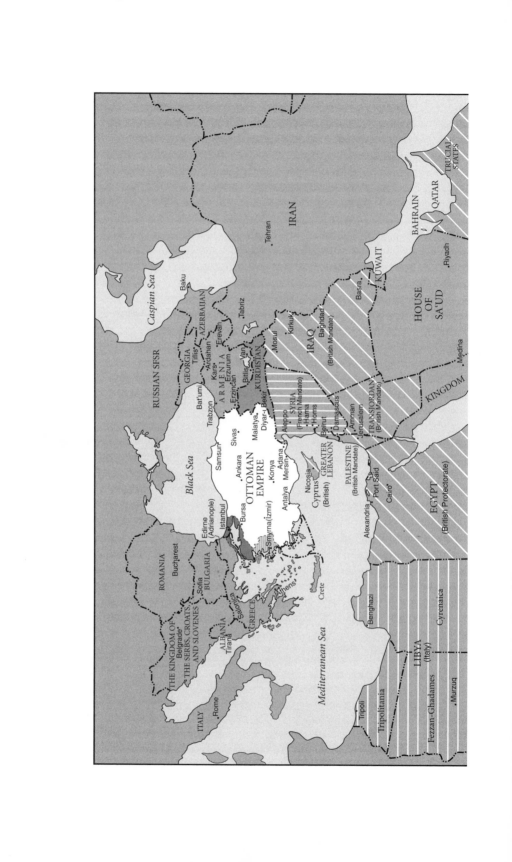

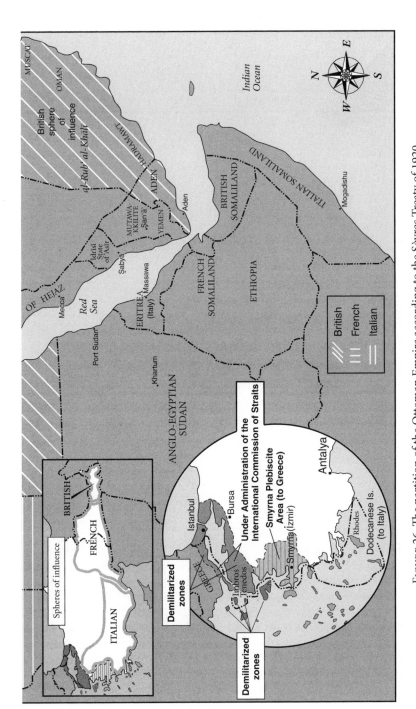

FIGURE 26. The partition of the Ottoman Empire according to the Sèvres Treaty of 1920

The harsh Treaty of Sèvres (August 1920), imposed upon the sultan's government by the victors, included provisions for the partition of Anatolia. The treaty foresaw the formation of French and Italian zones of occupation in the southeast and southwest, the cession of much of western Anatolia to Greece, and the establishment of two independent states, Armenia and Kurdistan, in the east and southeast. The residue of the territory was to remain Ottoman. Istanbul, while remaining the seat of the Ottoman government and Caliphate, was to become an international city, with free navigation through the Straits controlled by an international commission. The Ottoman state was to have a token army and navy without tanks, heavy artillery, airplanes, or battleships. The Ottoman budget was to be placed under the supervision of an Allied financial commission. Not surprisingly, Turkish nationalists, headed by the new Turkish Grand National Assembly and the nationalist government in Ankara, rejected these humiliating terms and resolved to fight to the bitter end to preclude their implementation.

In the ensuing Turkish War of Independence, the nationalist army defeated the Greeks and came to terms with the French and the Italians, thereby securing an independent Turkish state in Anatolia, and frustrating Armenian, Greek, and Kurdish aspirations. At the conclusion of the war, the Greek Orthodox population of Turkey was exchanged for the Muslim population of Greece (excluding the Greek Orthodox population of Istanbul and the Muslims of Western Thrace), thereby effectively ending Greek settlement in Anatolia. The borders set by the Treaty of Lausanne (1923) and the subsequent cession of Mosul to Iraq (1925) divided the Kurdish population of the empire between Turkey, Syria, and Iraq, thereby overturning the 62nd article of the Sèvres Treaty and shattering Kurdish aspirations for self-determination. Under the terms of the Treaty of Lausanne, the Armenians lost all hope of reestablishing a significant presence in Eastern Anatolia (as stipulated in the 89th article of the Sèvres Treaty); their sole consolation was a small homeland in Soviet Armenia which was established in 1920 and became part of the Transcaucasian Soviet Federated Socialist Republic in 1922.

Along with the myriad social problems bequeathed by the empire, the Ottoman successor states also inherited decades of imperial debt. The Treaty of Lausanne released Turkey from any obligations concerning Ottoman loans guaranteed on the basis of the Egyptian tribute, that is, the loans of 1855, 1891, and 1894. But the rest of the Ottoman debt was divided proportionally among the empire's heirs. An international referee later determined that, out of the debt of Lt 130 million (not including unpaid installments totaling Lt 30 million), Turkey would pay Lt 35 million, Greece, the Kingdom of the Serbs, Croats, and Slovenes, and Syria-Lebanon would each pay Lt 11 million, and the other heirs would incur relatively smaller amounts. ʿAsīr inherited the smallest amount, namely Lt 26,000.[107] Turkey made the last payment on the Ottoman debt in August 1948.

The abolition of the Ottoman sultanate on November 1/2, 1922 by the Turkish Grand National Assembly in Ankara dealt the *coup de grâce* to an empire that had long ceased to be one. The final institutional remnant of empire, the Caliphate, was abolished on March 3, 1924. To prevent any return to the Ottoman era, the government expelled all members of the royal family from Turkey.

The birth of numerous nation-states out of an old and vast empire, far from being a smooth natural evolution, was a messy, often painful process, which left many problems still unsolved in areas stretching from Sarajevo, Skopje, and Kosovo to Kirkuk, Nicosia, and Jerusalem. The emergence of new national boundaries left ethnic minorities stranded on either side; former communities of a multinational empire became majorities or minorities in ethnically defined nation-states with an unflinching desire for homogeneity. Social turmoil was often the result. The Bulgarian-Greek (1919–20) and the Turkish-Greek (1923–26) population exchanges, for example, involved the forced uprooting of more than two million individuals from their traditional homes and their transfer to so-called fatherlands. New borders also entailed radical changes to the socioeconomic structures of the new nation-states. For instance, the Armenian deportations and the Greek-Turkish population exchange produced an extreme scarcity in craftsmen and skilled industrial labor in Anatolia. Many important cities, such as Aleppo and Salonica, which lost their traditional hinterlands upon being detached from the empire, faced inevitable decline, and ultimately lost much of their significance. The collapse of the Ottoman Empire marked a sharp break with the past, producing an array of new structures that belong wholly to the post-Ottoman period. The problems underlying these new structures are nevertheless firmly rooted in the Ottoman legacy.

The CUP Era in Retrospect

Although it is commonly assumed that the Young Turk Revolution produced drastic changes in Ottoman domestic and foreign policy, there was far more continuity with Hamidian patterns than is generally recognized. The 1908 Revolution marked a watershed not because of the introduction of new policies in its wake, but because it made possible a sea-change in the structure of the ruling elite. Although the CUP began in stark opposition to

---

[107] İ. Hakkı Yeniay, *Yeni Osmanlı Borçları Tarihi* (Istanbul: İktisat Fakültesi Yayınları, 1964), pp. 130–33.

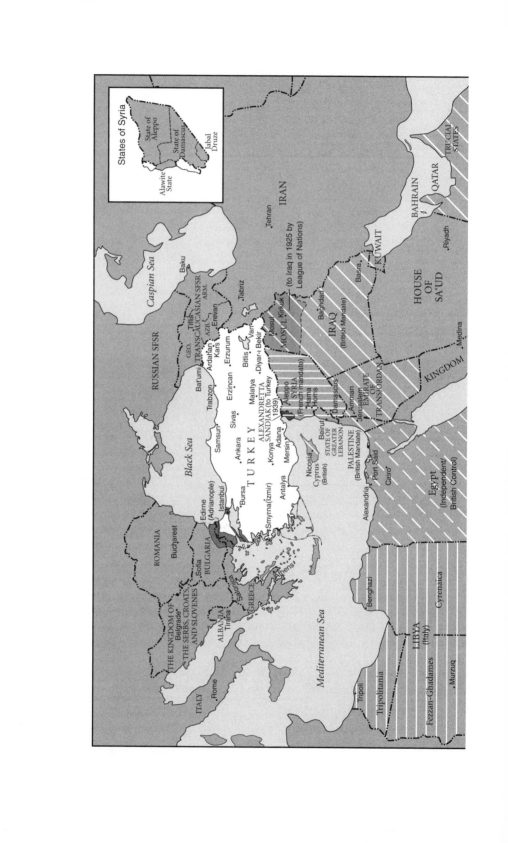

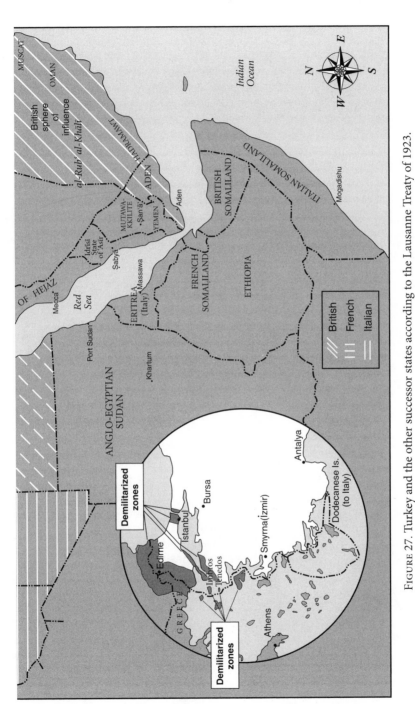

FIGURE 27. Turkey and the other successor states according to the Lausanne Treaty of 1923.

Abdülhamid II, the realities of power compelled it to follow his policies far more often than it would have liked. There is something symbolic in the famous picture taken at the state funeral of Abdülhamid II in 1918, in which the entire CUP leadership is seen following their deadly opponent's casket in solemn procession.

Politically, the most significant change that took place in this period was the introduction, however incomplete, of representation through party politics. For the first time in the history of the empire, politics was the business of political parties sponsoring competing policies and visions of the future. Although this political pluralism was not long-lasting, it caused a far more enduring change in the nature and composition of the Ottoman ruling elite. The revolution marked a changing of the guard, as new elites were swept up into politics both in the machinery of central government and in communal organization. The old elites that worked within the framework of Hamidian Ottomanism, such as the Armenian Amira class of bankers and rich artisans allied to the clergy, or the Albanian, Arab, and Kurdish notables who traded their loyalty for imperial privileges and a free hand in communal administration, lost power under the new regime. So did the religious establishments. Muslim, Christian, and Jewish religious leaders lost so much ground to the nationalist elites in the Ottoman heartlands that only in the most distant and loosely held regions of the empire in Arabia did successor states defining themselves in religious terms emerge. Even Sharif Ḥusayn of Mecca bowed to the slogans of the age, announcing his revolt on behalf of an imagined "Arab Nation." Members of the traditional elites who jumped on the nationalist bandwagon did so largely because they had no alternative.

The new elites empowered by the installation of a parliamentary system in a multinational empire were, for the most part, secular nationalists. It was mostly Turkish members of the CUP who rose to positions of prominence in the army and bureaucracy, while non-Turkish nationalists came to the fore as parliamentary deputies or regional leaders of separatist movements. Lacking the economic power and social status enjoyed by the traditional elites, the nationalist leaders exploited the new liberties of the postrevolutionary period to consolidate their power using newspapers, journals, and the ballot box. Through elections, they came to enjoy legitimacy as "the representatives of the people"—although they might disagree among themselves as to who "the people" really were—and they sought to assert the power conferred by this legitimacy in the struggle over the future of the empire.

Wars acted as a catalyst for the disintegration of the empire and the redrawing of the political map of the Balkans and Near East, giving birth to a host of successor states dominated by the elites formed during the Second Constitutional Period. In Turkey, the overwhelming majority of the Republican leaders were former CUP members; in the other successor states, nationalist elites speaking the anticolonial rhetoric pioneered by the CUP held a disproportionate share of power for many decades following the Ottoman collapse. Thus, the emergence of an intellectual, nationalist vanguard at the expense of the traditional religious and propertied elites stands out as the most significant sociopolitical legacy bequeathed by the Second Constitutional Period.

The revolution and its aftermath also saw the rise of the military in Ottoman society. Although defeat in war thwarted the late Ottoman project for building a nation in arms, the militarization of society and politics became a common feature of many of the Ottoman successor states, including Turkey. Along with the militarization of politics, the Second Constitutional Period left another lasting imprint on post-Ottoman polities: the creation of a hollow institutional façade legitimizing the ruling party. Once promoted and accepted, such fundamental tenets of a free society as elections, the right to representation, freedom of the press, and the right to assemble could not simply be suspended. But they could be largely emptied of content. In fact, the constitutional travesty that emerged during the Second Constitutional Period became the model for nearly all the nation-states that established themselves upon the ruins of the empire. One sees this pattern even in the most oppressive dictatorial regimes, such as Enver Hoxha's Albania, or the Ba'th leaderships in Syria and Iraq, which still felt it necessary to hold sham elections, maintain the illusion of an elected parliament, and sponsor a robust press tightly controlled by the state.

Ironically, the CUP's triumph in 1908 in the end proved as much of a victory for its political opponents. For four critical years, the leaders of the Committee struggled to maintain their grip on power, in part because they could not resolve their dilemma in choosing between the lofty principles of the revolution and the urge to dominate. The CUP's entire revolutionary platform rested on the case for a constitution. Immediate retreat from this goal would have been tantamount to betrayal of the people, and might have resulted in the loss of power. The "people" turned out to be at once a considerable force of legitimacy and a serious threat to CUP control. The restoration of the constitution and the institution of freely contested elections soon proved a boon to the CUP's challengers. The parliament was at once a legitimizing asset and an independent-minded body that hindered the CUP's freedom to implement their empire-saving program. Eventually, the constitutional regime was stripped of substance, even though it retained its form.

The conflict between the CUP's Turkist agenda and the multinational reality of the empire was another of many dilemmas that were resolved in an unsatisfactorily pragmatic fashion, resulting in the attenuation of revolutionary principle and the formulation of ambiguous policy. Just as the CUP's "Ottomanism" was supposed to appeal to non-Turkish communities while preserving the Turkist agenda, so too a secular interpretation of Islam was meant to pacify the ulema while maintaining the essentials of the scientistic platform. Perhaps a more uncompromising ideological attitude and the adoption of a supranational platform like that of the Bolsheviks in Russia might have saved the empire from these contradictions. But the sort of social upheaval openly espoused by the Bolsheviks was alien to the CUP worldview. In this respect, the CUP leaders resembled the Tanzimat statesmen who, by promoting the new while preserving the old, fostered an ambiguous dualism. They kept the sultan, but introduced the Committee; maintained the Islamic identity of the regime, yet endorsed secularism; espoused Turkism, yet professed Ottomanism; advocated democracy, but practiced repression; attacked imperialism, but courted empires; and proclaimed étatism while promoting liberal economics.

An uncharitable estimation of the CUP in power would attribute the ambivalence of their policies to a failure of imagination. A more generous evaluation would recognize that the CUP, like the leaders of the Tanzimat before them, and unlike the leaders of the Ottoman successor states that followed in their wake, had to come to terms with the fact that they ruled a multinational empire. They were not free to build a new state and society from scratch, primarily because they were not prepared to relinquish the empire. Ultimately, the revolutionaries of 1908 could not transcend the framework of the late Ottoman order bequeathed to them by the very Abdülhamid II they had come together to overthrow. It was up to a younger generation of revolutionaries, no longer burdened by the responsibilities of empire and the fissiparous challenge of nationalism, to abandon the Ottoman past and build something radically new.

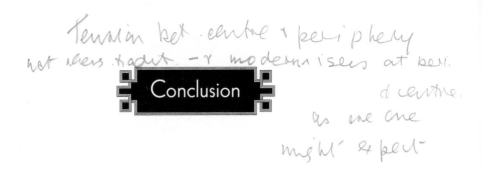

Conclusion

Tension bet. centre + periphery
not ideas trad't. — r modernises at best.
d centre.
As one one
might expect

THE HISTORY of the late Ottoman Empire exhibits several major dynamics that overlap and, at times, contradict each other. First among these is the struggle between center and periphery. Perhaps the principal theme of late Ottoman history is the attempt of the central government in the imperial capital to assert its control over a loosely held periphery which had gradually accumulated administrative, economic, and even diplomatic independence of the center. The seepage of power to the periphery peaked in 1808, when the center accorded brief legal recognition to this new balance of power. In its attempt to eradicate the old order, the center inevitably clashed with power brokers in the periphery who sought to preserve their autonomy and privileges. The crux of the center's problem with the outlying territories was not, as has often been suggested, ideological, but practical. The old order, under new circumstances, no longer afforded a cost-effective solution to the problem of ruling over a vast empire; it reduced the center to penury and powerlessness. Defense of the empire in the age of modern warfare demanded a large and professional army and navy equipped with advanced weaponry; the maintenance of such military focus depended on effective taxation; and effective taxation was not commensurate with the rule of local notables. Instead it required an effective, centralized bureaucracy. Hence the centralizing, bureaucratizing impulse that runs as a common thread through late Ottoman history.

This common-sense reaction had little to do with any struggle between "modernizers" (or "Westernizers") at the center and "reactionaries" in the periphery. In fact, in 1808 it was representatives of the periphery who attempted to impose modernization on the center. In 1839, the roles were reversed. Despite their varying ideological attitudes, *all* Ottoman administrations—from Selim III down to the CUP—strove to centralize the administration of the empire, while leaders in the periphery did their best to resist it. As the autonomous governors of Egypt and Baghdad in the early nineteenth century demonstrated, the periphery was quite capable of surpassing the center in applying European methods and technologies. For them, too, Westernization—the imitation of Europe—was not primarily an aim in and of itself, but rather an instrument for the improvement of government and society. Mehmed Ali's successful drive for European-style modernization did not automatically make him an ally of the center, despite the fact that it strove to achieve similar goals. The Ottoman central government supported Egyptian modernization as long as it enjoyed its fruits—the crushing of the rebels in the Morea, the overthrow of the Saudi state in the Arabian Peninsula, or increasing imperial tax revenues. But once Egyptian troops moved against the imperial army, and Egyptian wealth was channeled into local growth, the rulers of the empire lost any stake in Mehmed Ali's modernization policies. Similarly, the nationalist movements that later redrew the struggle along ethnic lines were led by Westernized elites fighting against a Westernized center.

Nor was the struggle between center and periphery primarily related to the rise of nationalism, although nationalism certainly intensified it. For one thing non-nationalist groups, like Zaydī insurgents in the highlands of Yemen or Ṣūfī rebels in ʿAsīr, made similar demands of the center on behalf of their regions. Images of captive nations engaged in a heroic struggle for freedom from Turkish domination only acquired relevance later. Clearly, nationalism served as a perfect ideological vehicle for mobilizing resistance in the periphery and articulating demands directed at the center and foreign powers. Adroit leaders mastered the new rhetoric to voice old, deep-rooted demands with greater vehemence and increasing success. It was tempting for historians of a nationalist orientation to recast an ambitious local ruler like Mehmed Ali as the founding hero who had forged a nation, with their very histories, in turn, contributing the foundation myths of nationhood. In reality, nationalism proved most effectual when other factors—particularly distance from the center—made its triumph feasible. Nationalist ideology enabled those seeking independence in the non-Turkish territories of the periphery to persevere in their struggle to the bitter end, while their counterparts in the Ottoman heartland—so thoroughly dominated by the hegemonic Turkish culture that they were unable to conceive of a viable entity independent of the revitalized center—quickly succumbed to force or the offer of minor concessions.

The second major feature of the late Ottoman period was the attempt to respond to the awe-inspiring challenges brought about by modernity. The Ottoman Empire was not unique in this respect. It began its journey later than most of its European counterparts, and hence initially had to rely more heavily on imitation and importation. But most of its problems were not peculiar to it; dealing with secularization, reconciling religion with scientific progress, confronting the traditional bases of society, coping with urbanization, responding to public opinion, digesting massive cultural transformation, incorporating technology into administration, adjusting to complex patterns of division of labor, defusing new tensions between center and periphery, staving off challenges to a supranational identity in the age of nationalism—all these were issues with which European counterparts of the empire also had to grapple, not to mention other Asian states.

The initial Ottoman responses to modernity can be broadly categorized under the heading of "Europeanization" (often termed "Westernization"). However, by the late nineteenth century the forging of an Ottoman modernity through a process of acculturation was almost complete. Even Islamist movements of the post-1908 period had long shed the categorical rejection of any imitation of Europe which characterized the Islamist response in earlier times. They had shifted their focus from practical questions to such abstract issues as the reconcilability of Islam with modern science and philosophy. Not unlike their counterparts the so-called Westernizers, who openly based their philosophical positions on the theses of Le Bon or Büchner, the Islamists drew on an arsenal that included not only Muḥammad ʿAbduh, but also Paul Janet and Gabriel Séailles. Thus, for all the importance of the rise of a militant materialism among the Ottoman elite, the picture of a perennial struggle between modernizers and reactionaries in the late Ottoman period is misleading.[1]

The third fundamental dynamic of late Ottoman history was the evolving relationship between the empire and the Great Powers of Europe. Writing in the wake of the tremendous growth in the power of the state in the twentieth century, it is difficult to overstress the extraordinary role played by old-fashioned diplomacy in mitigating foreign influence over domestic developments in a state as weak as the Ottoman Empire was in the nineteenth century. Still, Ottoman statesmen were able to deflect foreign demands only to a limited degree. Beyond that, they absorbed them as best they could. As a result, domestic policy in the late Ottoman Empire was related to foreign policy to an extent unparalleled before or since. In fact, it was the state's relations with European powers that provided the initial and sustaining impetus for the reforms aiming at centralization and modernization of the Ottoman administration. The primary weakness of the old order, in the eyes of the reformers, was its inability to respond effectively to external challenges. The old local armies, once summoned to arms only in times of crisis, were no longer of much use against European powers with modern military forces. Instead they served mainly as weapons in the hands of local leaders with which to defy the center. And central control over the tax base and resources of the provinces was precisely what was needed to finance military reform.

While the Ottoman government was busy trying to adapt to meet the new threats from abroad, the Great Powers were seeking to alter the empire from within. They had a host of moral and political reasons for doing so.

---

[1] Ottoman scientism was not only modern like other contemporary ideologies, but sought to monopolize modernity. This product of the late nineteenth century was not foreseen by the reformist statesmen. See my "II. Meşrutiyet Dönemi 'Garbcılığı'nın Kavramsallaştırılmasındaki Üç Temel Sorun Üzerine Not," *Doğu-Batı* 31 (February 2005), pp. 55–64.

The so-called Eastern Question was like a chameleon changing its colors with the environment. The moral argument for the liberation of oppressed Christians was not without links to domestic political considerations in the various European states that espoused it. It could also serve as a pretext for advancing expansionist ambitions, as was the case with Russia in the Balkans and the Caucasus, and with France and Italy in North Africa; or as a pretext for their deflection, as was most often the case with Austria in the Balkans. The British continually wavered between a moral perspective and a focus on the strategic need to block Russian expansion into the Near East by means of a strong Ottoman buffer. Every new crisis provided inspiration for the elaboration of new variations on these themes.

Much of the high-flown rhetoric in favor of reform emanating from the Great Powers was not genuine. By and large, European leaders opposed the wholesale transformation of the Ottoman Empire into an efficient, centralized state; they even feared the creation of a *Homo Ottomanicus*, equal to his fellow citizens and bound to them by a common identity that transcended religion, ethnicity, or tribe. Instead, they preferred a return to the administrative arrangements of the old order, in which a loose confederation— perhaps upheld by new humanistic principles and shorn of the traditional privileges accorded to Muslims—would guarantee them a continuation of the status quo. Preservation of the status quo was vital, in the eyes of European statesmen, because its collapse, whether through revolutionary change or otherwise, could trigger a serious European conflict. Moreover, the existing situation, in which favorable trade treaties guaranteed European industrial producers unrestricted access to the Ottoman market, was economically advantageous. The contradiction between strategic aims and moral rhetoric reflected the familiar tension between the demands of realpolitik and the pressure of public opinion. The artificial prolongation of Ottoman rule in the Balkans, for instance, was more the product of a desire for balance between Austria and Russia than the result of any Ottoman capabilities. Similarly, the preservation of the relative administrative unity of the Balkans under Ottoman rule owed much to the economic advantages it offered to European railroad companies eager to build extensive railroads, and to other corporations that sought the convenience of a single market with guaranteed low customs tariffs. At the same time, the fact that Ottoman rule in the Balkans allowed for an increasing measure of autonomy reflected European sensitivities to the issues of self-government and equal rights for non-Muslims.

Thus, the domestic opponents of Ottoman reform in the periphery shared their unease with powerful potential allies across the border. They looked upon every new measure of reform—including Ottoman constitutionalism— with the suspicion, if not the conviction, that it was insincere; in other words, that it represented a carefully disguised step toward Turkification. So, for instance, in 1876, both the representatives of the Great Powers and those of the Ottoman Slavs agreed that the appointment of Christian governors to administer the European provinces was preferable to the Ottoman solution of a constitution that made everybody equal before the law.

Ottoman statesmen, for their part, struggled to capitalize on the contradictions between the various European protagonists and to manipulate the rules of the European balance of power to their advantage. But the prize of second-class membership in the European club—the ultimate dividend of which was the guarantee of survival—came with a price attached, in the form of ceaseless demands for pro-Christian reform. The attempt to minimize the impact of these demands, to stave off the pressure for such reform, to stall and twist, deflect and renege, is the story of late Ottoman diplomacy.

In 1789, the Ottoman Empire, however weakened, was still in control of much of southeastern Europe; as such it was very much a European power. Yet it remained the quintessential "Other" in the eyes of the average European, and the perennial outsider vis-à-vis the major players of the great game of continental diplomacy. Several factors combined to alter this situation fundamentally. First and foremost was the reaction to the rise and fall of the Napoleonic threat to the peace of Europe. The new rules of European diplomacy after 1815 placed a premium on stability and equilibrium. To be sure, the preservation of the status quo was not meant to apply in principle to the Ottoman Empire, which was neither a signatory of any of the major treaties concluded at the end of the Napoleonic era, nor a member of the coalition that defeated Napoleon. However, in practice there was no getting around the fact that the Ottoman Empire was *European*—at least insofar as what happened in or to the Ottoman domains mattered to the European powers. In terms of the balance of power in Europe, the Ottoman Empire had only negative significance: although the empire itself could no longer threaten any of the major European powers, the prospect of its capitulation to any one Great Power posed a dreadful menace to all the others. The most serious and persistent threat came from neighboring Russia. As Russia made inroads into Ottoman sovereignty and territory in the first half of the nineteenth century, the resulting danger to British, Austrian and, to a certain degree, French strategic interests gained the Ottomans significant allies in the defense of the empire. It also highlighted the importance of the Ottoman role in the European balance against Russia. The common fear of a destabilization of the European balance of power as a result of Ottoman collapse was the empire's strongest diplomatic card in the last century of its existence. It provided Ottoman statesmen with an entry ticket into the European diplomatic arena, and gave them crucial leverage over foreign powers seeking territorial, strategic, or economic advantages at Ottoman expense.

At the same time, the French Revolution and the resultant sociopolitical changes in Europe, including the emergence of public opinion as an active force in the shaping of foreign policy, rendered obsolete the traditional view that Ottoman relations with the empire's Christian subjects were an internal Ottoman problem. Thus, a reformist interventionism crept into the dealings of many of the European powers with the empire. Additionally, European colonial powers inevitably developed an interest in the crumbling Ottoman periphery, especially in North Africa and at the strategic corners of the Arabian Peninsula. Like the Church of the pre-Reformation era, the Ottoman Empire was at once too rich (in strategic and economic terms) and too weak (in military terms) for its predators to leave it in peace. Moreover, the changes in production and transportation resulting from the industrial revolution dramatically increased the economic importance of the Ottoman market.

Thus, if the story of late Ottoman history is one of contraction in Europe and exposure to European encroachments in Asia and Africa, it is at the same time a tale of greater and more active Ottoman participation in the European concert, both politically and economically. That process continued into the twentieth century and proceeds even today.

These three major dynamics drove an astonishing transformation of the Ottoman state and society in the late nineteenth and early twentieth centuries: from a loose confederation to a relatively centralized state; from disparate administrative structures founded on ancient traditions and local arrangements to a reasonably standardized bureaucracy with a modern code of law; from a predominantly rural barter economy operating with pre-modern financial and fiscal arrangements to a monetary economy with modern budgets; from a formal organization of society along religious lines to exclusive recognition of a common Ottoman citizenship; from rule by the sultan and his court to constitutional government and ministerial responsibility; from a pre-modern army dependent on Janissaries and timariot cavalry to a professional military based on conscription; from a pre-modern system of land tenure to private ownership of property; and from a state that played the role of an aloof outsider in international affairs to one that actively participated in the European balance of power. At the end of the eighteenth century the Ottoman Empire was well on its way to becoming an anachronism; by the turn of the twentieth it was weak, militarily and financially, but by most standards modern.

If the absolute achievements of the Ottoman reforms appear impressive, it is the *relative* accomplishment of the Ottoman transformation effort that seems truly remarkable. The greatest difference between the Ottoman Empire in 1789 and its European contemporaries lay not in the nature of the challenge they faced, which was roughly equivalent, but in the enormous contrast in the existing structures that had to be revamped if the challenge were to be met. A heavy institutional inheritance stretching back to medieval times placed the Ottoman starting point perhaps several centuries behind Europe. Seen in this light, a comparison of late Ottoman history with the Japanese experience might be expected to yield more insight.[2] Yet there was a crucial difference: while Japan was free to develop its response to modernity in relatively insular security, the Ottoman state was in the middle of a predatory struggle for power on three continents.

No less daunting than the institutional deficit was the enormous gulf that separated the elite from the masses—a fissure that was far wider in the Ottoman case than in European societies, as literacy rates, for instance, suggest. This was especially true when it came to popular hostility toward many of the attributes of modernity, which in the Ottoman case was particularly closely linked to powerful aversions rooted in religion.

At the same time, a comparison of the Ottoman and European experiences in the modern age highlights the limits of the Ottoman transformation. Like the Austrians, the Ottomans ultimately failed to address the contradictions of a polyethnic empire in the age of nationalism. Clearly, a major failure of the Ottoman reform movement was the negligible progress it made toward the creation of a new political identity that could transcend traditional divisions by region, religion, or community, and thwart the rise of new ones founded on the idea of nationhood. Although Ottomanism made more headway than is commonly assumed, it failed to penetrate deeply into society and so proved ineffective in comparison with its rising competitor, nationalism. Additionally, while the administrative and economic aspects of the Ottoman transformation brought about substantial changes in Ottoman society, not least of which was a major reshuffling of the traditional social strata, the fact remains that the comparison with Europe underscores the weakness of industry, the consequent lack of an industrial working class, and the failure of a vital bourgeois class to emerge in the late Ottoman Empire. The haphazard, short-term, and often contradictory nature of Ottoman economic policy was partly to blame for this. Yet it should be remembered that Ottoman economic policies were implemented under conditions of near-constant turmoil caused by war, territorial loss, social upheaval, and heavy economic and political pressure from foreign powers. Moreover, the challenge of transforming the Ottoman economy was far greater than the equivalent challenges faced by the various Western European powers. Whereas the emergence of a bourgeoisie and industry in such European countries as Great Britain and Belgium was a

---

[2] This comparison was the subject of a major conference and a book published as its product. See *Political Modernization in Japan and Turkey*, eds. Robert E. Ward and Dankwart A. Rustow (Princeton: Princeton University Press, 1964).

result of unplanned economic, social, legal, and intellectual developments, Ottoman administrations set out to create them—a breathtaking challenge.

Finally, a few words on the role of ideas in history. The triumph in modern Turkey of a hybrid ideology made up of eighteenth-century French materialism and its vulgarized nineteenth-century German derivative should not mislead us into viewing late Ottoman history as a train with state-sponsored scientism as its final destination. Late Ottoman history, in other words, is not reducible to a prelude to the history of modern Turkey.[3] To be sure, the emergence of Republican ideology in the 1920s as a vehicle for mass-mobilization and state-building was not just an accident; but neither was it inevitable. The historical roots of the ideology of the republic may be traced back to the rise of Ottoman materialism—and its byproduct, Westernist (*Garbcı*) ideology—among the elites of the Second Constitutional Period; but its victory over the alternatives available at the time was surprising. Just as the prospect of Bolshevik victory would have struck contemporaries as improbable as late as 1917, so too the rise of Ottoman materialism from a fetish of the elites to the cornerstone of the state did not seem likely as late as 1922. And just as no historian could convincingly portray the last decades of Russian imperial history as a struggle between Bolsheviks and Tsarists, so too it is impossible to describe late Ottoman history as a simple battle between secularists and their religious opponents. As it happened, the collapse of the empire gave rise to a score of successor states;[4] only in one of them, the Republic of Turkey, did this particular ideology take root.

Scarcely less significant is the distinction between the enormous importance of this ideology, indeed of ideology in general, in the process of transformation initiated by the leaders of the Turkish Republic, and its far less salient role as an engine of historical change during the late Ottoman period. As this study has tried to demonstrate, the key processes of late Ottoman history can be explained above all, not by the logic of ideas, but by the structural constraints imposed on the leadership of the empire by geography, demography, institutions, and the examples set by European countries. This does not mean that one should approach late Ottoman history in a simple-mindedly historicist manner, seeing that the path of Ottoman history as predetermined. Rather, it means that one must begin with the recognition that the set of realistic choices that lay before the Ottoman leaders was not unlimited. One need not be a passionate Social

---

[3] Two edited volumes that appeared in the last decade of the twentieth century attempted to underscore this fact. See *Modernization in the Middle East: The Ottoman Empire and Its Afro-Asian Successors*, eds. Cyril E. Black and L. Carl Brown (Princeton: Darwin Press, 1992) and *Imperial Legacy: The Ottoman Imprint on the Balkans and the Middle East*, ed. L. Carl Brown (New York: Columbia University Press, 1996).

[4] There were, in fact, 27 successor states, if one begins the count in 1789.

Darwinist to recognize that modification of the old order became inescapable in the late eighteenth century, if the empire was to survive; or that the most logical source of inspiration for any new order was Europe. The vastness of the Ottoman state, the heterogeneous nature of its population, the magnitude and multiplicity of external threats, the relative weakness of its military institutions, and the patent inability of the old bureaucracy to marshal the financial means needed to wage modern war—all these made change imperative. At the same time, the gargantuan struggle that took place in Europe between 1789 and 1815 demonstrated the rising power of European ideas and institutions, and already hinted at the extent to which Europe would come to dominate the world economically, militarily, and politically. By and large, when Ottoman policy makers and intellectuals turned toward Europe, they did so not out of a clear, articulate ideological preference, as is often suggested by later scholars. Rather, they looked to Europe for answers because a return to the old order was thoroughly unattractive and because there was nowhere else to turn. Extreme reactionaries existed in late Ottoman society as elsewhere. But the sharp debate between them and the radical Westernizers distorts the historical reality of a consensus on the need for European-inspired change that was shared by a solid majority of the Ottoman elite from the nineteenth century onward.

A fundamental assumption underpinning this book has been that an enhanced understanding of late Ottoman history is indispensable not only to comprehend modern Turkey, or even the vast geographic area that was once ruled from Istanbul. It is also essential for the study of European and world history. The Ottoman experience provides a superb opportunity to examine the impact of modernity in a non-European setting. This brief account of this impact will have accomplished its goal if it succeeds in inspiring a new generation of scholars to take this endeavor further.

Further Reading in
Major European
Languages

THIS BOOK lays no claim to comprehensiveness. Readers who wish to read more on the topic of Ottoman history in general and late Ottoman history in particular should consult further studies. The selection given below will serve as a good starting point. For a more exhaustive list of virtually all important publications on all aspects of Ottoman history, readers are urged to consult Klaus Kreiser's meticulously compiled bibliography *Der osmanische Staat, 1300–1922* (Munich: R. Oldenbourg, 2001). For late Ottoman history more specifically, see the critical bibliographic survey in Erik J. Zürcher's *Turkey: A Modern History*, 3rd edition (London: I. B. Tauris, 2004, pp. 359–80).

Late Ottoman history is most often treated as a background for understanding modern Turkey. Less often, it is dealt with in the context of a narrative stretching from the late thirteenth century to the late twentieth. In either case, authors typically take a retrospective approach to history, attributing a teleological mission to the late Ottoman Empire. Too often it is assumed that Westernization and secularization propelled Ottoman history inexorably forward toward its ultimate goal: the modern, secular republic of Turkey. Despite this shortcoming, many such studies are valuable in terms of both factual content and analytical approach. Stanford J. Shaw's two-volume *History of the Ottoman Empire and Modern Turkey* (Cambridge: Cambridge University Press, 1976–77—the second volume was coauthored with Ezel Kural Shaw) contains numerous factual errors and a minimum of analysis, but offers a detailed description of Ottoman and Republican Turkish history until 1975. Among the books that bridge late Ottoman history and the early Republican era, Bernard Lewis's classic, *The Emergence of Modern Turkey*, 3rd edition (New York: Oxford University Press, 2002), provides a powerful analysis within the "Westernization and Modernization" paradigm, emphasizing intellectual and political history. Zürcher's aforementioned *Turkey: A Modern History* offers a stronger focus on modern Turkey, bringing the narrative up to 1980. Feroz Ahmad's *The Making of*

Modern Turkey (London: Routledge, 1993) takes the story up to 1991 in the framework of a hard-line Kemalist interpretation of late Ottoman and Republican history; it reads at times like a work of Republican propaganda from the 1930s. Shorter, less analytical, but more balanced texts with a focus on modern Turkey include Goeffrey Lewis's *Modern Turkey*, 2nd edition (London: Ernest Benn, 1974) and Roderic Davison's *Turkey: A Short History*, 3rd edition (Huntingdon, UK: Eothen Press, 1998). A much shorter survey that begins with the pre-Islamic past of the Turks and ends with an epilogue on Republican Turkey up to 1974 is Robert Mantran's *Histoire de la Turquie* (Paris: Press Universitaires de France, 1975). A readable journalistic book on Turkey with some discussion of the late Ottoman legacy is Nicole and Hugh Pope's *Turkey Unveiled: Atatürk and After* (London: John Murray, 1997).

There are several exceptions to the teleological approach to late Ottoman history. A well-researched and eloquently written book is Caroline Finkel's *Osman's Dream: The Story of the Ottoman Empire, 1300–1923* (London: John Murray, 2005). A similarly erudite but stylistically uneven work is the edited volume *Histoire de l'Empire ottoman*, ed. Robert Mantran (Paris: Fayard, 1989). Donald Quataert's *The Ottoman Empire, 1700–1922*, 2nd edition (Cambridge: Cambridge University Press, 2005) offers a concise history emphasizing social and economic affairs.

Another approach to the study of late Ottoman history is to situate it within the broader history of the Near East, though the empire was, of course, much more than a Near Eastern state. Well-written studies of the empire with a very strong emphasis on the Arab provinces include M[alcolm] E. Yapp, *The Making of the Modern Near East, 1792–1923* (London: Longman, 1987) and William L. Cleveland, *A History of the Modern Middle East*, 3rd edition (Boulder, CO: Westview Press, 2004). A recent, more analytical work including translations of key texts is James L. Gelvin, *The Modern Middle East: A History* (New York: Oxford University Press, 2005). Yet another approach to the topic has been to examine late Ottoman history within the framework of the history of the Turks, though it is problematic to reduce the history of a polyethnic empire to that of one of its chief components. A recent study along these lines is Carter Vaughn Findley's *The Turks in World History* (New York: Oxford University Press, 2005).

Those who wish to inquire further into major subfields of late Ottoman history should consult the following works. The second volume of *An Economic and Social History of the Ottoman Empire, 1300–1914* (Cambridge: Cambridge University Press, 1994), edited by Halil İnalcık and Donald Quataert, covers social and economic history. Kemal H. Karpat's *Ottoman Population, 1830–1914: Demographic and Social Characteristics* (Madison: University of Wisconsin Press, 1985) provides invaluable data on late Ottoman demographics. Donald Quataert's *Ottoman Manufacturing in the Age of the Industrial Revolution* (Cambridge: Cambridge University Press, 1993) is the standard reference on its subject. His edited volume, *Consumption Studies and the History of the Ottoman Empire, 1550–1922: An Introduction*, offers the beginnings of a treatment of the long-ignored history of consumption in the empire. Şevket Pamuk's *A Monetary History of the Ottoman*

Empire (Cambridge: Cambridge University Press, 2000) is the most comprehensive work on Ottoman monetary history in a Western European language. As for the fiscal history of the late Ottoman Empire, it has been thoroughly examined and masterfully portrayed by eminent Turkish scholars such as Halil Sahillioğlu, Yavuz Cezar, Tevfik Güran, and Coşkun Çakır. Unfortunately, their major works are in Turkish, leaving Pamuk's work, despite its monetary focus, the most relevant source in English. Valuable information may also be gleaned from A. du Velay's now century-old work, *Essai sur l'histoire financière de la Turquie depuis le règne du Sultan Mahmoud II jusqu'à nos jours* (Paris: A. Rousseau, 1903), which, for obvious reasons, omits the last two decades of the empire. Another useful source on Ottoman financial dealings with the West is Christopher Clay, *Gold for the Sultan: Western Bankers and Ottoman Finance 1856–1881: A Contribution to Ottoman and to International Financial History* (London: I. B. Tauris, 2000). As for intellectual history, Niyazi Berkes's *The Development of Secularism in Turkey* (Montreal: McGill University Press, 1964) provides detailed information about the main intellectual currents in the late imperial period, but its construction of late Ottoman history as a bipolar struggle between benevolent, well-informed "secularists" and malevolent, ignorant "religious fundamentalists" epitomizes the simplifications of the progressive school of history. *Late Ottoman Society: The Intellectual Legacy* (London: RoutledgeCurzon, 2005), edited by Elisabeth Özdalga, is informative but not methodical or highly analytical. There is no comprehensive text in a major European language on late Ottoman diplomatic history. M. S. Anderson's *The Eastern Question, 1774–1923: A Study in International Relations* (London: Macmillan, 1966) remains the best general source for understanding the European context of Ottoman foreign relations.

Bibliography

ARCHIVAL SOURCES

Archives of the Turkish Embassy in Paris
  Dossier 244

BOA [*Başbakanlık Osmanlı Arşivi/Prime Ministry Archives*] (Istanbul)
  Sections:
  A.AMD.MV (Amedî-Meclis-i Vükelâ)
  A.DVN.NMH (Amedî-Divân-ı Hümayûn, Nâme-i Hümayûn)
  Ayniyat
  BEO (Bâb-ı Âlî Evrak Odası)
  BEO/Mahremâne Müsveddat
  DH.EUM (Dahiliye Nezâreti Emniyet-i Umumiye Müdiriyeti Kalemi)
  DH.İD (Dahiliye İdarî)
  DH.KMS (Dahiliye Nezâreti Kalem-i Mahsus)
  DH.MB.HPS (Dahiliye Hapishaneler)
  DH.SYS (Dahiliye Siyasî)
  Divân-ı Hümayûn: Muharrerat-ı Umumîye
  DUİT (Dosya Usûlü İradeler Tasnifi)
  DVN (Divân-ı Hümayûn)
  HR.SYS (Hariciye Siyasî)
  HH (Hatt-ı Hümayûn)
  İrade-Dahiliye
  İrade-Meclis-i Mahsus
  MM (Maliyeden Müdevver)
  Muahede ve Mukavelenâme
  MV (Meclis-i Vükelâ Mazbataları)
  ŞD (Şûra-yı Devlet)
  YEE (Yıldız Esas Evrakı)
  Y.Mtv (Yıldız Mütenevvia)
  YP (Yıldız Perâkende)

This bibliography does not include all works cited in "Further Reading in Major European Languages."

Bundesarchiv (Berlin)
Nachlaß Fürsten von Bülow, nr. 82

İstanbul Müftülük Arşivi (Istanbul)
ŞS [*Şer'iye Sicilleri/ Sharī'a Court Records*], volumes 125–48, 150–52, 154, 159, 162, 167, 170, 173, 176, 178–93, 195, 203, 209, 211, 215, 226, 239, 243, 251, 256, 263, 269, 274, 276, 278, 281, 283, 285, 289, 291, 293, 297, 298, 302, 304, 308, 313, 317, 320, 322, 326–7, 329–30, 336, 338–9, 341, 343, 346, 351, 357, 363, 368, 373, 377, 380, 382, 386, 388, 390, 392, 395–6, 403–4, 410, 413, 417, 420, 426, 429, 432, 436, 440, 442, 447, 451–2, 458, 462, 468, 473, 478, 483, 487, 491, 493, 496–8, 501, 504, 507, 511, 514, 516, 523, 527, 531, 536, 540, 544, 549, 551, 556, 558, 560–61, 563, 565, 572, 576–7, 580, 582–3, 586, 590–91, 598, 601, 604, 608, 614–15, 618, 622, 624–5, 628, 631, 635, 639, 643–4, 647–8, 653–4, 660–61, 667, 672, 676, 679, 684, 687, 689, 691, 694, 696, 701, 707, 710, 715–16, 718, 720, 734, 736–8, 740, 743–4, 1478, 1642, 1658, 1657, 1664, 1677, 1698, 1706, 1715, 1743, 1785, and 1819.

National Archives (Washington, DC)
Dispatches from U.S. Ministers to Turkey (1818–1906), 72 (July 1–December 29, 1902)

PRO [Public Record Office] (London)*
F.O. [Foreign Office]
    371: General Correspondence: Turkey
    424/37, 46: Confidential Print
    800/79: Sir (Viscount) Grey's Private Papers, Turkey, 1905–10
CAB [*Cabinet Papers*]
    38

Royal Archives, Windsor Castle (Windsor, Berkshire)
(M) H.

TSA (Topkapı Sarayı Arşivi/ Topkapı Palace Archives) (Istanbul)
E. 1518/1

TSentralen Dürzhaven Arkhiv (Sofia)
Fond. 3 K: Monarkhicheski institut

PRIVATE PAPERS

Private Papers of Ahmed Rıza (in the author's private collection)
Private Papers of Dr. Bahaeddin Şakir (in the author's private collection)
Ernst Jäckh Papers, Yale University (New Haven), MSS 466

*Since the merger of the Public Record Office of the United Kingdom with the Historical Manuscripts Commission and the Office of Public Sector Information forming the National Archives in 2003–2004, the title "Public Record Office" has not been used officially. Like many other scholars, I preferred to use it to avoid confusion with the National Archives in Washington, D.C.

Manuscripts

[Abdülhamid Ziyaüddin]. *Ziya Paşa'nın Rüyanâmesi*, IUL, İbnülemin Mahmud Kemal İnal Mss., no. 2461.

[Abdullah Tatarcıkzâde]. *Lâyiha-i Tatarcıkzâde Abdullah Molla Efendi*, IUL, Turkish Mss., no. 6930.

Ahmed Salâhi. *Osmanlı ve Avrupa Politikası ve Abdulhamid-i Sanî'nin Siyaseti*, IUL, Turkish Mss., D. 2/9521 (1303 [1885]).

1247 Senesi'nde Memâlik-i Şâhâne'de Mevcud Nüfûs Defteri, IUL, Turkish Mss., no. 8867.

Devlet-i Aliyye-i Osmaniye'nin Bin Üç Yüz On Üç Senesine Mahsus İstatistik-i Umumîsidir, IUL, Turkish Mss., no. 9184.6.

Ebubekir Ratib. *Tuhfet'ül-Sefaret fi'l-Ahvâl-i Asâkir el-Nasara ve'l-İdare*, TPL, H. 613.

İbrahim Kâmi. *Humbara Risâlesi*, TPL, H. 619.

İsmail Çınarî. *Humbara İrtifa'at ve Mesafât Cedveli*, TPL, H. 640.

[Mahmud Nedim]. *Sadr-ı âzâm Mahmud Nedim Paşa'nın Âyine-i Devlete Dair Kitabı*, Fatih Millet Library Mss., no. Trh. 1022.

Mehmed bin Süleyman. *Risâle-i Humbara*, TPL, H. 631.

Mehmed Emin Behic. *Sevânih el-Levâyih*, TPL, H. 370.

[Rasih Mustafa]. *Sefaretnâme-i Rasih Efendi*, IUL, Turkish Mss., no. 3887.

Risâle der Beyân-ı Lüzûm-ı Temeddün ve İctima'-i Beni Âdem, Süleymaniye Library, Halet Efendi Mss., no. 765/13 [1815–16].

Spinoza Mektebine Reddiye, TPL, H. 372.

Su'al-i Osmanî ve Cevab-ı Nasranî [a copy made in 1719], TPL, H. 1634.

Tercüme-i Risâle-i Fenn-i Harb, tr. Constantinos Ypsilanti, TPL, H. 615.

Vauban, Sébastien Le Prestre de. *Darben ve Def'an Muhasara ve Muharese-i Kıla' ve Husun*, tr. Constantinos Ypsilanti, TPL, H. 614.

Official Publications and Collections of Documents

Düstûr
First Series:
1 (Istanbul: Matbaa-i Âmire, 1289 [1872])
2 (Istanbul: Matbaa-i Âmire, 1289 [1872])
3 (Istanbul: Matbaa-i Âmire, 1289 [1872])
4 (Istanbul: Matbaa-i Âmire, 1295 [1880])
Second Series:
1 (Istanbul: Matbaa-i Osmaniye, 1329 [1911])
4 (Istanbul: Matbaa-i Âmire, 1331 [1913])

6 (Istanbul: Matbaa-i Âmire, 1334 [1916])

7 (Istanbul: Matbaa-i Âmire, 1336 [1918])

8 (Istanbul: Evkaf Matbaası, 1928)

9 (Istanbul: Evkaf Matbaası, 1928)

Documents diplomatiques: Les affaires balkaniques, 1912–1914, 1 (Paris: Imprimerie nationale, 1922).

Die Große Politik der europäischen Kabinette, 38: Neue Gefahrenzonen im Orient, 1913–1914 (Berlin: Deutsche Veragsgesellschaft für Politik und Geschichte, 1926).

Muʿaddel Kanun-i Esasî ve İntihab-ı Mebʿusan Kanunu, ed. Tevfik Tarık (Istanbul: İkbal Kütübhanesi, 1327 [1912]).

The Parliamentary History of England, ed. William Cobett, 29 (London: R. Bagshaw, 1817).

Recueil des traités, conventions, protocoles, arrangements et déclarations signés entre l'Empire ottoman et les Puissances étrangères, 1903–1922, 1 (*1903–1916*), ed. Sinan Kuneralp (Istanbul: The Isis Press, 2000).

MAJOR OTTOMAN WORKS OF HISTORY

Ahmed Âsım. *Âsım Tarihi,* 1-2 ([Istanbul]: Ceride-i Havâdis Matbaası, [1867]).

Ahmed ʿAtaullah (Tayyarzâde). *Tarih-iʿAta,* 4 (Istanbul: s.n., 1293 [1877]).

Ahmed Cevdet. *Maʿrûzât,* ed. Yusuf Halaçoğlu (Istanbul: Çağrı Yayınları, 1980).

———.*Tezâkir,* 1, ed. Cavid Baysun (Ankara: Türk Tarih Kurumu Yayınları, 1953).

———.*Tarih-i Cevdet,* 1–2, 4–12 (Istanbul: Matbaa-i Osmaniye, 1309 [1891]).

Ahmed Lûtfî. *Tarih-i Lûtfî,* 1 (Istanbul: Matbaa-i Âmire, 1290 [1873]); 3 (Istanbul: Matbaa-i Âmire, 1875), 5 (Istanbul: Mahmud Bey Matbaası, 1292 [1875]); 6 (Istanbul: Mahmud Bey Matbaası, 1302 [1885]); 7 (Istanbul: Mahmud Bey Matbaası, 1306 [1889]); 8 (Istanbul: Sabah Matbaası, 1328 [1910]).

Ahmed Vâsıf. *Mehasinü'l-Âsâr ve Hakaikü'l-Ahbâr,* ed. Mücteba İlgürel (Ankara: Türk Tarih Kurumu Yayınları, 1994).

Mahmud Celâleddin. *Mir'at-ı Hakikat,* 1 (Istanbul: Matbaa-i Osmaniye, 1326 [1908]).

Mehmed ʿAtaullah (Şânizâde). *Şânizâde Tarihi,* 1–2 ([Istanbul]: Süleyman Efendi Matbaası, 1290 [1873]); 3 ([Istanbul]: s.n., 1291 [1874]).

Mehmed Raşid. *Tarih-i Raşid,* 2 (Istanbul: s.n., [1865]).

Mustafa Nuri. *Netayicü'l-vukuʿat,* 4 (Istanbul: Uhuvvet Matbaası, 1327 [1909]).

Raşid Belgradî. *Tarih-i Vakʿa-i Hayretnüma Belgrad ve Sırpistan,* 1 ([Istanbul]: Tatyos Divitçiyan Matbaası, 1291 [1874]).

BOOKS

Abdurrahman Vefik. *Tekâlif Kavâidi*, 1 (Istanbul: Kanaat Kütübhanesi, 1328 [1910]); 2 (Istanbul: Kanaat Kütübhanesi, 1330 [1912]).

Adıvar, Abdülhak Adnan. *Osmanlı Türklerinde İlim* (Istanbul: Maarif Matbaası, 1943).

[Ahmed Cemal]. *Cemal Paşa Hâtıratı, 1913–1922* (Istanbul: Ahmed İhsan ve Şürekâsı, 1339 [1922]).

Ahmed Midhat. *Avrupa Âdâb-ı Muaşereti yahud Alafranga* (Istanbul: İkdam Matbaası, 1312 [1894]).

———. *Üss-i İnkılâb*, 2 (Istanbul: Takvim-i Vekayiʿ Matbaası, 1295 [1878]).

Ahmed Naʿim. *İslâmda Daʿva-yı Kavmiyyet* (Istanbul: Tevsiʿ-i Tıbaʿat Matbaası, 1332 [1914]).

Ahmed Niyazi. *Hâtırat-ı Niyazi yahud Tarihçe-i İnkılâb-ı Kebîr-i Osmanîden Bir Sahife* (Istanbul: Sabah Matbaası, 1324 [1908]).

Ahmed Refik. *İnkılâb-ı Azîm* (Istanbul: Asır Matbaası, 1324 [1908]).

[Altınay], Ahmet Refik. *Hicrî On Üçüncü Asırda Istanbul Hayatı, 1200–1255* (Istanbul: Istanbul Matbaacılık, 1932).

Anderson, M[atthew] S[mith]. *The Eastern Question, 1774–1923: A Study in International Relations* (London: Macmillan, 1966).

Autheman, André. *La Banque Impériale Ottomane* (Paris: Ministère de l'économie et des finances, 1996).

Bağış, Ali İhsan. *Osmanlı Ticaretinde Gayrî Müslimler: Kapitülasyonlar, Avrupa Tüccarları, Beratlı Tüccarlar, Hayriye Tüccarları, 1750–1839* (Ankara: Turhan Kitabevi, 1983).

[Beauchamp, Alphonse de]. *The Life of Ali Pacha of Janina, Vizier of Epirus, Surnamed Aslan, or the Lion from Various Authentic Documents* (London: Lupton Relfe, 1822).

Beşir Fu'ad. *Victor Hugo* (Istanbul: Ceb Kütübhanesi, 1302 [1885]).

Bilge, M. Sadık. *Osmanlı Devleti ve Kafkasya: Osmanlı Varlığı Döneminde Kafkasya'nın Siyasî-Askerî Tarihi ve İdarî Taksimatı, 1454–1829* (Istanbul: Eren, 2005).

Bilgegil, M. Kaya. *Yakın Çağ Türk Kültür ve Edebiyatı Üzerinde Araştırmalar*, 1: *Yeni Osmanlılar* (Ankara: Atatürk Üniversitesi Yayınları, 1976).

Biliotti, Adrien. *La Banque Impériale Ottomane* (Paris: Henri Jouve, 1909).

Birinci, Ali. *Hürriyet ve İtilâf Fırkası: II. Meşrutiyet Devrinde İttihat ve Terakki'ye Karşı Çıkanlar* (Istanbul: Dergâh Yayınları, 1990).

Blaisdell, Donald C. *European Financial Control in the Ottoman Empire: A Study of the Establishment, Activities, and Significance of the Administration of the Ottoman Public Debt* (New York: Columbia University Press, 1929).

[Burckhardt, John Lewis]. *Johann Ludwig Burckhardt's Reisen in Nubien* (Weimar: Landes-Industrie-Comptoirs, 1820).

Bogorov, I[van] A[ndraev]. *Niakolko dena razkhodka po bŭlgarskite mesta* (Bucharest: K. N. Radulescu, 1868).

Büchner, Louis [Ludwig]. *Madde ve Kuvvet*, 1–3, tr. Baha Tevfik and Ahmed Nebil (Istanbul: Teceddüd-i İlmî ve Felsefî Kütübhanesi, [1911]).

Byron, [George Gordon]. *Childe Harold's Pilgrimage*, ed. A. H. Thompson (Cambridge: Cambridge University Press, 1931).

Çakır, Serpil. *Osmanlı Kadın Hareketi* (Istanbul: Metis Yayınları, 1994).

Çankaya, Mücellidoğlu Ali. *Son Asır Türk Tarihinin Önemli Olayları ile Birlikde Yeni Mülkiye Tarihi ve Mülkiyeliler*, 1: *Mülkiye Tarihi, 1859–1968* (Ankara: Mars Matbaası, 1968–69).

Cezar, Mustafa. *Osmanlı Tarihinde Levendler* (Istanbul: Güzel Sanatlar Akademisi Yayınları, 1965).

Cezar, Yavuz. *Osmanlı Maliyesinde Bunalım ve Değişim Dönemi: XVIII. yy dan Tanzimat'a Mali Tarih* (Istanbul: Alan Yayıncılık, 1986).

Commins, David Dean. *Islamic Reform: Politics and Social Change in Late Ottoman Syria* (New York: Oxford University Press, 1990).

Davison, Roderic H. *Reform in the Ottoman Empire, 1856–1871* (Princeton: Princeton University Press, 1963).

Deringil, Selim. *The Well-Protected Domains: Ideology and the Legitimation of Power in the Ottoman Empire, 1876–1909* (London: I.B. Tauris, 1998).

Devereux, Robert. *The First Ottoman Constitutional Period: A Study of the Midhat Constitution and Parliament* (Baltimore: Johns Hopkins Press, 1963).

Dinekov, Petŭr. *Sofiia prez XIX vek do osvobozhdenieto na Bŭlgariia*, 9: *Materiali za istoriiata na Sofiia* (Sofia: Bŭlgarski arkheologicheski institut, 1937).

Eldem, Vedat. *Osmanlı İmparatorluğunun İktisadi Şartları Hakkında Bir Tetkik* (Istanbul: Türkiye İş Bankası Kültür Yayınları, 1970).

Engelhardt, Ed[ouard]. *La Turquie et le Tanzimat; ou Histoire des réformes dans l'Empire ottoman depuis 1826 jusqu'à nos jours*, 1 (Paris: A. Cotillon, 1882).

Ergin, Osman. *Türkiye Maarif Tarihi*, 2: *Tanzimat Devri Mektepleri* (Istanbul: Osmanbey Matbaası, 1940).

Fortna, Benjamin J. *Imperial Classroom: Islam, the State, and Education in the Late Ottoman Empire* (Oxford: Oxford University Press, 2002).

Freidenberg, M[aren] M[ikhailovich]. *Dubrovnik i Osmanskaia Imperiia* (Moscow: Izdatel'stvo Nauka, 1989).

Genç, Mehmet. *Osmanlı İmparatorluğunda Devlet ve Ekonomi* (Istanbul: Ötüken, 2000).

Gencer, Ali İhsan. *Bahriye'de Yapılan Islahât Hareketleri ve Bahriye Nezâreti'nin Kuruluşu, 1789–1867* (Istanbul: Edebiyat Fakültesi Yayınları, 1985).

Georgeon, François. *Abülhamid II: Le sultan calife, 1876–1909* (Paris: Librairie Arthème Fayard, 2003).

Gladstone, W[illiam] E[wart]. *The Gladstone Diaries with Cabinet Minutes and Prime-Ministerial Correspondence*, 9 (January 1875–December 1880), ed. H.C.G. Matthew (Oxford: Clarendon Press, 1986).

———. *Bulgarian Horrors and the Question of the East* (London: John Murray, 1876).

Gordlevskii, V[ladimir] A[leksandrovich]. *Izbrannye sochineniia*, 2 (Moscow: Izdatel'stvo Vostochnoi Literaturi, 1961).

Hammer [-Purgstall], Joseph von. *Geschichte der osmanischen Dichtkunst*, 4: *von der Regierung Sultan Suleiman's II bis auf unsere Zeit, 1687–1838* (Pest: Hartleben's Verlag, 1838).

———. *Geschichte des osmanischen Reiches*, 7: *vom Carlowiczer bis zum Belgrader Frieden, 1699–1739* (Pest: Hartleben's Verlage, 1831).

Hanioğlu, M. Şükrü. *Preparation for a Revolution: The Young Turks, 1902–1908* (New York: Oxford University Press, 2001).

———. *The Young Turks in Opposition* (New York: Oxford University Press, 1995).

Hasan Ferid. *Nakd ve İ'tibar-ı Malî*, 2: *Evrak-ı Nakdiye* (Istanbul: Matbaa-i Âmire, 1334 [1918]).

Heller, Joseph. *British Policy towards the Ottoman Empire, 1908–1914* (London: Frank Cass, 1983).

Helmreich, E[rnst] Christian. *The Diplomacy of the Balkan Wars, 1912–1913* (Cambridge, MA: Harvard University Press, 1938).

Hisar, Abdülhak Şinasi. *Boğaziçi Yalıları, Geçmiş Zaman Köşkleri* (Istanbul: Bağlam Yayınları, 1997).

[İbrahim] Şinasi. *Fransız Lisanından Nazmen Tercüme Eylediğim Bâzı Eş'ar* (Istanbul: Press d'Orient, 1859).

İğdemir, Uluğ. *Kuleli Vak'ası Hakkında Bir Araştırma* (Ankara: Türk Tarih Kurumu Yayınları, 1937).

İhsanoğlu, Ekmeleddin. *Mısır'da Türkler ve Kültürel Mirasları* (Istanbul: IRCICA, 2006).

Imperial Legacy: The Ottoman Imprint on the Balkans and the Middle East, ed. L. Carl Brown (New York: Columbia University Press, 1996).

İnal, İbnülemin Mahmud Kemal. *Osmanlı Devrinde Son Sadrıazamlar*, 2, 4, 6, 9 (Istanbul: Millî Eğitim Basımevi, 1940).

İskit, Server. *Türkiyede Matbuat İdareleri ve Politikaları* (Istanbul: Başvekâlet Basın Yayın Umum Müdürlüğü, 1943).

———. *Türkiyede Neşriyat Hareketleri Tarihine Bir Bakış* (Istanbul: Maarif Vekâleti, 1939).

İttihad-ı Anâsır-ı Osmaniye [Istanbul]: 1327 [1911].

Karal, Enver Ziya. *Selim III'ün Hat-tı Hümayunları: Nizam-ı Cedit, 1789–1807* (Ankara: TTK Yayınları, 1946).

———. *Selim III.ün Hatt-ı Humayunları* (Ankara: TTK Yayınları, 1942).

Karpat, Kemal H. *Ottoman Population, 1830–1914: Demographic and Social Characteristics* (Madison: University of Wisconsin Press, 1986).

Kaynar, Reşat. *Mustafa Reşit Paşa ve Tanzimat* (Ankara: Türk Tarih Kurumu Yayınları, 1954).

Khristomatiia po istoriia na Bŭlgariia, 2, eds. Khristo A. Khristov and Nikolai Genchev (Sofia: Nauka i izkustvo, 1969).

Kressenstein, [Friedrich] Kreß von. *Mit den Türken zum Suezkanal* (Berlin: Otto Schlegel, 1938).

Kushner, David. *The Rise of Turkish Nationalism, 1876–1908* (London: Frank Cass, 1977).

Kütükoğlu, Mübahat S. *Osmanlı-İngiliz İktisâdî Münâsebetleri*, 1 (*1580–1838*) (Ankara: TKAE Yayınları, 1974).

Kuveyt Mes'elesi (Istanbul: Matbaa-i Âmire, 1334 [1917]).

Larcher, M[aurice]. *La guerre turque dans la guerre mondiale* (Paris: E. Chiron, 1926).

Lemke, Mikh[ail]. *Ocherki po istorii Russkoi tsenzury i zhurnalistiki XIX stolietiia* (St. Petersburg: Knigoizdatel'stvo M.V. Pirozhkova, 1904).

Lewis, Bernard. *The Muslim Discovery of Europe* (New York: W.W. Norton, 1982).

MacFarlane, Charles. *Turkey and Its Destiny: The Result of Journeys Made in 1847 and 1848 to Examine into the State of That Country*, 2 (London: John Murray, 1850).

Mahmud Muhtar. *Maziye Bir Nazar: Berlin Mu'ahedesi'nden Harb-i Umumî'ye Kadar Avrupa ve Türkiye Münâsebâtı* (Istanbul: Matbaa-i Ahmed İhsan ve Şürekâsı, 1341 [1925]).

Mardin, Ebül'ulâ. *Medenî Hukuk Cephesinden Ahmet Cevdet Paşa* (Istanbul: Hukuk Fakültesi Yayınları, 1946).

Mardin, Şerif. *The Genesis of Young Ottoman Thought: A Study in the Modernization of Turkish Political Ideas* (Princeton: Princeton University Press, 1962).

Mehmed Cavid. *İlm-i İktisad*, 1 (Istanbul: Matbaa-i Âmire, 1326 [1910]).

[Mehmed Emin Âlî]. *Réponse à son altesse Moustapha Fazil Pacha au sujet de sa lettre au Sultan* ([Paris]: Imprimerie Jouaust, 1867).

Mehmed Es'ad. *Üss-i Zafer* ([Istanbul]: Matbaa-i Süleyman Efendi, 1293 [1876]).

[Mehmed Kâmil]. *Hâtırat-ı Sadr-ı Esbak Kâmil Paşa* (Istanbul: Matbaa-i Ebüzziya, 1329 [1911]).

[Mehmed] Mourad. *Le palais de la Yildiz et la Sublime Porte: Le véritable mal d'Orient* (Paris: Imprimerie Centrale, 1895).

Mehmed Nâbi and Rumbeyoğlu Fahreddin. *Gümrük Resmi'nin Yüzde On Beşe İblâğı, Ecnebî Postaları ve Kapitülâsyon* (Istanbul: Matbaa-i Âmire, 1334 [1917]).

———. *Hadramut Mes'elesi* (Istanbul: Matbaa-i Âmire, 1334 [1917]).

———. *Maskat Mes'elesi* (Istanbul: Matbaa-i Âmire, 1334 [1917]).

Mehmed Nuri and Mahmud Naci. *Trablusgarb* (Istanbul: Tercüman-ı Hakikat Matbaası, 1330 [1912]).

[Mehmed] Rıza. *Hülâsa-i Hâtırat* (Istanbul: s.n., 1325 [1909]).

[Mehmed] Sa'id. *Gazeteci Lisanı* (Istanbul: Sabah Matbaası, 1327 [1909]).

Memâlik-i Osmaniye Ceb Atlası: Devlet-i Aliyye-i Osmaniye'nin Ahvâl-i Coğrafiyye ve İstatistikiyyesi, eds. Tüccarzâde İbrahim Hilmi and Binbaşı Subhi (Istanbul: Kütübhane-i İslâm ve Askerî, 1323 [1905]).

Midhat Paşa: Hayat-ı Siyasiyesi, Hidemâtı, Menfa Hayatı, 1: *Tabsıra-i İbret*, ed. Ali Haydar Midhat (Istanbul: Hilâl Matbaası, 1325 [1909]).

Miller, A[natolii] F[ilippovich]. *Mustafa Pasha Bairaktar: Ottomanskaia imperiia v nachale XIX veka* (Moscow: Izdatel'stvo Akademii Nauk, 1947).

Modernization in the Middle East: The Ottoman Empire and Its Afro-Asian Successors, eds. Cyril E. Black and L. Carl Brown (Princeton: Darwin Press, 1992).

Mosse, W. E. *The Rise and Fall of the Crimean System, 1855–71: The Story of a Peace Settlement* (London: MacMillan, 1963).

Mustafa Fâzıl. *Paris'den Bir Mektub: Sultan Abdülaziz Han'a Cemiyet-i Ahrar Re'isi Mısırlı Mustafa Fâzıl Paşa Merhum Tarafından Gönderilen Mektubun Tercümesidir* (Istanbul: Artin Asadoryan Matbaası, 1326 [1908]).

Nevsâl-ı Millî: 1330, ed. T. Z. (Istanbul: Artin Asadoryan, 1330 [1914]).

Okay, M. Orhan. *Beşir Fuad: İlk Türk Pozitivist ve Natüralisti* (Istanbul: Hareket Yayınları, 1969).

Orhonlu, Cengiz. *Osmanlı İmparatorluğu'nun Güney Siyaseti: Habeş Eyaleti* (Istanbul: Edebiyat Fakültesi Yayınları, 1974).

———. *Osmanlı İmparatorluğunda Aşiretleri İskân Teşebbüsü, 1691–1696* (Istanbul: Edebiyat Fakültesi Yayınları, 1963).

Ortaylı, İlber. *İmparatorluğun En Uzun Yüzyılı* (Istanbul: Hil Yayın, 1987).

———. *Tanzimattan Sonra Mahalli İdareler, 1840–1878* (Ankara: TODAİE, 1974).

Osmanlı İttihad ve Terakki Cemiyeti Program ve Nizamnâmesidir: 1329 Senesi Umumî Kongresi'nde Tanzim ve Kabul Olunmuşdur (Istanbul: Matbaa-i Hayriye ve Şürekâsı, 1329 [1913]).

Özkaya, Yücel. *Osmanlı İmparatorluğu'nda Âyânlık* (Ankara: Türk Tarih Kurumu Yayınları, 1994).

———. *Osmanlı İmparatorluğunda Dağlı İsyanları, 1791–1808* (Ankara: A. Ü. Dil ve Tarih-Coğrafya Fakültesi Yayınları, 1983).

Pamuk, Şevket. *İstanbul ve Diğer Kentlerde 500 Yıllık Fiyatlar ve Ücretler, 1469–1998* (Ankara: Devlet İstatistik Enstitüsü, 2000).

Philipp, Thomas. *Acre: The Rise and Fall of a Palestinian City, 1730–1831* (New York: Columbia University Press, 2001).

Political Modernization in Japan and Turkey, eds. Robert E. Ward and Dankwart A. Rustow (Princeton: Princeton University Press, 1964).

[Qemali, Ismail]. *The Memoirs of Ismail Kemal Bey*, ed. Sommerville Story (London: Constable, 1920).

Quataert, Donald. *Ottoman Manufacturing in the Age of the Industrial Revolution* (Cambridge: Cambridge University Press, 1993).

Ranke, Leopold von. *Die serbische Revolution: Aus serbischen Papieren und Mittheilungen* (Berlin: Duncker und Humblot, 1844).

Rauf Ahmed and Ragıb Raif. *Boğazlar Mes'elesi* (Istanbul: Matbaa-i Osmaniye, 1334 [1918]).

———. *Mısır Mes'elesi* (Istanbul: Matbaa-i Âmire, 1334 [1918]).

Rudūd al-ʿulamāʾ ʿalā madhhab Darwin fīʾl-irtiqāʾ (Beirut: Maṭbaʿat al-Mursalīn al-Yasūʿīyīn, 1886).

S. M. *Alafranga Bir Hanım: Ahlâk-ı Nisvâniyeyi Musavvir Romandır* (Istanbul: Artin Asadoryan, 1329 [1911]).

Saʿid Halim. *Buhranlarımız: Meşrutiyet* (Istanbul: Şems Matbaası, 1335 [1919]).

Saint-Denys, A[ntoine] de Jucherau de. *Révolutions de Constantinople en 1807 et 1808*, 1 (Paris: Brissot-Thivars, 1819).

Sanders, [Otto] Liman von. *Fünf Jahre Türkei* (Berlin: August Scherl, 1920).

Şerafeddin Mağmumî. *Başlangıç* (Istanbul: İstepan Matbaası, 1307 [1888–1890]).

Shaw, Stanford J. *Between Old and New: The Ottoman Empire under Sultan Selim III, 1789–1807* (Cambridge, MA: Harvard University Press, 1971).

———. *Ottoman Egypt in the Age of the French Revolution by Ḥuseyn Efendî* (Cambridge, MA: Harvard University Press, 1964).

———. *The Financial and Administrative Organization and Development of Ottoman Egypt, 1517–1798* (Princeton: Princeton University Press, 1962).

Shiblī Shumayyil. *al-Ḥaqīqah wa-hiya risālah tataḍamman rudūdan li-ithbāt madhhab Darwin fī al-nushūʾ waʾl-irtiqāʾ* (Cairo: al- Muqtaṭaf, 1885).

Şiir Tahlilleri: Âkif Paşadan Yahya Kemalʾe Kadar, ed. Mehmed Kaplan (Istanbul: Anıl Yayınevi, 1958).

Söylemezoğlu, Galip Kemali. *Hariciye Hizmetinde Otuz Sene, 1892–1922*, 1 (Istanbul: Şaka Matbaası, 1950).

Subhi Edhem. *Darwinizm* (Monastir: Beynʾel-milel Ticaret Matbaası, 1327 [1911]).

Sulaymān Musā. *al-Ḥusayn ibn ʿAlī waʾl-thawra al-ʿArabīya al-kubrā* (Amman: Lajnat Tārīkh al-Urdunn, 1992).

Süleyman Sûdî. *Usûl-i Meskûkât-ı Osmaniye ve Ecnebiye* (Istanbul: A. Asadoryan, 1311 [1893]).

———. *Defter-i Muktesid*, 3 (Istanbul: Mahmud Bey Matbaası, 1307 [1889]).

Tanpınar, Ahmet Hamdi. *19 uncu Asır Türk Edebiyatı Tarihi* (Istanbul: Çağlayan Kitabevi, 1982).

Taşkıran, Cemalettin. *Ana Ben Ölmedim: Birinci Dünya Savaşı'nda Türk Esirleri* (Istanbul: Türkiye İş Bankası Kültür Yayınları, 2001).

Temperley, Harold. *England and the Near East: The Crimea* (London: Longmans [1936]).

Tevfik Fikret. *Rubab-ı Şikeste* (Istanbul: Tanin Matbaası, 1327 [1911]).

Toprak, Zafer. *Türkiye'de Ekonomi ve Toplum, 1908–1950: İttihat-Terakki ve Devletçilik* (Istanbul: Yurt Yayınları, 1995).

———. *Türkiye'de "Milli İktisat," 1908–1918* (Ankara: Yurt Yayınları, 1982).

Tunaya, Tarık Zafer. *Türkiye'de Siyasal Partiler*, 3: *İttihat ve Terakki, Bir Çağın, Bir Kuşağın, Bir Partinin Tarihi* (Istanbul: Hürriyet Vakfı Yayınları, 1989).

Tunçay, Mete. *Türkiye'de Sol Akımlar, 1908–1925*, 1 (Istanbul: BDS Yayınları, 1991).

Türkgeldi, Ali Fuat. *Mesâil-i Mühimme-i Siyasiye,* 1, ed. Bekir Sıtkı Baykal (Ankara: Türk Tarih Kurumu Yayınları, 1960).

Urquhart, David. *How Russia Tries to Get into Her Hands the Supply of Corn of the Whole Europe: The English Turkish Treaty of 1838* (London: R. Hardwicke, 1859).

Us, Hakkı Tarık. *Meclis-i Meb'usan, 1293–1877,* 2 (Istanbul: Vakit Kütüphanesi, 1954).

al-Usra al-'Aẓmīya, ed. 'Abd al-Qādir al-'Aẓm (Damascus: Maṭba'at al-Inshā', 1960).

Uzun, Ahmet. *Tanzimat ve Sosyal Direnişler: Niş İsyanı Üzerine Ayrıntılı Bir İnceleme* (Istanbul: Eren, 2002).

Vartan Paşa [Yovsep Vardanean]. *Akabi Hikyayesi: İlk Türkçe Roman (1851),* ed. A. Tietze (Istanbul: Eren, 1991).

Webster, Charles. *The Foreign Policy of Palmerston, 1830–1841: Britain, the Liberal Movement and the Eastern Question,* 1 (London: G. Bell, 1951).

Wilson, Woodrow. *Woodrow Wilson: The Essential Political Writings,* ed. Ronald J. Pestritto (Lanham, MD: Lexington Books, 2005).

Winter, Michael. *Egyptian Society under Ottoman Rule, 1517–1798* (London: Routledge, 1992).

Yasamee, F[eroz] A[bdullah] K[han]. *Ottoman Diplomacy: Abdülhamid II and the Great Powers, 1878–1888* (Istanbul: Isis Press, 1996).

Yeniay, İ. Hakkı. *Yeni Osmanlı Borçları Tarihi* (Istanbul: İktisat Fakültesi Yayınları, 1964).

Yüceer, Nâsır. *Birinci Dünya Savaşı'nda Osmanlı Ordusu'nun Azerbaycan ve Dağıstan Harekâtı: Azerbaycan ve Dağıstan'ın Bağımsızlığını Kazanması, 1918* (Ankara: Genelkurmay ATASE Yayınları, 1996).

Yusuf Akçura. *Üç Tarz-ı Siyaset* (Cairo: Matbaa-i İctihad, 1907).

Ziya Gökalp. *Türkleşmek, İslâmlaşmak, Mu'asırlaşmak* (Istanbul: Yeni Matbaa, 1918).

ARTICLES AND CHAPTERS IN BOOKS

Abadan, Yavuz. "Tanzimat Fermanının Tahlili." *Tanzimat I* (Istanbul: Maarif Vekâleti, 1940), pp. 31–58.

Barkan, Ömer Lûtfi. "Türk Toprak Hukuku Tarihinde Tanzimat ve 1274 (1858) Tarihli Arazi Kanunnamesi." *Tanzimat I* (Istanbul: Maarif Vekâleti, 1940), pp. 321–421.

Baykal, Bekir Sıtkı. "Midhat Paşa'nın Gizli Bir Siyasî Teşebbüsü." *III. Türk Tarih Kongresi* (Ankara: Türk Tarih Kurumu Yayınları, 1948), pp. 470–77.

Çadırcı, Musa. "Türkiye'de Muhtarlık Teşkilâtının Kurulması Üzerine Bir İnceleme." *Belleten* 34/135 (1970), pp. 409–20.

Clark, Edward C. "The Ottoman Industrial Revolution." *IJMES* 5/1 (January 1974), pp. 65–76.

Elliot, Henry. "The Death of Abdul Aziz and of Turkish Reform." *The Nineteenth Century and After* 23/132 (February 1888), pp. 276–96.

Groc, G[érard]. "La presse en français à l'époque ottomane." *La presse française de Turquie de 1795 à nos jours: Histoire et catalogue*, eds. G. Groc and İ. Çağlar (Istanbul: Isis Press, 1985), pp. 3–26.

Güran, Tevfik. "Tanzimat Dönemi'nde Osmanlı Maliyesi: Bütçeler ve Hazine Hesapları, 1841–1861." *Belgeler* 13/17 (1988), pp. 213–362.

Hanioğlu, M. Şükrü. "II. Meşrutiyet Dönemi 'Garbcılığı'nın Kavramsallaştırılmasındaki Üç Temel Sorun Üzerine Not." *Doğu-Batı* 31 (February 2005), pp. 55–64.

Ibrahim Hakki. "Is Turkey Progressing?" *The Imperial and Asiatic Quarterly Review and Oriental and Colonial Record* 3/2 (April 1892), pp. 265–78.

İhsanoğlu, Ekmeleddin. "Cemiyet-i İlmiye-i Osmaniye'nin Kuruluş ve Faaliyetleri." *Osmanlı İlmî ve Meslekî Cemiyetleri* (Istanbul: IRCICA, 1987), pp. 197–220.

İnalcık, Halil. "Application of the Tanzimat and Its Social Effects." *Archivum Ottomanum* 5 (1973), pp. 99–127.

———. "Sened-i İttifak ve Gülhane Hatt-i Hümâyûnu." *Belleten* 28/112 (1964), pp. 603–22.

———. "Osmanlı Hukukuna Giriş: Örfi-Sultanî Hukuk ve Fatih'in Kanunları." *Ankara Üniversitesi Siyasal Bilgiler Fakültesi Dergisi* 13/2 (1958), pp. 102–26.

Issawi, Charles. "Population and Resources in the Ottoman Empire and Iran." *Studies in Eighteenth Century Islamic History*, eds.Thomas Naff and Roger Owen (Carbondale: Southern Illinois University Press, 1977), pp. 152–64.

Kütükoğlu, Mübahat S. "Sultan II. Mahmud Devri Yedek Ordusu: Redif-i Asâkir-i Mansûre." *Tarih Enstitüsü Dergisi* 12 (1981–82), pp. 127–58.

Mehmed Galib. "Tarihden Bir Sahife: Âlî ve Fu'ad Paşaların Vasiyetnâmeleri." *Tarih-i Osmanî Encümeni Mecmuası* 1/2 [June 14, 1910], pp. 70–84.

[Mehmed Şerif]. "Sultan Selim Han-ı Sâlis Devrinde Nizâm-ı Devlet Hakkında Mütalâ'at." *Tarih-i Osmanî Encümeni Mecmuası* 7/38 [June 14, 1916], pp. 74–88.

Mehmet, Mustafa A. "O nouă reglementare a raporturilor Moldovei şi Ţării Româneşti faţă de Poartă la 1792 (O carte de lege—*Kanunname*—în limba turcă)." *Studii* 20/4 (1967), pp. 695–707.

Panayotopoulos, A. J. "The 'Great Idea' and the Vision of Eastern Federation: A Propos of Views of I. Dragoumis and A. Souliotis-Nicolaïdis." *Balkan Studies* 21/2 (1980), pp. 331–65.

Persignac, Comte Am. de. "Les gaîétes de la censure en Turquie." *La Revue* 67/2 (1907), pp. 384–94 and 521–37.

Quataert, Donald. "Dilemma of Development: The Agricultural Bank and Agricultural Reform in Ottoman Turkey, 1888–1908." *IJMES* 6/2 (April 1975), pp. 210–27.

Salzmann, Ariel. "An Ancien Régime Revisited: 'Privatization' and Political Economy in the Eighteenth-Century Ottoman Empire." *Politics and Society* 21/4 (December 1993), pp. 393–423.

Strauss, Johann. "Who Read What in the Ottoman Empire (19th–20th Centuries)?" *Arabic Middle Eastern Literatures* 6/1 (2003), pp. 39–76.

Suvla, Refii-Şükrü. "Tanzimat Devrinde İstikrazlar." *Tanzimat I* (Istanbul: Maarif Vekâleti, 1940), pp. 263–88.

Yazıcı, Nesimî. "II. Mahmud Döneminde Menzilhaneler: 'Refʿ-i Menzil Bedeli'." *Sultan II. Mahmud ve Reformları Semineri* (Istanbul: Edebiyat Fakültesi Yayınları, 1990), pp. 157–91.

Zafer Toprak. "İttihat ve Terakki'nin Para-Militer Gençlik Örgütleri." *Boğaziçi Üniversitesi Beşeri Bilimler Dergisi* 7 (1979), pp. 93–113.

Unpublished Dissertation

Aksakal, Mustafa. "Defending the Nation: The German-Ottoman Alliance of 1914 and the Ottoman Decision for War." Unpublished Ph.D. thesis, Princeton University, 2003.

Journals and Newspapers

Alafranga (Istanbul, 1910)
American Journal of International Law (Washington, DC, 1912)
Ceride-i Mahakim (Istanbul, 1890)
Genc Kalemler (Salonica), 1 (1911)
Güneş (Istanbul), 1 (1883)
Hayâl (Istanbul, 1874)
Hürriyet (London, 1868–69)
İbret (Istanbul, 1872)
İctihad (Istanbul, 1913–14).
İkdam (Istanbul, 1908)
The Imperial and Asiatic Quarterly Review and Oriental and Colonial Record (Woking), 3 (1892)
İslâm Mecmuası (Istanbul), 1–2 (1914–15)
İstikbâl (Istanbul, 1875–76)
İttihad Gazetesi (Cairo, 1899)
Kanun-i Esasî (Cairo, 1899)
Kashf al-Niqāb (Paris, 1895)
Kurdistan/Kürdistan (Cairo, London, 1898, 1900)
La Liberté (Paris, 1867)
Mecmua-i Fünûn (Istanbul, 1862–4)
Muʿahedat Mecmuası (Istanbul), 1 (1877); 4 (1881)
Muhbir (London, 1868)
Musavver Salnâme-i Servet-i Fünûn (Istanbul), 1 (1910)
New York Herald (Paris, 1896)

Niles' Weekly Register (Baltimore), 7 (1832)
Ruznâme-i Ceride-i Havâdis (Istanbul, 1874)
Sabah (Istanbul, 1876)
Sabah (Istanbul, 1908–1909)
Sebil'ür-Reşad (Istanbul), 11–12 (1914)
Servet-i Fünûn (Istanbul, 1909)
Şûra-yı Ümmet (Paris, 1907, Istanbul, 1908) (also published as *Haftalık Şûra-yı Ümmet*) (Istanbul, 1909)
Takvim-i Vekayiʿ
Terakki (Istanbul, 1868–9)
Terakki (Paris, 1907)
Tercüman-ı Hakikat (Istanbul, 1878)
Türk (Cairo, 1904–1906)
Türk Yurdu (Istanbul), 4 (1913)
Turkiyyā al-fatāt (Paris, 1896)
Ulûm Gazetesi (Paris, 1870)
Vakit (Istanbul, 1876)

Index

MUSLIM OTTOMANS did not normally have family names. An individual might be known by his personal name (as "Mehmed"), by a combination of his birth-name and personal name (e.g., "Ahmed Rıza"), by a combination of an adjective indicating his place of birth and his personal name (e.g., Çatalcalı Ali Efendi, born in Çatalca), by a combination of an honorific and his personal name (e.g., Alemdar Mustafa), or by a combination of a patronymic indicating the geneaology of his family and his personal name (e.g., Çaparoğlu Süleyman or Karaosmanzâde Ömer, descended from Çapar and Karaosman respectively). In this index Muslim Ottoman names are therefore alphabetized by personal name: "Ahmed Rıza" and not "Rıza, Ahmed"; "Ali Efendi Çatalcalı" and not "Çatalcalı Ali Efendi"; "Mustafa Alemdar" and not "Alemdar Mustafa"; and "Süleyman Çaparoğlu" rather than "Çaparoğlu Süleyman". An exception is made for those individuals who survived long enough into the Republican period to adopt family names in accordance with the "Surname Law" of June 21, 1934. This law required all citizens of the Turkish Republic to adopt a family name by January 1, 1935. Such individuals are alphabetized by family name, e.g., "Uşaklıgil, Halid Ziya" and not "Halid Ziya".